Get the eBook FREE!

(PDF, ePub, Kindle, and liveBook all included)

We believe that once you buy a book from us, you should be able to read it in any format we have available. To get electronic versions of this book at no additional cost to you, purchase and then register this book at the Manning website.

Go to https://www.manning.com/freebook and follow the instructions to complete your pBook registration.

That's it!
Thanks from Manning!

Data Engineering on Azure

Data Engineering on Azure

VLAD RISCUTIA

MANNING
SHELTER ISLAND

For online information and ordering of this and other Manning books, please visit
www.manning.com. The publisher offers discounts on this book when ordered in quantity.
For more information, please contact

Special Sales Department
Manning Publications Co.
20 Baldwin Road
PO Box 761
Shelter Island, NY 11964
Email: orders@manning.com

Manning Publications Co.
20 Baldwin Road
PO Box 761
Shelter Island, NY 11964

Development editor:	Elesha Hyde
Technical development editor:	Danny Vinson
Review editor:	Mihaela Batinić
Production editor:	Keri Hales
Copy editor:	Frances Buran
Proofreader:	Katie Tennant
Technical proofreader:	Karsten Strøbaek
Typesetter:	Gordan Salinovic
Cover designer:	Marija Tudor

ISBN 9781617298929
Printed in the United States of America

To my daughter, Ada

brief contents

contents

preface

This is the book I wish I had available to refer to over the past few years, while scaling out the big data platform of the Customer Growth and Analytics team in Azure. As our data science team grew and the insights generated by the team became more and more critical to the business, we had to ensure that our platform was robust.

The world of big data is relatively new, and the playbook is still being written. I believe our story is common: data teams start small with a handful of people, who first prove they can generate valuable insights. At this stage, a lot of work happens ad hoc, and there is no immediate need for big engineering investments. A data scientist can run a machine learning (ML) model on their machine, generate some predictions, and email the results.

Over time, the team grows and more workloads become mission critical. The same ML model now plugs into a system serving live traffic and needs to run on a daily basis with more than a hundred times the data it was originally prototyped with. At this point, solid engineering practices are critical; we need scale, reliability, automation, monitoring, etc.

This book contains several years of hard-learned lessons in data engineering. To name a few examples:

- Empowering every data scientist on the team to deploy new analytics and data movement pipelines onto our platform while maintaining a reliable production environment
- Architecting an ML platform to streamline and automate execution of dozens of ML models

- Building a metadata catalog to make sense of the large number of available datasets
- Implementing various ways to test the quality of the data and sending alerts when issues are identified

The underlying theme of this book is DevOps, bringing the decades-old best practices of software engineering to the world of big data. Data governance is another important topic; making sense of the data, ensuring quality, compliance, and access control are all a critical part of governance.

The patterns and practices described in this book are platform agnostic. They should be just as valid regardless of which cloud you use. That said, we can't be too abstract, so I provide some concrete examples through a reference implementation. The reference implementation is Azure. Even here, there is a wide selection of services we can pick from.

The reference implementation uses a set of services, but keep in mind, the book is less about the particular set of services and more about the data engineering practices realized through them. I hope you enjoy the book, and that you find some best practices you can apply to your environment and business space.

acknowledgments

Many thanks to my wife, Diana, and daughter, Ada, for their support. Thanks for bearing with me for a second round!

This book wouldn't be what it is without the great input and advice from Michael Stephens and Elesha Hyde. Also, thanks go to Danny Vinson for reviewing the early draft and to Karsten Strøbæk for checking all the code samples. I thank all the reviewers for their time and feedback: Albert Nogués, Arun Thangasamy, Dave Corun, Geoff Clark, Glenn Swonk, Hilde Van Gysel, Jesús A. Juárez Guerrero, Johannes Verwijnen, Kelum Senanayake, Krzysztof Kamyczek, Luke Kupka, Matthias Busch, Miranda Whurr, Oliver Korten, Peter Kreyenhop, Peter Morgan, Phil Allen, Philippe Van Bergen, Richard B. Ward, Richard Vaughan, Robert Walsh, Sven Stumpf, Todd Cook, Vishwesh Ravi Shrimali, and Zekai Otles.

Many thanks go to the Customer Growth and Analytics leadership team for their support and for giving me the opportunity to learn: Tim Wong, Greg Koehler, Ron Sielinski, Merav Davidson, Vivek Dalvi, and everyone else on the team.

I was also fortunate to partner with many other teams across Microsoft. I want to thank the IDEAs team, especially Gerardo Bodegas Martinez, Wayne Yim, and Ayyappan Balasubramanian; the Azure Data Explorer team, Oded Sacher and Ziv Caspi; the Azure Purview team, Naga Krishna Yenamandra and Gaurav Malhotra; and the Azure Machine Learning team, especially Tzvi Keisar.

And I thank the Manning team, who helped put this book together from development through production and everything in between.

about this book

Just as software engineering brings engineering rigor to software development, data engineering aims to bring the same rigor to working with data in a reliable way. This book is about implementing the various aspects of a big data platform in a real-world production system: data ingestion, running analytics and machine learning (ML), and distributing data, to name a few. The focus of this book is on the operational aspects such as DevOps, monitoring, scale, and compliance. Examples are provided using Azure services.

Who should read this book?

A typical reader is a data scientist, software engineer, or architect with several years of experience who has become a data engineer looking into building and scaling a production data platform. Readers should have a basic knowledge of the cloud and some experience working with data.

How this book is organized: A roadmap

This book is divided into three parts, and each part looks at a data platform through a different lens. Chapter 1 introduces the overall architecture of a data platform, gives an overview of the Azure services we'll use for the reference implementation, and defines some of the key terms (such as what we mean by data engineering and infrastructure as code, etc.) to lay some common groundwork. Then, part 1 covers the core infrastructure of a data platform:

- Chapter 2 discusses storage infrastructure, the heart of a big data platform.
- Chapter 3 covers DevOps, the key ingredient that brings engineering discipline to the realm of data.
- Chapter 4 talks about orchestration, how data movement and processing is scheduled and executed throughout the platform.

Part 2 covers the main workloads a data platform needs to support:

- Chapter 5 deals with processing data, reshaping it to better support various analytical scenarios.
- Chapter 6 covers analytics and how we can apply good engineering practices to recurring reporting and analysis.
- Chapter 7 shows how we can support end-to-end machine learning workloads (also known as MLOps).

Part 3 cover various aspects of governance:

- Chapter 8 focuses on metadata (data about the data) and how to make sense of all the assets in a big data platform.
- Chapter 9 discusses data quality and different types of tests that we can run against our datasets.
- Chapter 10 covers an important topic—compliance—including how we classify and handle different types of data.
- Chapter 11 talks about data distribution and the various way data is shared with other teams downstream.

The chapters can be read in any order, as these each touch on different aspects of data engineering. Part 1, however, is a prerequisite if you want to run the code examples. These chapters also set up the foundational pieces of the infrastructure, but otherwise, feel free to skip around and focus on the chapters that sound most interesting to you.

About the code

This book contains many examples of source code both in numbered listings and in line with normal text. In both cases, source code is formatted in a `fixed-width font`, `like this` to separate it from ordinary text.

Also, in many cases, the original source code has been reformatted; we've added line breaks and reworked indentation to accommodate the available page width in the printed book. In some cases, even this was not enough, and listings include line-continuation markers (➡). Additionally, code annotations accompany many of the listings, highlighting important concepts.

All the code samples in this book are available on GitHub at https://github.com/vladris/azure-data-engineering. The code was thoroughly tested, but because the Azure cloud and surrounding tooling continuously evolves, check appendix C if you run into issues trying any of the code samples.

liveBook discussion forum

Purchase of *Data Engineering on Azure* includes free access to a private web forum run by Manning Publications where you can make comments about the book, ask technical questions, and receive help from the author and from other users. To access the forum, go to https://livebook.manning.com/#!/book/data-engineering-on-azure/discussion. You can also learn more about Manning's forums and the rules of conduct at https://livebook.manning.com/#!/discussion.

Manning's commitment to our readers is to provide a venue where a meaningful dialogue between individual readers and between readers and the author can take place. It is not a commitment to any specific amount of participation on the part of the author, whose contribution to the forum remains voluntary (and unpaid). We suggest you try asking him some challenging questions lest his interest stray! The forum and the archives of previous discussions will be accessible from the publisher's website as long as the book is in print.

about the author

VLAD RISCUTIA is a software engineer at Microsoft, where he oversees development of the data platform supporting the central data science team for Azure. He spent the past few years as an architect on the Customer Growth and Analytics team, building out a big data platform used by Azure's data science organization. He has headed up several major software projects and mentors up-and-coming software engineers.

about the cover illustration

The figure on the cover of *Data Engineering on Azure* is captioned "Femme Tartar," or Tartar woman. The illustration is taken from a collection of dress costumes from various countries by Jacques Grasset de Saint-Sauveur (1757–1810), titled *Costumes de Différents Pays,* published in France in 1797. Each illustration is finely drawn and colored by hand. The rich variety of Grasset de Saint-Sauveur's collection reminds us vividly of how culturally apart the world's towns and regions were just 200 years ago. Isolated from each other, people spoke different dialects and languages. In the streets or in the countryside, it was easy to identify where they lived and what their trade or station in life was just by their dress.

The way we dress has changed since then and the diversity by region, so rich at the time, has faded away. It is now hard to tell apart the inhabitants of different continents, let alone different towns, regions, or countries. Perhaps we have traded cultural diversity for a more varied personal life—certainly for a more varied and fast-paced technological life.

At a time when it is hard to tell one computer book from another, Manning celebrates the inventiveness and initiative of the computer business with book covers based on the rich diversity of regional life of two centuries ago, brought back to life by Grasset de Saint-Sauveur's pictures.

Introduction

1

With the advent of cloud computing, the amount of data generated every moment reached an unprecedented scale. The discipline of data science flourishes in this environment, deriving knowledge and insights from massive amounts of data. As data science becomes critical to business, its processes must be treated with the same rigor as other components of business IT. For example, software engineering teams today embrace DevOps to develop and operate services with 99.99999% availability guarantees. Data engineering brings a similar rigor to data science, so data-centric processes run reliably, smoothly, and in a compliant way.

For the past few years, I've had the privilege of being a software architect for Microsoft's Customer Growth and Analytics team. Our team's motto is "Using Azure to understand Azure." We connect many datapoints across the Microsoft business to better understand our customers and to empower teams across the company. Privacy is important to us, so we never look at our customers' data, but we do have access to telemetry from Azure, commercial transactions, and other operational pipelines. This gives us a unique perspective on Azure in understanding how customers can get the most value from our offerings.

As a few examples, we help marketing, sales, support, finance, operations, and business planning with key insights, while simultaneously providing operational excellence recommendations to our customers through Azure Advisor. While our data science and machine learning (ML) teams focus on the insights, our data engineering teams ensure we can operate at the scale of an Azure business with high reliability because any outage in our platform can impact our customers or our business.

Our data platform is fully built on Azure, and we are working closely with service teams to preview features and give product feedback. This book is inspired by some of our learnings over the years. The technologies presented are close to what my team uses on a day-to-day basis.

1.1   What is data engineering?

This book is about practical data engineering in a production environment, so let's start by defining data engineering. But to define data engineering, we first need to talk about data science.

"Data is the new oil," as the saying goes. In a connected world, more and more data is available for analysis, inference, and ML. The field of data science deals with extracting knowledge and insights from data. Many times, these insights prove invaluable to a business. Consider a scenario like the movies Netflix recommends to a customer. The better the recommendations, the more likely to retain a customer.

While many data science projects start as exploratory, once these show real value, they need to be supported in an ongoing, reliable fashion. In the software engineering world, this is the equivalent of taking a research, proof-of-concept, or hackathon project and graduating it into a fully production-ready solution. While a hack or a prototype can take many shortcuts and focus on "the meat of the problem" it addresses, a production-ready system does not cut any corners. This is where the engineering part of software engineering comes into play, providing the rigor to build and run a reliable system. This includes a plethora of concerns like architecture and design, performance, security, accessibility, telemetry, debuggability, extensibility, and so on.

> **DEFINITION** *Data engineering* is the part of data science that deals with the practical applications of collecting and analyzing data. It aims to bring engineering rigor to the process of building and supporting reliable data systems.

The ML part of data science deals with building a model. In the Netflix scenario, the data model recommends, based on your viewing history, which movies you are likely to enjoy next. The data engineering part of the discipline deals with building a system that continuously gathers and cleans up the viewing history, then runs the model at scale on the data of all users and distributes the results to the recommendation user interface. All of this provided in an automated fashion with monitoring and alerting build around each step of the process.

Data engineering deals with building and operating big data platforms to support all data science scenarios. There are various other terms used for some of these aspects: DataOps refers to moving data in a data system, MLOps refers to running ML at scale as in our Netflix example. (ML combined with DevOps is also known as MLOps.) Our definition of data engineering encompasses all of these and looks at how we can implement DevOps for data science.

1.2 Who this book is for

This is a book for data scientists, software engineers, and software architects turned data engineers and tasked with building a data platform to support analytics and/or ML at scale. You should know what the cloud is, have some experience working with data and code, and not mind using a shell. We'll touch on the basics of all of these, but the focus for this book will be on data platform building.

Data engineering is surprisingly similar to software engineering and frustratingly different. While we can leverage a lot of the lessons from the software engineering world, as we will see in this book, there is a unique set of challenges we will have to address. Some of the common themes are making sure everything is tracked in source control, automatic deployments, monitoring, and alerting. A key difference between data and code is that code is static: once the bugs are worked out, a piece of code is expected to work consistently and reliably. On the other hand, data moves continuously into and out of a data platform, and it is likely failures will occur due to various external reasons. Governance is another major topic that is specific to data: access control, cataloguing, privacy, and regulatory concerns are a big part of a data platform.

The main theme of the book is bringing some of the lessons learned from software engineering over the past few decades to the data space so you can build a data platform exhibiting the properties of a solid software solution: scale, reliability, security, and so on. This book tackles some of these challenges, goes over patterns and best practices, and provides examples of how these could be applied in the Azure cloud. For the examples, we will use the Azure CLI (CLI stands for command-line interface), KQL (the Kusto Query Language), and a little bit of Python. The focus won't be on the services themselves though. Instead, we will focus on data engineering challenges (and solutions) in a production environment.

1.3 What is a data platform?

Just as many data science projects start as an exploration of a data space and what insights can be derived from the data, many data science teams start in a similar exploratory fashion. A small team comes up with some good insights at first, and then as the team grows, so do the needs of the underlying platform supporting the team.

What first used to be an ad hoc process now requires automation. Once there were just two data scientists on the team, so who got to see which data was not as much of a concern as it is now, when there are 100 data scientists, some interns, and some external vendors. What used to be a monthly email is now a live system integrated with the company's website. Different scenarios that used to be achieved through different means must now be supported by a robust data platform.

> **DEFINITION**   A *data platform* is a software solution for collecting, processing, managing, and sharing data for strategic business purposes.

Let's look at an analogy to software engineering. You can write code on your laptop (for example, a web service like GIPHY) that, when given some keywords, returns a set of topical animations. Even if the code does exactly what it is meant to, that doesn't mean it can scale to a production environment. If you want to host the same service at web scale and expect that anyone around the world can access it at any time, there is an additional set of concerns to consider: performance, scaling to millions of users, low latency, a failover solution in case things go wrong, a way to deploy an update without downtime, and so on. We can call the first part, writing code on your laptop, software development or coding. The second part, operating a production service, we can call software engineering.

The same applies to data engineering. Running a data platform at scale comes with a unique set of challenges to consider and address. Data science deals with writing queries and developing ML models. Data engineering takes these and scales them to millions of rows of data, provides automation and monitoring, ensures security and compliance, and so on. These aspects are the main focus of this book.

1.3.1   *Anatomy of a data platform*

The data platform grows to support all these new production scenarios, converting ad hoc processing into automated workflows and applying best practices. At this scale, certain patterns emerge. Figure 1.1 shows the anatomy of such a platform. Because we are dealing with data, many of the visuals focus on data flows.

Part 1 of the book focuses on infrastructure, the core services of a data platform. These include storage and analytics services, automatic deployment and monitoring, and an orchestration solution.

We'll start with storage—the backbone of any data platform. Chapter 2 covers the requirements and common patterns for storing data in a data platform. Because our focus is on production systems, in chapter 3, we'll discuss DevOps and what DevOps means for data. Data is ingested into the system from multiple sources. Data flows into and out of the platform, and various workflows are executed. All of this needs an orchestration layer to keep things running. We'll talk about orchestration in chapter 4.

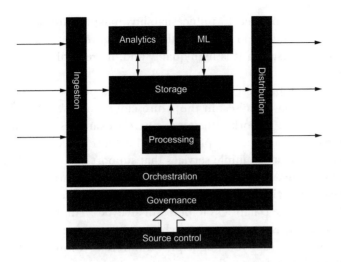

Figure 1.1 On the left, data is ingested into the system and persisted in a storage layer. Processing aggregates and reshapes the data to enable analytics and ML scenarios. Orchestration and governance are cross-cutting concerns that cover all the components of the platform. Once processed, data is distributed to other downstream systems. All components are tracked by and deployed from source control.

Part 2 focuses on the three main workloads that a data platform must support. These are

- *Processing*—Encompasses aggregating and reshaping the data, standardizing schema, and any other processing of the raw input data. This makes the data easier to consume by the other two main processes: analytics and machine learning. We'll talk about data processing in chapter 5.
- *Analytics*—Covers all data analysis and reporting, thereby deriving knowledge and insights on the data. We'll look at ways to support this in production in chapter 6.
- *Machine learning*—Includes all ML models training on the data. We'll cover running ML at scale in chapter 7.

Part 3 covers governance, a major topic with many aspects. Chapters 8, 9, and 10 touch on these key topics:

- *Metadata*—Cataloguing and inventorying the data, tracking lineage, definitions, and documentation is the subject of chapter 8.
- *Data quality*—How to test data and assess its quality is the topic of chapter 9.
- *Compliance*—Honoring compliance requirements like the General Data Protection Regulation (GDPR), handling sensitive data, and controlling access is covered in chapter 10.

After all the processing steps, data eventually leaves the platform to be consumed by other systems. We'll cover the various patterns for distributing data in chapter 11. Data governance is a pretty loose term, so let's work with the following definition:

DEFINITION *Governance* is the process of managing the availability, usability, integrity, regulatory compliance, and security of the data in a data system. Effective data governance ensures that data is consistent and trustworthy and doesn't get misused.

On one hand, governance is needed to reduce liability, making sure data complies with regulations, is secure, and so on. On the other hand, governance also includes making data discoverable, ensuring it is high-quality and, in general, increasing the usability of the platform.

Infrastructure-wise, the topics discussed apply to any data platform, regardless of whether it is implemented on premises, in the Azure cloud, in AWS (Amazon Web Services), and so on. We need to work with some concrete examples, though, so this book covers the implementation of a data platform in the Azure cloud.

Even within Azure, there are multiple services that support analytics, ML, and so on. For example, we can use Azure Databricks, Azure Machine Learning (AML), or Azure HDInsight/Spark to train ML models, and we can use Azure Synapse, Azure Data Explorer (ADX), or Azure Databricks to perform analytics. This book covers one possible implementation but, as every software architect knows, there are always trade-offs. Depending on your scenario, you might pick a different technology to implement your data platform. There is no *right* way.

Many factors inform the technology choice: existing assets, what the users of the platform are familiar with, portability, performance for various workloads, and so on. We will look at some of these key differences and zoom in on one possible implementation. As you read, keep in mind that the underlying patterns are more important than the particular technology choice, and you might choose to materialize these on a different technology stack.

1.3.2   *Infrastructure as code, codeless infrastructure*

Because we are dealing with production systems, we'll focus a lot on DevOps and best practices. This includes avoiding interactive configuration tools and automating everything via scripts and machine-readable configurations, also known as infrastructure as code.

> **DEFINITION**   *Infrastructure as code* is the process of managing and provisioning infrastructure through automation by relying on configuration files and automation scripts as opposed to manual and interactive configurations.

Surprisingly, focusing on infrastructure as code doesn't mean we will have to write thousands of lines of code to build a data platform. In fact, most of the components we need are readily available and only need to be configured and stitched together to support our scenarios. Such an infrastructure using mostly off-the-shelf components and a little glue is called a codeless infrastructure.

> **DEFINITION**   *Codeless infrastructure* is an infrastructure built by configuring existing services and connecting them to achieve the required scenarios. This is done with as little custom code as possible.

In general, code is not an asset; rather, it is a liability. What the code does, the scenarios it enables, is the real asset. The code itself needs maintenance, has bugs, requires updates, and in general, consumes engineering time and resources. When possible, it's better to let others worry about this maintenance. Today, most of the infrastructure we need is offered as services by cloud providers like Microsoft and Amazon. We will use Azure, Microsoft's cloud offering, to implement the examples in this book.

With these services, a small engineering team can achieve a (surprising) lot. Focus moves from developing infrastructure to configuring, deploying, and monitoring it, and then focusing on solving some of the higher-level challenges of the domain. In our case, these challenges are around scaling out data workloads and governance concerns.

1.4 Building in the cloud

Big data comes from operating at scale. The amount of data grows with the number of people and devices connected to the internet and the information these generate. As infrastructure becomes commoditized in the cloud, data platforms are built in the cloud too. We used to run analytics on SQL Servers hosted on premises with over hundreds of megabytes, maybe even gigabytes, of data. Now we can run analytics on hundreds of gigabytes or even terabytes of data in the cloud, using specialized storage and distributed querying solutions. We can rent these solutions from multiple cloud providers like Microsoft, Amazon, or Google.

1.4.1 IaaS, PaaS, SaaS

Cloud solutions are usually categorized into infrastructure as a service (IaaS), platform as a service (PaaS), and software as a service (SaaS). IaaS provides virtualized computing resources like networking, storage, and virtual machines (VMs). Instead of buying computers, networking equipment, and ensuring that these are properly set up and running, we can rent them from a cloud provider. If we suddenly need more capacity, we can easily request more. If we need less capacity, we can free that up almost instantly. This ends up being much cheaper than building and maintaining a small data center. But it doesn't stop here.

PaaS provides higher-level abstractions than just the basic computing resources. Instead of renting infrastructure on which we install an SQL Server, we can rent a fully managed Azure SQL instance. This is a database handled by Azure that includes high availability, automatic installation of software updates, threat detection, and many other features that we otherwise would've had to handle ourselves.

Finally, SaaS goes one step beyond that and offers full applications in the cloud. An example of SaaS is Power BI, an interactive data visualization and business intelligence solution. We can just sign in and start working, nothing to configure, nothing to manage.

When building a data platform, we mostly operate at the PaaS level; we leverage the data solutions offered by our cloud, in this case Azure, to enable all of our scenarios with as little custom code as possible. This aligns with our principle of codeless infrastructure—the less time we need to spend maintaining infrastructure, the more time we can spend adding value to the business.

1.4.2   *Network, storage, compute*

Another common way to categorize services is by their function: network, storage, and compute. Network resources deal with connectivity and security, connecting on-prem networks to the cloud, and so on. While not a major focus of this book, network is important for a data platform from the perspective of data movement. Copying giga-bytes or terabytes of data from one storage solution to another incurs network costs, and moving data across regions increases latency. On the other hand, in some cases, we do need to move data from one service to another because different services are built for different workloads, and there is no single service that can efficiently support all of our needs. We need to keep in mind these aspects while building our data platform.

Storage resources are concerned with data. Services like Azure Blob Storage and Azure Data Lake Storage (ADLS) can store virtually infinite amounts of data. Capacity, access times, and security features are some of the relevant properties of storage solu-tions. For example, a question we might want to ask ourselves when making a technol-ogy choice is, how fast can we scan/retrieve the data from our storage solution?

Compute resources are services that handle processing; VMs, containers, Azure Functions, and Azure Web Apps are all compute resources. Environments that run ML training and analytics are also compute resources. Scaling is a key aspect for com-pute resources in a data platform. Can our compute handle millions of rows of data? Can our ML infrastructure train dozens of models in parallel? These are questions we need to ask ourselves to make informed technology choices.

Some Azure services cover both storage and compute. For example, Azure Data Explorer provides an integrated environment to both ingest data and perform analyt-ics on it. Other services cover a single aspect; we can put data in a data lake, but we need to connect some compute resource like Azure Machine Learning to it in order to use the data.

1.4.3   *Getting started with Azure*

If you are new to Azure, you can sign up for a free account at https://azure.microsoft .com/en-us/free/. An Azure free account gives you access to the Azure platform, including 12 months free for several services and $200 in credit to explore paid ser-vices for 30 days. This should be more than enough to work through the examples in this book.

Do keep in mind that some services are charged on a per-use or consumption basis, although others incur costs for as long as they are running. For example, Azure Functions, the serverless compute offering, allows 1 million free invocations per month. Additional invocations are charged based on the number of executions and resources used. That means that a function that doesn't get called doesn't cost any-thing. On the other hand, if we provision a virtual machine and leave it running, it incurs costs even if we don't touch it.

> **NOTE** When you are done with the examples in this book, make sure to clean things up to avoid unnecessary charges.

1.4.4 *Interacting with Azure*

There are three main ways to interact with Azure. These include

- Using the Azure portal UI at https://azure.microsoft.com/
- Using the Azure REST API
- Using the command line

Because we are focusing on DevOps and automation, we will avoid UI interaction as much as possible and instead rely on scripting, which we can more easily transition from ad hoc to automated. In most cases, this means using the command line. It should also make working through the examples in the book easier. Instead of pages of screenshots, you can clone the GitHub repo with the examples and copy and paste them into your shell. We will fall back to UI screenshots for the few places where automation doesn't work; for example, signing up to new services like Azure DevOps (ADO).

To interact with Azure using the command line, we will use PowerShell Core and the Azure CLI.[1] You can use a different shell if you prefer, but using PowerShell makes it easier to run the code samples in this book without modification.

In many cases, Azure resources have a URL that needs to be unique. If we name such a resource AzureDataEngineering, the first reader to run the example will create the URL and it will be unavailable for others. To avoid this issue, for this type of resources, we will use a unique suffix. We will store this suffix in a PowerShell variable in your profile.

In PowerShell, `$PROFILE` should show you the path of the PowerShell profile script that runs when you start the shell. Open it in your favorite text editor by calling, for example, `notepad $PROFILE` and adding the line from the following listing. Replace `<unique suffix>` with your nickname.

Listing 1.1 Setting up `$suffix` in your PowerShell profile

```
...$suffix = "<unique suffix>"
```

We will append this string to Azure resources that need to be unique. Now, when we launch the shell, we'll have this handy in the `$suffix` variable.

> **NOTE** Remember to set `$suffix` in your profile; otherwise, many examples in this book that rely on this won't work.

The `$suffix` variable should be unique but fairly short, and it should contain only alphanumeric characters. Various services have restrictions on what characters are allowed in their names. For example, I used my alias, `"vladris"`. With that out of the way, let's go ahead and install Azure CLI.

Azure CLI is a multiplatform command line for interacting with Azure. It's used for configuration and task automation. For the types of automation in this book, like

---

[1] PowerShell Core is a cross-platform shell you can get from https://github.com/PowerShell/Powershell.

provisioning resources and configuring services, this is easier to work with than going to the REST API. For programmatic access, we should get the Azure SDK for our particular language (C#, Python, and so on), which will call into the REST API, but let's just get the command-line tools for now.

You can get Azure CLI for any platform by following the instructions here: https://docs.microsoft.com/en-us/cli/azure/install-azure-cli. For Windows, run the command in the following listing from PowerShell launched in Administrator mode.

Listing 1.2 Installing Azure CLI from PowerShell

```
Invoke-WebRequest -Uri https://aka.ms/installazurecliwindows -OutFile
➡ .\AzureCLI.msi; Start-Process msiexec.exe -Wait -ArgumentList
➡ '/I AzureCLI.msi /quiet'; rm .\AzureCLI.msi
```

This command downloads and installs the Azure CLI tools that you can then access on any shell by invoking `az`. After running the installer, you might need to run `refreshenv` for the environment to pick up the Azure CLI tools. The first step before using Azure CLI is logging into Azure. From the shell, call `az login` as shown in the next listing.

Listing 1.3 Logging into Azure using Azure CLI

```
az login
```

You should be prompted to log in, after which you can interact with Azure by using the command line. The general format of an `az` command is

```
az <group> [<subgroup>] <command> <arguments>
```

For example, to create a new resource group, which is a container for Azure resources, we would invoke the command in the following listing.

Listing 1.4 Creating an Azure resource group

The <group> in this case is group (Azure CLI short for Azure Resource Group); the command is create.

A new resource group needs a location. For this example, we use Central US.

```
az group create `
--location "Central US" `
--name "MyResourceGroup"
```

A new resource group also needs a name. We'll call this one MyResourceGroup.

The listing can actually be a one-liner, but here we use a backtick (`` ` ``), which is the PowerShell way to split a command across multiple lines. This will make the command easier to read and annotate. If you are using a different shell, you might need to use a different separator or, better yet, just make it a one liner.

A couple of notes on the examples in this book: at the time of writing, some of the Azure CLI extensions that we will use are in an experimental stage. You might get a warning saying the same. You can ignore this. The latest code examples can be found in the book's GitHub repository here: https://github.com/vladris/azure-data-engineering. Also, see appendix C for some troubleshooting steps in case you get stuck when running any of the examples in the book.

1.5 *Implementing an Azure data platform*

As we work through the topics in this book, we will look into implementing a data platform. Figure 1.2 shows this implementation.

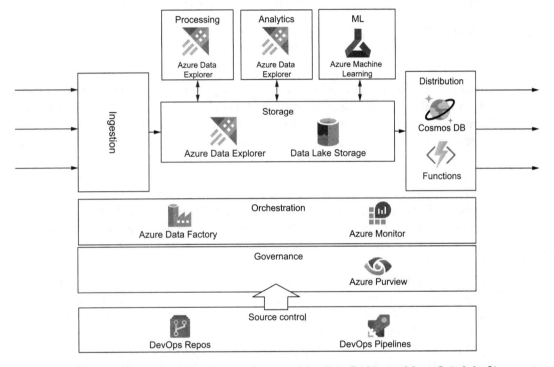

Figure 1.2 Implementation of a data platform. Here we use Azure Data Explorer and Azure Data Lake Storage as the main data stores. We then run processing and analytics on Azure Data Explorer and ML on Azure Machine Learning. Data distribution is from storage and through an API implemented via Cosmos DB and Azure Functions. Orchestration is handled by Azure Data Factory, and we implement monitoring using Azure Monitor. We use Azure Purview for metadata management, Azure DevOps Repos for source control, and Azure DevOps Pipelines for deployment.

The large boxes in figure 1.2 are the same as in figure 1.1, just slightly rearranged to better fit the services used. Don't worry if you are not familiar with these services; we'll go over a quick rundown in this section and then focus on each in the following chapters.

In part 1, we discuss storage, DevOps, and orchestration. For storage, we will use Azure Data Explorer and Azure Data Lake Storage. Azure Data Explorer excels at ingesting data with high throughput and can query millions of rows of data within seconds, making it ideal for analytics and exploration scenarios. Azure Data Lake Storage provides virtually infinite storage space. Unlike Azure Data Explorer, which is an integrated storage and analytics solution, Azure Data Lake Storage is a purely storage solution. Other compute services, like Azure Data Lake Analytics, Azure Databricks, or Azure Machine Learning can connect to Azure Data Lake Storage and provide processing for it. We will go over more of the details in chapter 2.

We will rely on Azure DevOps Repos and Azure DevOps Pipelines, both part of the Azure DevOps offerings, for source control, code flow processes, and automated deployments. Chapter 3 focuses on DevOps. For orchestration, we will use Azure Data Factory (ADF). Azure Data Factory is the main Azure serverless ETL solution.

> **DEFINITION** *ETL* (short for extract, transform, load) is the general process of copying data from one or more sources into a destination, while applying any required transformation.

Moving data around and running various processes on a schedule is a complex topic, which we will cover in chapter 4. We will also cover monitoring and introduce Azure Monitor, a service that provides real-time alerts if any issues are encountered.

Part 2 of the book focuses on the three main workloads we need to run on a data platform: modeling, analytics, and machine learning. Modeling focuses on reshaping and curating the data such that users of the data platform can more easily consume it in their processes. Analytics includes all reporting and insights derived from the data. For both topics, we will rely on the compute capabilities of Azure Data Explorer with orchestration provided by Azure Data Factory, monitoring through Azure Monitor, and other DevOps concerns covered by Azure DevOps. We will cover these topics in chapters 5 and 6.

ML is a bit different. Although both processing and analytics focus on directly shaping and querying the data, ML workloads focus on training models that can automatically provide classifications, predictions, and so on. For these types of workloads, we will look at Azure Machine Learning (AML). Azure Machine Learning is Azure's fully managed platform for ML model management, which we will discuss in chapter 7.

Part 3 of the book focuses on governance. First, we will look at metadata management, which helps us explore our data space. We will see how we can inventory our data, term definitions in our business domain, lineage, and other such concerns. Chapter 8 is all about metadata, or data about our data. Azure Purview is the metadata-as-a-service solution offered by Azure.

Data quality is another important aspect that ensures data is available on time, is complete, is not corrupted, and so on. Unfortunately, we currently don't have an out-of-the-box solution for data quality, so we will look at how we can implement something on Azure. This is the subject of chapter 9.

Chapter 10 is all about governance, so we will leverage the capabilities of our storage layer to properly secure data and implement requirements like GDPR compliance. We'll also talk about data classification and proper data handling.

Chapter 11 covers data distribution. We will look at different ways of sharing data from our data platform. We will look at sharing data via an API, instead of directly at the storage layer, and discuss the benefits of this. To build a low-latency, scalable API, we will leverage Cosmos DB as our serving-layer storage and Azure Functions for building a REST API over this storage. We'll also look at sharing data for bulk copy directly from the storage layer using Azure Data Share.

You might have noticed some technologies are missing from this picture. For example, we haven't mentioned Azure SQL, Azure Synapse Analytics, or Azure Databricks. Each of these services, much like the ones we are going to use in this book, deserve their own book if you want to deep-dive and understand all the pros, cons, and nuances. Appendix A provides a quick overview, but again, this is not a book about Azure services. This is a book about implementing a data platform, so the main focus is the scenarios we want to achieve and the workloads we want to support.

We can think of the set of services we pick for the job as an implementation detail. Of course, we want to make an informed decision about our implementation. As mentioned earlier, everyone's particular scenario will bring different decision points, so the platform covered in this book is just one possible implementation out of many. The underlying concepts are the same. In part 1 we will look at the core infrastructure of our data platform, starting with our storage layer in chapter 2.

Summary

- Data engineering aims to bring engineering rigor to the process of building and supporting data systems.
- Data governance deals with availability, usability, integrity, regulatory compliance, and security of a data system.
- Cloud providers enable us to rent their services, which frees us from having to manage infrastructure.
- Infrastructure as code is the practice of managing and provisioning infrastructure through automation.
- Codeless infrastructure refers to the use of existing services to implement an infrastructure as opposed to custom code.
- Cloud services can be categorized as infrastructure as a service (IaaS), platform as a service (PaaS), and software as a service (SaaS).
- Cloud services can also be categorized as network, storage, and compute with some solutions providing integrated storage and analytics.
- You can interact with Azure in three ways: through the web UI, through REST APIs, and through command-line tools.

Part 1

Infrastructure

In part 1, we'll set up the core infrastructure of our data platform. All other topics discussed in the book (running various workloads, aspects of governance) will be built on top of this infrastructure.

- Chapter 2 discusses storage and various patterns of ingesting and storing data. We'll look at two Azure services: Azure Data Explorer and Azure Data Lake Storage.
- Chapter 3 covers DevOps and introduces Azure DevOps, as this is a book about data engineering and bringing engineering rigor to data. We'll see how we can store everything in Git and use automated pipelines for deployment.
- Chapter 4 describes orchestration: how data moves through our platform and how we can schedule various processes. For orchestration and data movement, we'll use Azure Data Factory. For monitoring, we'll use Azure Monitor.

Storage

This chapter covers

- Storing data in a data platform
- Using Azure Data Explorer for ingestion and analytics
- Using Azure Data Lake Storage for big data storage
- Applying data ingestion patterns

Data storage is the core piece of a data platform around which everything else is built. The focus of this chapter is storage solutions and trade-offs. We'll also introduce two Azure services that we will use and discuss how these integrate. Figure 2.1 recaps the high-level view from chapter 1, highlighting the component discussed in this chapter.

Because data moves continuously in and out of the data platform, this chapter focuses on storage and the need to accommodate multiple storage solutions, both external and inside the data platform. We will sketch out the storage layer of our data platform, then stand up the corresponding Azure services.

In this chapter, we will deploy an Azure Data Explorer (ADX) cluster, Microsoft's big data analytics platform. We will create a table, ingest some data into it, and

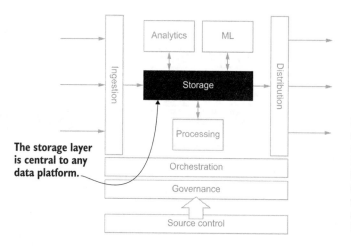

The storage layer is central to any data platform.

Figure 2.1   Storage is the core piece of a data platform around which everything else is built. Data gets ingested into the storage layer and is distributed from there. All workloads (data processing, analytics, and machine learning) access this layer.

then we'll look at a few basics KQL queries, the Kusto Query Language used by Azure Data Explorer. Kusto was the code name of Azure Data Explorer before it launched as a public service. You sometimes might encounter "Kusto" instead of "Azure Data Explorer," but know these are the same service.

Next, we'll configure an Azure Data Lake Storage (ADLS) instance, the highly scalable data lake solution. We'll see how we can upload data to the data lake and look at some of the integration options with Azure Data Explorer. We'll export data from Azure Data Explorer into Azure Data Lake Storage and then read it back as an external table.

Finally, we will talk about data ingestion patterns. We'll see how data can be ingested at various frequencies, and how it can be fully or incrementally loaded into our platform. We will also look at what happens if the data gets corrupted and we need to reload it to fix the issues.

2.1   *Storing data in a data platform*

Let's say we are building a data platform for a website that sells data engineering books. We want to pull together website traffic logs from our website team, sales from our payments team, and customer support data from our customer success team. This allows us to correlate, for example, how different website features impact customer retention and customer satisfaction. Web telemetry data, sales data, and customer issues data are datasets that we'll bring into our platform.

> **DEFINITION**   A *dataset* is a collection of data. In the case of tabular data, a dataset corresponds to one or more tables.

The website is quite popular, so our website team collects a lot of telemetry datapoints. To scale to the incoming traffic, it uses Azure Data Explorer to quickly store and query the website visits. (We will talk more about Azure Data Explorer later in this chapter.) On the other hand, our payments team deals with a smaller scale and uses an SQL database to store payments data. The customer success team uses a third-party solution, and

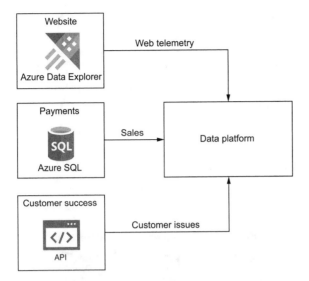

Figure 2.2 Different teams in the organization use different technologies to store data. The website team uses Azure Data Explorer, the payments team uses Azure SQL, while the customer success team uses a third-party solution from which we can get data via an API.

the developers suggest calling an API to retrieve the data in that system. Figure 2.2 shows how all these teams provide data to our data platform.

Let's define each of these environments that store data (website, payments, customer success) as a data fabric.

> **DEFINITION** A *data fabric* is an environment for storing and managing data. From a consumer perspective, it represents a single storage technology—the "fabric" on which the data persists. Examples of data fabrics in Azure are SQL, Azure Data Explorer, Blob Storage, and so forth.

If all the data that your data platform needs resides on the same data fabric, you can count yourself lucky. In most cases, as in our previous example, a data platform needs to stitch together data from multiple fabrics. Different teams across the enterprise might be using different storage solutions, or maybe we are ingesting data from an external company. A large data platform needs to accommodate heterogenous data storage. By *heterogenous data storage*, we mean data spread across multiple data fabrics.

2.1.1 Storing data across multiple data fabrics

We need to embrace having data across multiple storage solutions, not only for ingestion. Different workloads might perform better on different data fabrics as we will see throughout this book. For example, Azure Data Explorer excels at querying millions of rows in a matter of seconds, which identifies anomalies or produces aggregates. Suppose we want to keep a large amount of data for historical reasons or simply to allow other teams within our enterprise to copy the data to their systems. In this case, Azure Data Explorer with its high-performance indexing and caching capabilities might be overkill, so we can park the data in a cheap storage like Azure Data Lake Storage. We will cover these two data fabrics in this chapter.

On the other hand, Cosmos DB, the Azure globally distributed NoSQL solution, provides turnkey *geo-replication* (meaning data can be replicated across different worldwide data centers with a simple configuration change) and retrieves one particular document in milliseconds. This makes it ideal as a storage layer behind a data API (more on this in chapter 11). Figure 2.3 expands on figure 2.2 to show the different data fabrics within our data platform.

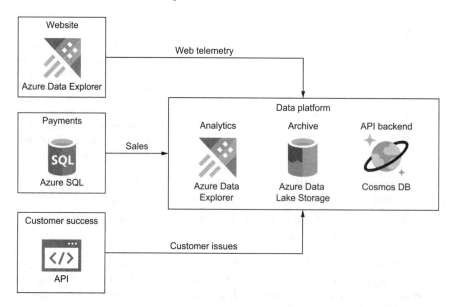

Figure 2.3   Different teams use different data fabrics, even within one data platform. In our data platform, we use different data fabrics for different workloads: Azure Data Explorer for analytics, Azure Data Lake Storage for long-term storage, and Cosmos DB as an API backend.

Again, this is a reference implementation for a data platform storage, but keep in mind, it is one option out of many. Depending on your scenario, your team's needs, skill sets, data volumes, and latency requirements, other solutions might be better suited. For example, Azure Stream Analytics can perform real-time analysis on streaming data, while Azure Databricks can run big data analytics on top of Azure Data Lake Storage.

2.1.2   *Having a single source of truth*

While we should embrace supporting multiple data fabrics, there is value in having a "single source of truth"—one storage solution through which all data in the system flows. Figure 2.4 shows Azure Data Explorer as such a single source of truth for our data platform.

One reason for flowing everything through Azure Data Explorer is that we have all data in our platform in one place, where we can perform analysis across multiple datasets coming from different upstream teams. If data is spread around different services, it becomes harder to build comprehensive views.

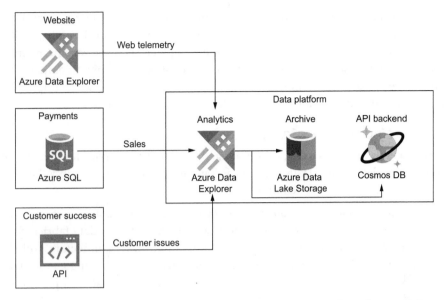

Figure 2.4 Data flows into the data platform to Azure Data Explorer. From there, certain datasets are copied to Azure Data Lake Storage and Cosmos DB. Azure Data Explorer becomes the "single source of truth" for our data platform.

> **DEFINITION** Upstream and downstream are data flow terms that help us understand where a system stands in relation to our data platform. *Upstream systems* are systems from which we ingest data into our platform. *Downstream systems* are systems that consume data from our data platform.

Another advantage of such a setup is that it makes it easier to repair data. In many situations, data will need to be fixed. An example of this might be a data issue upstream. Once the issue is identified and corrected, we need to re-ingest the data. The single source of truth helps because once we know the data has been updated there, the updates flow seamlessly throughout the system. Contrast this with a setup in which various datasets land in different data fabrics. We would have to track the data flow of a single dataset to make sure a fix is propagated correctly.

The trade-off to be aware of is that the more data we move around, the more latency and costs we incur and the more failure points we introduce into the system. For example, if we ingest data from the payments team into Azure Data Explorer, then we copy it to Azure Data Lake Storage, either of the steps could fail; we might run into an issue ingesting into Azure Data Explorer, or we might run into an issue copying into Azure Data Lake Storage. If we ingest the data directly into Azure Data Lake Storage, we have just one failure point, although it will be harder to tie this data together with the data available in Azure Data Explorer. We need to find the right balance between placing the data in the optimal storage solution for the processing we are trying to do and for keeping things at a reasonable cost and complexity level.

Also keep in mind that the setup we are using (Azure Data Explorer as a single source of truth with other storage services downstream) is not the only possible one. Depending on your particular scenario, scale, budget, service-level agreement (SLA), etc., you might end up with a different set of services. Appendix A compares the various Azure services and trade-offs. In the next two sections, we will set up Azure Data Explorer and Azure Data Lake Storage for our data platform.

2.2   *Introducing Azure Data Explorer*

Azure Data Explorer is a fast, fully managed data analytics service for analysis on large volumes of data. Azure Data Explorer is a great choice for storage in a data platform due to some of its unique features:

- *Data ingestion, both by batching and streaming, with up to 200 MB per second per node.* Data can be ingested in numerous ways from different data fabrics. Some fabrics are supported natively by the engine, others offer connectors, and SDKs are available for programmatic ingestion across multiple languages. Data from Azure Event Grids, Event Hubs, or IoT Hubs can be stream ingested in real time.
- *Automatic compression and indexing.* Unlike SQL, we don't need to worry about explicitly creating indexes and tuning those to improve query performance. Azure Data Explorer automatically indexes all data on ingestion.
- *Extremely fast queries.* Billions of rows of data can be queried within seconds, much faster than other solutions at this scale.

Another neat feature of Azure Data Explorer is its support of the MS-TDS protocol. *MS-TDS* stands for Microsoft Tabular Data Stream, the communication protocol used by Microsoft's SQL servers and clients. This allows an SQL client to connect to Azure Data Explorer, and Azure Data Explorer then pretends to be an SQL engine. Data can then be queried using SQL. Unfortunately, Azure Data Explorer had to make some trade-offs to enable such fast ingestion/analytics. Some of the key limitations to be aware of include

- *Azure Data Explorer doesn't update data in place.* Data can be appended to and dropped from a table, but there is no support for modifying rows once ingested.
- *A query can only return a maximum of 500,000 rows and 64 MB.* If either is exceeded, the query fails. There are also limits on how much memory and CPU resources queries can consume. There is also a limit on time; if a query takes more than 4 minutes, the engine aborts it.

Query limits might not seem like a big deal, but a data platform processing huge volumes of data might run into these. There are workarounds, of course, like partitioning the data and improving filtering. These are limitations to keep in mind when deciding whether to use Azure Data Explorer in your data platform. We'll see how we can work around these limitations once we deploy Azure Data Explorer and connect to it.

Figure 2.5 shows the anatomy of an Azure Data Explorer instance. At an infrastructure layer, the cluster runs on a set of virtual machines (VMs) that handle data caching and query execution. Ingested data is stored in Azure Storage. At a logical layer, a cluster has one or more databases. Each database contains tables and functions. Tables store data and have schemas. Functions are queries that we can parameterize and persist in a database so that they can be easily reused.

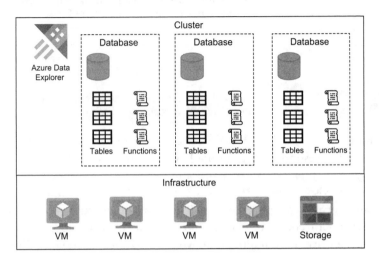

Figure 2.5 At the infrastructure level, an Azure Data Explorer cluster runs on one or more virtual machines (VMs) or nodes and stores data in Azure Storage. At the logical level, an Azure Data Explorer cluster contains databases. Databases contain tables and functions.

Because we'll use Azure Data Explorer as the backbone of our data platform, let's go ahead and deploy an instance. You can also do this using the Azure web UI, but we'll stick to the command line.

2.2.1 Deploying an Azure Data Explorer cluster

We'll use Azure CLI to set up an Azure Data Explorer cluster to use throughout this book. If you'd rather not work through the setup steps in this section, you can run the setup.ps1 script in the Chapter2 folder of this book's GitHub repository and skip to section 2.2.2. I do, however, recommend running the individual commands, as you will gain a good understanding of the required setup steps.

First, we'll install the Kusto extension for Azure CLI, create a resource group, and then create an Azure Data Explorer cluster in that resource group. The following listing shows how.

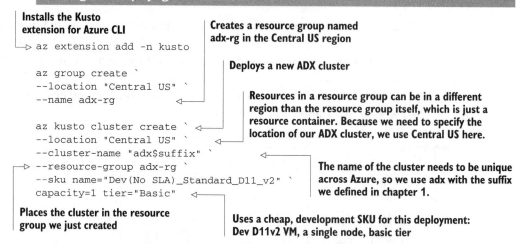

Listing 2.1 Deploying a Kusto cluster

Installs the Kusto extension for Azure CLI

```
az extension add -n kusto

az group create `
--location "Central US" `
--name adx-rg

az kusto cluster create `
--location "Central US" `
--cluster-name "adx$suffix" `
--resource-group adx-rg `
--sku name="Dev(No SLA)_Standard_D11_v2" `
capacity=1 tier="Basic"
```

Creates a resource group named adx-rg in the Central US region

Deploys a new ADX cluster

Resources in a resource group can be in a different region than the resource group itself, which is just a resource container. Because we need to specify the location of our ADX cluster, we use Central US here.

The name of the cluster needs to be unique across Azure, so we use adx with the suffix we defined in chapter 1.

Places the cluster in the resource group we just created

Uses a cheap, development SKU for this deployment: Dev D11v2 VM, a single node, basic tier

Note that running the `az kusto cluster create` command takes some time because it provisions the Azure resources. Azure Data Explorer clusters can be provisioned on different SKUs. A SKU includes the VM size and the number of nodes. This can be adjusted based on needs: the higher the VM size and the higher the number of nodes, the faster we can query and support concurrent access from multiple users. Also keep in mind that Azure CLI comes out of the box with a set of Kusto commands (`az kusto`, etc.), but these are more limited than what the extension provides. The syntax is also different.

> **NOTE** In order for the code examples to work, first run the `az extension add -n kusto` command. At the time of writing, the extension is considered experimental, so when you invoke the command, you'll see a warning. You can ignore this.

Of course, the more performant SKUs are more expensive. For the examples in this book, we will use a low-end dev SKU and a single node. Even so, I suggest stopping the cluster when not working through the examples so it doesn't needlessly eat up your Azure credit. Listing 2.2 shows how to stop and restart the cluster. The `stop` and `start` commands, like the `cluster create` command, take a little bit of time to complete.

Listing 2.2 Stopping and starting an Azure Data Explorer cluster

```
az kusto cluster stop `
--cluster-name "adx$suffix" `
--resource-group adx-rg

az kusto cluster start `
--cluster-name "adx$suffix" `
--resource-group adx-rg
```

Both commands require the cluster name and the resource group.

Let's keep the cluster running for now as we finish the setup, but remember to stop it when not needed. Now, let's create a telemetry database in this cluster, which we'll use to store the telemetry from our website team. The following listing shows how to create a database through the Azure CLI.

Listing 2.3 Creating a database

```
az kusto database create `
--cluster-name "adx$suffix" `
--database-name telemetry `
--resource-group adx-rg `
--read-write-database location="Central US"
```

Supplies the cluster name, the new database name, and the resource group

Creates a read/write database. Another option is a read-only follower database (see sidebar).

Follower databases

Azure Data Explorer supports creating follower databases. A follower database in a cluster has all the data of the leader database in another cluster. This allows data sharing between clusters without requiring any explicit data movement (the data replication is handled by the Azure Data Explorer engine).

The main advantage of this is that it enables different clusters to run queries against the same data using different compute resources. Because data needs to be the same, the follower database is read-only, so only the leader can modify the data.

A leader database can have any number of followers. Leader/follower is implemented at the database level, so two clusters can follow databases from each other. One limitation with this setup is that the cluster following a database must be in the same region as the leader. We'll talk more about follower databases in chapter 11, when we look at data distribution.

The next step is to grant yourself permissions for the cluster. Even if you are the owner of the Azure subscription, which allows you to provision and tear down Azure resources, you won't be able to connect and query the data in the cluster. That's because Azure Data Explorer maintains its own list of permissions (just like an SQL database does).

An Azure account includes an Azure Active Directory tenant. Azure Active Directory is the Microsoft identity solution, which manages the identities of users and applications that can access the Azure resources under the account. Azure Active Directory also allows us to define and manage security groups.

To grant yourself permissions for Azure Data Explorer, you need to supply your principal ID, principal type (User in this case, but it can also be Group or App), and tenant ID. Azure Data Explorer uses this information to look up the principal ID in the appropriate Azure Active Directory instance (based on tenant ID).

Azure Data Explorer has various roles including Administrator (can grant others user permissions), User (read/write access), and Viewer (read-only access). Permissions are set at the database level. We can also assign a couple of special permissions at the cluster level. These propagate to all databases. In our case, let's get the cluster's AllDatabasesAdmin role, which translates to having Administrator rights on all databases. As a resource owner, you have the right to grant yourself Azure Data Explorer–level access. Listing 2.4 shows how to do this.

Listing 2.4   Granting Azure Data Explorer–level permissions

Retrieves your Azure Active Directory object
ID and stores it in the $me variable

```
$me = az ad signed-in-user show --query objectId

$tenantId = az account show --query tenantId

az kusto cluster-principal-assignment create `
--cluster-name "adx$suffix" `
--resource-group adx-rg `
--principal-id $me `
--principal-type User `
--tenant-id $tenantId `
--role AllDatabasesAdmin `
--principal-assignment-name admin1
```

Retrieves the tenant ID
of your Azure account

As with other Kusto commands,
we need to provide the cluster
name and resource group.

The principal ID, type, and tenant
ID together define an identity.

Gives the assignment a
name; in this case, admin1

Grants the AllDatabasesAdmin role

Now that you have permissions to the cluster, you can connect to it using a client. If you prefer the native experience, you can download the Kusto Explorer tool from https:// aka.ms/ke. Otherwise, you can use the web experience at https://dataexplorer.azure .com/ or in the Azure portal. If you use the Azure Data Explorer instance, you should see a Query tab on the left.

2.2.2   *Using Azure Data Explorer*

Assuming you go with the web experience, log in at https://dataexplorer.azure.com/. You will probably have to switch tenants. By default, if you are using a Microsoft identity like an @outlook.com email, you would be using the Microsoft public tenant. Click the top-right corner of the screen on your username or picture, and you should see the menu in figure 2.6.

Click Switch Directory and enter the value $tenantId from listing 2.4. If you have the PowerShell session open, you can type $tenantId to get the value; otherwise, you can call az account show --query tenantId again.

Now Azure Data Explorer can use your identity to connect to the cluster we just created. Click Add Cluster and enter the URI of the cluster we just provisioned in listing 2.2. The URI has the following format:

```
https://<cluster name>.<region>.kusto.windows.net/
```

This is an example of a name that needs to be unique across Azure. You can find this URI in the Azure portal if you navigate to your Azure Data Explorer cluster on the Overview tab.

Figure 2.6 **The top right brings up the identity card. The Switch Directory option lets us switch tenants to our Azure account.**

NOTE Although multiple people can create a resource group named `adx-rg` in different subscriptions, cluster names need to be unique.

Go ahead and connect to the cluster you just provisioned. After connecting, click the telemetry database to select it. You should see something like figure 2.7.

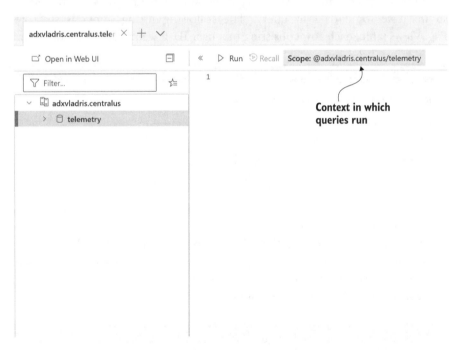

Figure 2.7 **After connecting to the Azure Data Explorer cluster, select the telemetry database. Now you can type queries and commands and execute them. On the top right, called Scope here, we can see the context in which queries will run.**

You need to select the telemetry database because all Azure Data Explorer queries run within a database context. To view the database context, see Scope on the top right of figure 2.7. In my case, Scope is @adxvladris.centralus/telemetry. I used my alias vladris as the $suffix, so my cluster is named adxvladris. The full URI is https://adxvladris.centralus.kusto.windows.net. Your cluster will have a different name and URI.

> **DEFINITION** *Scope* is the context in which a query is executed. When we, for example, create a table, Azure Data Explorer uses this scope to figure out in which database to place the new table.

Let's create a PageViews table to store the website telemetry. This table will have three columns: a User ID column of type `long` (a 64-bit number), a Page column of type `string` that tracks the page visited, and a Timestamp column of type `datetime` that tracks the time of visit. The following listing shows how to create this table.

Listing 2.5 Creating a telemetry table

```
.create table PageViews(UserId: long, Page: string, Timestamp: datetime)
```

Now, let's simulate some telemetry data for our table. In the real world, this data would be ingested into our system from the website team, but we'll add a few rows just so we have some data to query. The following listing appends six rows to the PageViews table, each row consisting of a user ID, a web page, and a timestamp.

Listing 2.6 Simulating telemetry data

```
.ingest inline into table PageViews <|
57000,'/',          datetime(2020-06-30 10:01:05)
12345,'/about/',    datetime(2020-06-30 10:06:00)
57000,'/products/',datetime(2020-06-30 10:07:15)
89943,'/',          datetime(2020-06-30 10:15:43)
89943,'/products',  datetime(2020-06-30 10:21:50)
24566,'/',          datetime(2020-06-30 10:25:37)
```

Don't worry if you are not familiar with the syntax used by Azure Data Explorer. We'll go over a few basics in this chapter, and you can use appendix B as a handy cheat sheet. In general, a query in Azure Data Explorer starts with a table name, and then we use the pipe operator (|) to pipe data to various filters and transformations. For example, we can query our PageViews table to get all distinct users on 2020-06-03 between 10:00 and 10:30 with the query in the next listing.

Listing 2.7 Getting distinct users

```
PageViews              ⟵—— Starts with the PageViews table
| where Timestamp between
```

```
        (datetime(2020-06-30 10:00)
➡    ..datetime(2020-06-30 10:30))        ⟵
┌⟶ | distinct UserId
```

The where operator filters rows to return only those with a Timestamp within our time range.

The distinct operator dedupes user IDs.

Let's try another example: counting the page views by user. The next listing shows how to do that using the `summarize` operator to aggregate the data.

Listing 2.8   Page view count by user

```
PageViews
| where Timestamp between                    Starts with the PageViews table,
    (datetime(2020-06-30 10:00)              where we filter for time range
➡    ..datetime(2020-06-30 10:30))  ⟵
| summarize count() by UserId   ⟵            Uses the summarize operator with the
                                             count() aggregation function by user ID
```

If we want to find the user with the most visits, we can enhance the query in listing 2.8. The following listing shows how this is done.

Listing 2.9   Top user by page views

```
PageViews
| where Timestamp between
    (datetime(2020-06-30 10:00)..datetime(2020-06-30 10:30))
| summarize Visits = count() by UserId    ⟵
┌⟶ | top 1 by Visits
```

We add Visits = before count() to rename the resulting column Visits, which we refer to on the next line.

Picks the top row by the value of Visits

As you can see, Azure Data Explorer borrows a lot of concepts from SQL, but its syntax is closer to stream processing. With stream processing, each step does some filtering, transformation, or aggregation, and then the result is piped to the next step. Data from multiple tables can also be joined or unioned using the `join` and `union` operators.

In this book, we will use Azure Data Explorer as our single source of truth and backend for our analytical workloads. The high-throughput ingestion capabilities and great query performance make Azure Data Explorer an ideal candidate for core data platform storage.

2.2.3   Working around query limits

Before moving on, let's make sure we have the know-how to work around some of the limitations of the platform. While we won't hit these limits with the small examples we'll use throughout this book, you might run into these in the real world. Let's recap the query limits:

- A query can return a maximum of 500,000 rows and 64 MB of data.
- A query can't take more than 4 minutes to execute.
- A query has limits on how much memory and CPU resources it can consume.

As the size of the data grows, we might start hitting these limits. Microsoft documentation covers some of the best practices for running queries; see http://mng.bz/XYZp. Some of these best practices include making sure to apply filters first (using `where`) and putting the table with the fewest rows on the left side of a join.

Partitioning is another strategy to reduce the number of rows we can process with a given query. Azure Data Explorer provides the `hash()` function to help with this. This function takes as its first argument a value, and as an (optional) second argument, a modulo value to apply to the result.

Listing 2.10 shows how we can partition PageViews data based on a hash of the timestamp. In the Azure Data Explorer UI, you can only execute a single query at one time. Depending on where your cursor is, the UI highlights the query it will execute. For this example, highlight the first query and run it, then highlight the second query and run it.

Listing 2.10   Partitioning data using `hash()`

```
PageViews
| where hash(Timestamp, 2) == 0   ◁──┐   The first partition uses hash() by timestamp and
                                          takes only the rows for which hash mod 2 is 0.

PageViews
| where hash(Timestamp, 2) == 1   ◁──┐   The second partition uses hash() by timestamp
                                          and takes only the rows for which hash mod 2 is 1.
```

As the number of rows increases, we can enlarge the mod value of the hash to generate smaller partitions. The hashing function distributes the input values evenly over the output range, so if we pick a column with an even distribution of values, we will get roughly equal partitions.

We can integrate this concept into various other scenarios. For example, if we want to process a large dataset that would exceed the limits, we can partition it and process each partition in sequence. Next, let's go over the second storage solution we will use in our data platform, Azure Data Lake Storage.

2.3   *Introducing Azure Data Lake Storage*

Azure Data Lake Storage (ADLS) is a highly scalable and cost-efficient big data storage solution. Unlike Azure Data Explorer, which we looked at in the previous section, Azure Data Lake Storage deals exclusively with storage. You can think of Azure Data Lake Storage as a filesystem in the cloud. Reading and processing data stored in the data lake requires an additional service to provide compute. Before diving deeper into the capabilities of Azure's data lake solution, let's define data lake.

> **DEFINITION**   A *data lake* is a system or repository of data, usually object blobs or files, stored in its natural, raw format. Data lakes store structured, semi-structured, and unstructured data, which is available for users and other systems to read and process.

As the definition implies, data lakes are meant to store huge amounts of data. In our example, we will look at Azure Data Lake Storage Gen2, the second generation of

Azure Data Lake Storage. Azure Data Lake Storage Gen2 combines the filesystem semantics and granular access control of Azure Data Lake Storage Gen1 with the low-cost hyperscale of Azure Blob Storage.

2.3.1 Creating an Azure Data Lake Storage account

Let's create a resource group called `adls-rg` and then provision an Azure Data Lake Storage account using the Azure CLI. The following listing shows how to do that.

Listing 2.11   Creating an ADLS account

```
az group create `
--location "Central US" `
--name adls-rg

az storage account create `
--name "adls$suffix" `
--resource-group adls-rg `
--enable-hierarchical-namespace true
```

Creates a new resource group for the ADLS account

Enables hierarchical namespaces on the storage account

Another resource that needs a unique URI, so we use $suffix in the name.

Azure Data Lake Storage Gen2 is built on top of the basic Azure Storage account (https://azure.microsoft.com/en-us/services/storage/) with additional filesystem capabilities. We create an Azure Data Lake Storage Gen2 instance the same way as a storage account with an additional setting to enable hierarchical namespaces. We won't talk about Azure Storage here. If you have worked with Azure at all, you are probably familiar with Azure Storage. If not, follow the previous link to learn more about it. Next, we can provision a filesystem in this storage account as the following listing shows.

Listing 2.12   Provisioning a filesystem

```
az storage fs create `
--account-name "adls$suffix" `
--name fs1
```

When running the code in listing 2.12, you might receive a warning that credentials are not being provided in the environment and have to be queried from the service. You can ignore this.

We are all set. We have a storage account and a filesystem in which we can start putting data. The setup is easier than for Azure Data Explorer because we don't need to worry about VM SKUs, node count, and such.

2.3.2 Using Azure Data Lake Storage

Let's upload a file to our storage account. First, confirm that we don't have anything in it by listing the filesystem. The following listing retrieves all files in the `fs1` filesystem of our account.

Listing 2.13   Listing files in a filesystem

```
az storage fs file list `
--account-name "adls$suffix" `
--file-system fs1
```

The response should be an empty array ([]). Now, let's create a file on our machine and upload it to the storage account. The following listing creates a hello.txt file containing "Hello world!" and uses Azure CLI to upload it.

Listing 2.14   Uploading a file to Azure Data Lake Storage

```
echo "Hello world!" | Out-File -FilePath hello.txt     ◁─── In PowerShell, this is how
                                                             we output the result of
az storage fs file upload `                                  the echo command to the
--account-name "adls$suffix" `        Provides the storage   hello.txt file.
--file-system fs1 `                   account and filesystem
--path hello.txt `
--source hello.txt     ◁─────────────  --path is the destination
                                       path under the filesystem.
--source is the source path on our machine.
```

The file should have now made its way to the cloud. If you run the code in listing 2.13 again to retrieve the content of the filesystem, you'll no longer get an empty array. You should see one item with some metadata for the file you just uploaded.

As mentioned, Azure Data Lake Storage is ideal for storing huge amounts of data, and for distributing it downstream and plugging in different compute solutions if needed. The granular access control enables secure data sharing, and virtually all Azure compute services can read from Azure Data Lake Storage.

2.3.3   *Integrating with Azure Data Explorer*

Many Azure services can connect to one another to streamline scenarios. Azure Data Explorer and Azure Data Lake Storage are no exception. We can easily export data from Azure Data Explorer to Azure Data Lake Storage, and we can similarly ingest data from Azure Data Lake Storage into Azure Data Explorer. Not only that, Azure Data Explorer can query data stored in Azure Data Lake Storage directly, without ingesting it first. Performance is obviously not as good as ingested and indexed data, but that capability exists.

Let's export our web telemetry table to Azure Data Lake Storage. First, let's get the URL of our filesystem and an account key, which we'll need to provide to Azure Data Explorer. The following listing shows how to print these to the command line.

Listing 2.15   Getting an ADLS URL and key

```
echo "https://adls$suffix.blob.core.windows.net/fs1/;"     ◁───
                                          Outputs the URL of your ADLS instance, where the format is
az storage account keys list `   ◁───   <account name>.blob.core.windows.net/<filesystem>. Here
--account-name "adls$suffix" `           the account name contains $suffix and the filesystem is fs1.
--query [0].value
                                         The storage account keys list command
The query extracts from the result the value    retrieves the access keys for the account.
of the first access key. Ignore the quotes.
```

The next listing shows how we can export data using the `.export` command. We need to run this in the Azure Data Explorer web UI, not on the command line.

Listing 2.16   Exporting from Azure Data Explorer to Azure Data Lake Storage

Exports data in CSV format. Other supported formats are TSV, JSON, Parquet, and SQL.

You need to provide the URL of your filesystem and the account key as retrieved in listing 2.12.

```
.export to csv (
    h@"https://<Account name>.blob.core.windows.net/fs1/;<Key>"
)
with (
    namePrefix="PageViews",
    extension="csv"
)
<| PageViews
```

Prefixes the output with PageViews. ADX generates one or more files during export.

Uses the .csv extension

Exports the result of a query. Our query returns all the rows from PageViews.

Now you can check that a file prefixed with PageViews and with a .csv extension shows up in Azure Data Lake Storage. You can use the Azure CLI `fs file list` command in listing 2.13, or you can use the Azure portal to browse the resource and explore the storage.

Now, let's flip this around. Let's create an external table in Azure Data Explorer pointing to the Azure Data Lake Storage file. The following listing shows how we can do this in the Azure Data Explorer web UI.

Listing 2.17   Creating an external table in Azure Data Explorer

Creates an external table, PageViewsADLS

Provides a schema that is the same as PageViews, our original table

```
.create external table PageViewsADLS
    (UserId: long, Page: string, Timestamp: datetime)
kind = blob
dataformat = csv (
    h@"https://<Account name>.blob.core.windows.net/fs1/PageViews;<Key>"
)
```

Points to blob storage in CSV format

Appends /PageViews to the storage URL, the prefix for our files. Remember to update the account name and access key.

Now we have a view on top of the Azure Data Lake Storage data that we can query in Azure Data Explorer and, if needed, join with other ingested data. The following listing shows how we can get distinct users from this external table.

Listing 2.18   Getting distinct users from Azure Data Lake Storage

```
external_table("PageViewsADLS")
| where Timestamp between
    (datetime(2020-06-30 10:00)..datetime(2020-06-30 10:30))
| distinct UserId
```

The difference between listing 2.7 and this one is that we query the external table PageViewsADLS instead of the native PageViews table.

Figure 2.8 shows our data flow. The PageViews table is exported to Azure Data Lake Storage as one or more CSV files. The external table, PageViewsADLS, reads directly from the CSV files when queried.

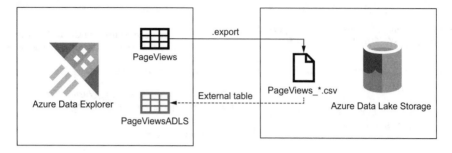

Figure 2.8   We export the PageViews table from Azure Data Explorer to Azure Data Lake Storage using `.export`. We then create an external table, PageViewsADLS, that reads data directly from the Azure Data Lake Storage PageViews file(s).

Azure Data Explorer can also export data and define external tables in SQL. Again, query performance is significantly impacted in these situations because data is not ingested and indexed. It is a useful feature nonetheless.

Azure Data Explorer can also continuously export data to an external table. We won't get into the details of that here, but know that you can set things up so that data is automatically published as it is being ingested. Now that we have deployed two storage solutions, we'll spend the remainder of the chapter talking about ingesting datasets into our platform.

2.4   Ingesting data

In this section, we'll look at the following aspects of data ingestion, frequency and load type, and how we can handle corrupted data. We'll stick to Azure Data Explorer for our examples, but keep in mind that the same concepts apply regardless of the data fabric we use. Let's start by looking at the frequency with which we ingest data.

2.4.1   Ingestion frequency

Frequency defines how often we ingest a given dataset. This can range from continuous ingestion for streaming data to yearly ingestion with a dataset that we only need to update once a year. For example, our website team produces web telemetry that we can, if we want, ingest in real time. If our analytics scenarios include some real-time or near-real-time processing, we can bring the data into our data platform as it is being generated. Figure 2.9 shows this streaming ingestion setup.

The Azure Event Hub is a service that can receive and process millions of events per second. An event contains some data payload sent by the client to the event hub. A high-traffic website, for example, can treat each page view as an event and pass the user ID, URL, and timestamp to the event hub. From there, data can be routed to various

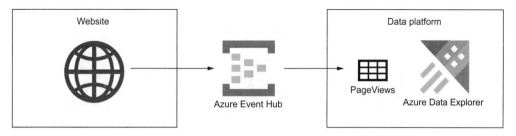

Figure 2.9 As users visit website pages, each visit is sent as an event to an Azure Event Hub. Then Azure Data Explorer ingests the data into the PageViews table in real time.

other services. In our case, it can be ingested in Azure Data Explorer in real time. Another option if we don't have any real-time requirements is to ingest the data on some regular cadence; for example, every midnight we load the logs for the day. Figure 2.10 shows this alternative setup.

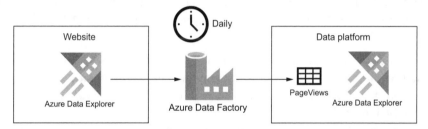

Figure 2.10 Logs get copied from the website's dedicated Azure Data Explorer cluster to the data platform's Azure Data Explorer cluster using an Azure Data Factory. Copying the data happens on a daily basis.

In this case, the website team stores its logs in a dedicated Azure Data Explorer cluster. The cluster only stores data for the past 30 days because it is only used to measure the website performance and to debug issues. Because we want to keep data longer for analytics, we want to copy it to our cluster and preserve it there.

Azure Data Factory (ADF) is the Azure ETL service that enables serverless data integration and transformation. We can use Azure Data Factory to coordinate when and where data gets moved. In our case, we copy the logs of the previous day every night and append those to our PageViews table. We will cover Azure Data Factory in much more detail in chapter 4 when we discuss orchestration.

Let's take another example: the sales data from our payments team. We use this data to measure revenue and other business metrics. Because not all transactions are settled, it doesn't make sense to ingest this data daily. Our payments team curates this data and officially publishes the financials for the previous month on the first day of each month. This is an example of a monthly dataset (one we ingest once it becomes available; in our scenario, on the first of each month). Figure 2.11 shows this ingestion.

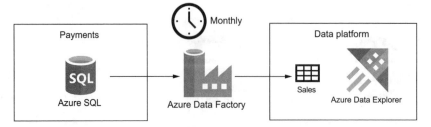

Figure 2.11   Sales data gets copied from the payments team's Azure SQL to our Azure Data Explorer cluster on a monthly cadence.

This is similar to our previous Azure Data Factory ingestion of page view logs, the difference being the data source. In this case, we ingest data from Azure SQL, and the ingestion cadence is monthly instead of daily. Let's define the cadence of when a dataset is ready for ingestion as its grain.

> **DEFINITION**   The *grain* of a dataset specifies the frequency at which new data is ready for consumption. This can be continuous for streaming data or hourly, daily, weekly, and so on.

We ingest a dataset with a weekly grain on a weekly cadence. The grain is usually defined by the upstream team producing the dataset. Partial data might be available earlier, but the upstream team can usually tell us when the dataset is complete and ready to be ingested.

While some data (like the logs in our example) can be ready in real time or at a daily grain, there are datasets that get updated once a year. For example, businesses use fiscal years for financial reporting, budgeting, and so on. These datasets only change once a year. Another ingestion parameter is the type of data load.

2.4.2   Load type

Outside of streaming data, where data gets ingested as it is produced, we have two options for updating a dataset in our system. We can perform a full load or an incremental load.

> **DEFINITION**   A *full load* means we fully refresh the dataset, discarding our current version and replacing it with a new version of the data. An *incremental load* means we append data to the dataset. We start with the current version and periodically enhance it with additional data.

For example, our customer success team has a list of active customer issues. As these issues get resolved and new issues appear, we can perform a full load when we ingest the active issues into our system. The usual pattern is to ingest the updated data into a staging table, then swap it with the destination table as figure 2.12 shows.

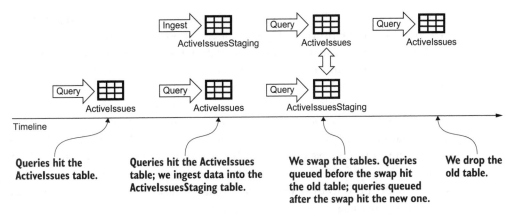

Figure 2.12   Queries run against the ActiveIssues table as we ingest the data into the ActiveIssuesStaging table. Then we swap the two tables. Queries already started before the swap run against the old table; queries started after the swap run against the new table. Finally, we can drop the old table.

Listing 2.19 shows how we would do this in Azure Data Explorer. Highlight each command in turn and run it.

Listing 2.19   Performing a full load of active customer issues

Maintains an ActiveIssues table with the customer ID,
issue type, and timestamp for when an issue opens

```
.create table ActiveIssues(CustomerId: long,
    IssueType: string, Timestamp: datetime)

.create table ActiveIssuesStaging(CustomerId: long,
    IssueType: string, Timestamp: datetime)

.ingest inline into table ActiveIssuesStaging <|
20044,'Login issue',    datetime(2020-06-30 11:05:03),
57403,'Refund request', datetime(2020-06-30 16:32:10),
63911,'Login issue',    datetime(2020-06-30 19:26:42)

.rename tables ActiveIssues=ActiveIssuesStaging,
    ActiveIssuesStaging=ActiveIssues

.drop table ActiveIssuesStaging
```

The first step in a full load creates a staging table. We call ours ActiveIssuesStaging.

Ingests data into the staging table from upstream, but for this example, we generate a few rows inline.

Once we populate the staging table, we swap it with the destination table.

Drops the staging table

Most storage solutions offer some transactional guarantees on renaming tables to support scenarios like this. This means if someone is running a query against the ActiveIssues table, there is no chance of the query failing due to the table not being found or of the query getting rows from both the old and the new tables. Queries running in parallel with a rename are guaranteed to hit either the old or the new table. Now, let's look at the other type of data load—incremental.

Let's take as an example our PageViews table. Because the website team only keeps logs for 30 days and we want to maintain a longer record when we ingest the data into our system, we can't fully refresh the PageViews table. Instead, every night we take the page view logs of the previous day and append those to the table.

One challenge of incremental loads is to figure out exactly what data is missing (the data we need to append) and what data we already have. We don't want to append data we already have as it would create duplicates.

There are a couple of ways we can go about determining the delta between upstream and our storage. The simplest one is contractual: the upstream team guarantees that data will be ready at a certain time or date. For example, the payments team promises that the sales data for the previous month will be ready on the first of each month, by noon. Then, say, on July 1st, we load all sales data with a timestamp for June and append it to the existing sales data we have in our system. In this case, the delta is the June sales.

Another way to determine the delta is to keep track on our side of what is the last row we ingested and only ingest from upstream data after this row. This is also known as a *watermark*. Whatever is under the watermark is data we already have in our system. Upstream can have data above the watermark, which we need to ingest.

Depending on the dataset, keeping track of the watermark can be simple or complex. In the simplest case, if the data has a column where values always increase, we can see what the latest value is in our dataset and ask upstream for data with values greater than our latest. For example, if page view data contains a timestamp and the timestamp always increases, we can get the last timestamp from our system using the query in the following listing.

Listing 2.20 Determining the watermark for page view data

```
PageViews                                    The max() aggregation function returns
| summarize max(Timestamp)          ◁─┘      the maximum value across the column.
```

We can then ask for page views with a timestamp greater than the watermark when we append data in our system. Other examples of ever-increasing values are auto-incrementing columns, like the ones we can define in SQL.

Things get more complicated if there is no easy ordering of the data from which we can determine our watermark. In that case, the upstream system needs to keep track of what data it already gave us and hand us a watermark object. When we hand back the object, upstream can determine what is the delta we need. Fortunately, this scenario is less common in the big data world. We usually have simpler ways to determine delta, like timestamps and auto-incrementing IDs.

What happens, though, when a data issue makes its way into the system? For example, we got the sales data from our payments team on July 1st, but the next day we get notified that there was an issue; somehow a batch of transactions is missing. They fixed the dataset upstream, but we already loaded the erroneous data into our platform. Let's talk about restatements and reloads as a way to resolve this.

2.4.3 Restatements and reloads

In a big data system, it is inevitable that at some point data gets corrupted or is incomplete. The owners of the data fix the problem, then issue a restatement.

> **DEFINITION** A *restatement* of a dataset is a revision and re-release of a dataset after one or more issues were identified and fixed.

Once data is restated, we need to reload it into our data platform. This is obviously much simpler if we perform a full load for the dataset. In that case, we simply discard the corrupted data previously loaded and replace it with the restated data.

Things get more complicated if we load this dataset incrementally. In that case, we need to drop only the corrupted slice of the data and reload that from upstream. Let's see how we can do this in Azure Data Explorer.

Azure Data Explorer stores data in extents. An *extent* is a shard of data, a piece of a table that contains some of its rows. Extents are immutable. Once written, they are never modified. When we ingest data, one or more extents are created. Periodically, Azure Data Explorer merges extents to improve query performance. This is handled by the engine in the background. Figure 2.13 shows how extents are created during ingestion, then merged by Azure Data Explorer.

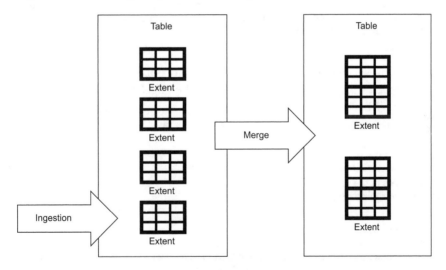

Figure 2.13 Extents are created during ingestion, then merged by Azure Data Explorer to improve query performance.

While we can't modify an extent, we can drop it. Dropping an extent removes all data stored within. Extents support tagging, which enables us to attach metadata to them. A best practice is to add the `drop-by` tag to extents on creation. This tag has special meaning for Azure Data Explorer: it only merges extents with the same `drop-by` tag. This ensures that all data ingested into an extent with a `drop-by` tag is never grouped with data ingested with another `drop-by` tag. Figure 2.14 shows how we can use this tag to ensure data doesn't get mixed, and then we can drop extents with that tag to remove corrupted data.

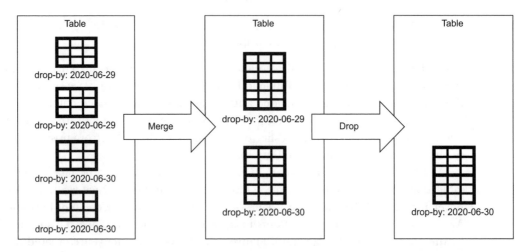

Figure 2.14 We ingest two extents with the `drop-by` tag `2020-06-29` and two extents with `drop-by` tag `2020-06-30`. These get merged into one extent with the `drop-by` tag `2020-06-29` and one extent with the `drop-by` tag `2020-06-30`. We can ask Azure Data Explorer to drop all extents tagged with `2020-06-29` to remove a part of the data.

Let's see how we can do the extent tagging and dropping in the Azure Data Explorer UI. Listing 2.21 ingests a few more rows into the PageViews table. This time we add a `drop-by` tag. Each row consists of a user ID, a web page, and a timestamp. We can inspect our extents and drop them based on this tag.

Listing 2.21   Tagging extents on ingestion and then dropping them

**Ingests more rows in the PageViews table,
but this time, we apply a drop-by tag.**

```
.ingest inline into table PageViews with (tags =
  '["drop-by:2020-06-29"]') <|
89943,'/',          datetime(2020-06-29 11:09:45),
89943,'/about/',    datetime(2020-06-29 11:09:52),
89943,'/products/',datetime(2020-06-29 11:10:16),
89943,'/',          datetime(2020-06-29 11:12:05),

PageViews    ◄——— Querying PageViews should now show the newly ingested rows.

.show table PageViews extents    ◄——┐ Shows the data extents ADX created
                                     │ with the .show table extents command
.show table PageViews extents where
tags has "drop-by:2020-06-29"    ◄——┘
                                     Queries the extents and filters by a given tag

.drop extents <|
```

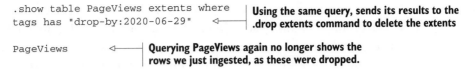

```
.show table PageViews extents where
tags has "drop-by:2020-06-29"
```
Using the same query, sends its results to the .drop extents command to delete the extents

```
PageViews
```
Querying PageViews again no longer shows the rows we just ingested, as these were dropped.

The `drop-by` tag ensures that extents with different values for the tag never get merged together, so we don't risk dropping more data than what we want dropped. The value of the tag is arbitrary; we can use anything, but a good practice is to use an ingestion timestamp. For example, when we load data on 2020-06-29, we use the `drop-by:2020-06-29` tag. If we later learn that the data we loaded is corrupt and upstream restates the data, we can drop the extents containing corrupted data and re-ingest from upstream to repair our dataset.

Obviously, this process is more complicated than if we do a full load of the data every time. In general, if we can afford a full load, we should use that. Maintenance-wise, it is a much simpler approach. Sometimes, though, this is impossible. For example, if we want to maintain page view logs beyond the 30-day retention period upstream has, we can't keep reloading the data. Other times, full load is just too expensive; we end up moving the same gigabytes of data again and again with minor differences. For these situations, we have to look at an incremental load and manage the additional complexity.

Now that we have storage figured out for our data platform, we'll talk about DevOps in the next chapter. We'll bring the great engineering practices from software engineering to the world of data science.

Summary

- A data fabric is an environment like SQL, Azure Data Explorer, or Azure Data Lake Storage for storing and managing data.
- We should embrace working with multiple data fabrics, both from an ingestion perspective and for internal storage inside our data platform.
- Even when using multiple data fabrics, it's good to have a single source of truth—one data fabric in which we ingest everything. This helps with both analytics, where we want to correlate different datasets, and with repairs, in case the data is corrupted.
- Azure Data Explorer is a great option for a data platform core storage solution as it is optimized for quickly ingesting huge volumes of data and querying that in seconds.
- Azure Data Lake Storage is a cheap, hyper-scalable solution for storing data. The service doesn't offer any compute capabilities, but most other Azure services including Azure Data Explorer can connect to it.
- We can ingest data continuously (streaming) or at a certain regular cadence (daily, weekly, monthly, or yearly).

- When we ingest data, we can either discard our existing data and perform a full reload, or we can perform an incremental load of only the data we are missing.
- It is inevitable for some data to get corrupted. Once repaired upstream, we need a way to discard the corrupted data from our system and reload the updated data.

DevOps

This chapter covers

- Bringing DevOps to data engineering
- Introducing Azure DevOps
- Deploying infrastructure
- Deploying analytics

This key chapter puts the "engineering" in data engineering. DevOps practices allow us to build reliable, reproducible systems. One of the principles you will see repeated throughout the book is tracking everything in source control and deploying everything automatically. Figure 3.1 highlights the layer we will cover in this chapter.

In this chapter, we will talk about DevOps and how it became an industry standard for software engineering. We'll see what learning we can take from that and apply it to the world of data and data platforms. We'll explore Azure DevOps, the Azure offering in the DevOps space, which provides an integrated, one-stop-shop service for all our needs.

First, we will apply DevOps to infrastructure and see how we can deploy Azure Data Explorer (ADX) automatically from source control, including all the configuration we went through in the previous chapter. Next, we will apply DevOps to analytics and

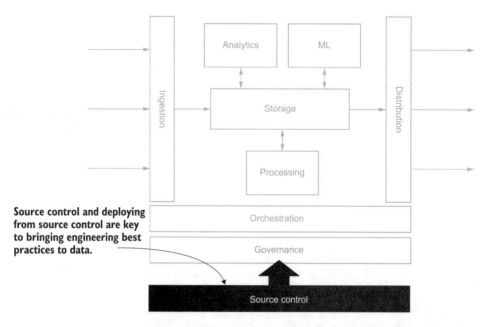

Figure 3.1   Tracking everything in source control and automatically deploying is foundational to a robust system.

see how we can deploy tables and queries from source control. Let's start with a discussion on DevOps: what it is and why it matters.

3.1   What is DevOps?

The standard across the software industry used to be for the development team (Dev) to implement services and for the operations team (Ops) to deploy them in the production environment and then monitor them. The thinking behind this was that the production environment needed to be locked down, and operational concerns like provisioning machines, configuration, and monitoring required a different set of skills than the design and development of services. DevOps, on the other hand, lets software engineers take charge of the end-to-end process.

> **DEFINITION**   A *DevOps team* owns their solution end to end, from requirements gathering and design through development and testing to deployment, monitoring, and fixing production issues.

Two major shifts in the industry caused the emergence of DevOps. The first is the broad adoption of agile software development practices, which aim to optimize the time it takes for software delivery, from requirements to production. DevOps removes the coordination overhead between the two teams and the issues this overhead produces. For example, a deployment fails and the developer says, "It works on my machine." Then the developer works with the ops counterpart to identify the issue.

The second major shift is the move to the cloud. This can be a cloud offering from one of the major providers like Microsoft or Amazon, but it can also be a private data center run by a company. The key change is the move from individual servers, which require a lot of maintenance and attention, to infrastructure that can be provisioned and deprovisioned on demand. This concept is also known as "cattle, not pets." Pets have names and require a lot of attention, and losing one is tragic. All cattle, on the other hand, receive the same treatment, and losing one is no big deal.

The shift to the cloud created a renewed focus on automation for deployment and configuration, which is an invaluable tool in the DevOps toolbox. The infrastructure-as-code process of managing and provisioning infrastructure makes deployment and operational concerns much more like software development. Some of the key software tools that enable DevOps follow:

- *Source code management*—Includes source control, code navigation and search, and code review tools
- *Build automation*—An environment to host and execute builds for continuous integration, test execution, and status
- *Packaging*—Facilitates versioning and packaging build artifacts
- *Release automation*—Pipelines for deploying services to various environments (preproduction, production), either continuously (continuous delivery), on some schedule, or on demand
- *Monitoring and alerting*—Tools to collect telemetry from running services and, in case of failure detection, to alert owners of a potential outage

We'll cover source code management and release automation in this chapter, and monitoring and alerting as part of orchestration in chapter 4. We don't have any code to build (codeless infrastructure), so we'll skip build automation and packaging.

3.1.1 DevOps in data engineering

A key premise of this book is that the data engineering discipline brings the same engineering processes and rigor found in software engineering to the realm of data science. We can take the lessons learned from software engineering and the best practices developed there and apply these to data and data platforms.

Let's say we want to produce a report for monthly active users on our website. Our website telemetry is stored in Azure Data Explorer. The first question we need to ask is whether the Azure Data Explorer cluster and database can be created automatically or only manually through the Azure Portal UI or Azure CLI. How easy would it be to recreate this setup if, for example, we need to deploy in a different region or a different subscription? This is the first part of DevOps for data engineering—DevOps for the infrastructure. Figure 3.2 shows how we would deploy infrastructure from source control. We'll cover DevOps Repos and Pipelines in the following sections.

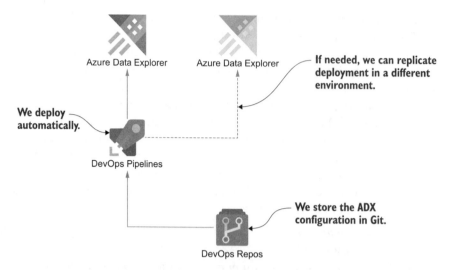

Figure 3.2   We store our configuration in DevOps Repos (Git) and deploy using a pipeline. If needed, we can replicate the deployment in a different environment.

Next, let's say Mary, a data scientist on the team, produces the following Azure Data Explorer query, which looks at the number of page views during the past month. The following listing shows the query.

Listing 3.1   Total page views over the past month

```
PageViews
| where Timestamp > startofmonth(now())
| count
```

If you run the query in listing 3.1, you won't get any rows because, in the previous chapter, we just ingested a few rows of dummy data into the PageViews table; in fact, all of the rows for June, 2020. In the real world, a query like this would return thousands or millions of rows. For the purposes of our chapter, the actual result of the query is not important.

Mary uses this query to produce a report, but she realizes the numbers are slightly off. It turns out there is some test traffic that is automatically generated by the known user ID 12345. It turns out the website team always tags test traffic as coming from user 12345, which we shouldn't count as page views (after all, this is not a real website user). She updates the query to ignore the test traffic as the following listing shows.

Listing 3.2   Updated total page views over the past month

```
PageViews
| where Timestamp > startofmonth(now())
    and UserId != 12345          ←
| count                              Filters out the known test user ID 12345
```

Now Mary can run this query any time and report on the total number of page views the website sees. From a pure analytics point of view, we can say we're done. Mary produced her report. From an engineering rigor point of view, we need to consider a few more scenarios.

What happens if Mary is out on vacation when this report is needed? Will someone else produce the report? Would they know to filter out the test traffic? If they get the query handed over, would they know what ID 12345 is?

We can store this query in source control, such that everyone on the team can access it. The commit history should log the addition of the ID 12345 filter with an explanation of why it is needed. We can also deploy this query by packaging it into an Azure Data Explorer function and storing it inside the database itself. Figure 3.3 extends figure 3.2 and shows how we can deploy, not only infrastructure, but also analytics from source control.

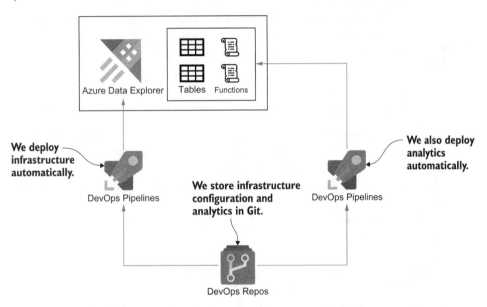

Figure 3.3 We don't deploy only the Azure Data Explorer cluster automatically, we do the same for table schemas and queries (packaged as functions).

It might seem like a lot of extra effort, but we know from software engineering the value of automation. It might be easier to, for example, test some code manually once or twice, but with a small investment in test automation, we save a lot of time in the long run. We can run tests much more frequently and catch issues as early as they appear, and that ends up saving us a lot of manual testing time.

The same goes for the page view count scenario: yes, setting up a deployment pipeline takes a bit of work, but then we can reuse it for all sorts of other queries and reports. It also helps to avoid issues like having a single person who knows how to produce a certain report and that person is currently unavailable.

A big part of data engineering is operationalizing data science and automating tasks like reporting, analytics, and machine learning at scale and with high quality standards like we would expect from a software system. Let's now look at the technology our reference implementation uses to achieve this, Azure DevOps.

3.2 *Introducing Azure DevOps*

Azure DevOps is the Microsoft DevOps solution that we will use throughout this book. It includes

- A set of tracking and project management features, which are worth mentioning but will not be the focus of this book.
- Azure Pipelines, which we will use to automate build, validation, and deployment
- Source control, also known as Azure Repos, which includes Git hosting, code review, and policies.

  Note that we can just as well use GitHub, which also integrates with Azure Pipelines, but we'll stick to Azure Repos for convenience so we can keep all DevOps concerns in one place.
- Azure Artifacts, which is an artifact repository where we can package and store build outputs.
- Many other features, including a hosted Wiki, dashboarding capabilities, and so on.

This book is about what engineering practices like DevOps bring to the realm of data. These practices can be applied to any data platform, on any cloud, and using any DevOps tools. Azure DevOps is not the only solution for any of the topics covered in this book, but we must choose some concrete implementation to provide practical examples.

Because we will be working with the Azure cloud, Azure DevOps is the best solution as it provides the best integration. You can start a free account for Azure DevOps at the following URL: https://azure.microsoft.com/en-us/services/devops/. You should see something like that shown in figure 3.4.

Click Start Free and set up your organization. Make sure you are authenticated against your tenant so the DevOps service is provisioned under your Azure account. Like we did in chapter 2 for the Azure Data Explorer web UI, choose Switch Directory if needed.

The free tier includes all we need to work through the examples in this book, including source control and hosted Azure Pipelines. Once you start, a DevOps organization is provisioned for you. Click Organization Settings and change the name to `dataengineering-$suffix`, where `$suffix` is the variable we set up in the PowerShell profile to ensure uniqueness. As a reminder, we did this in chapter 1, section 1.4.4, where we added the following line to our PowerShell profile: `$suffix = "<unique suffix>"`. The name of the organization becomes part of the URL, so it needs to be globally unique. We'll use this organization in the following examples.

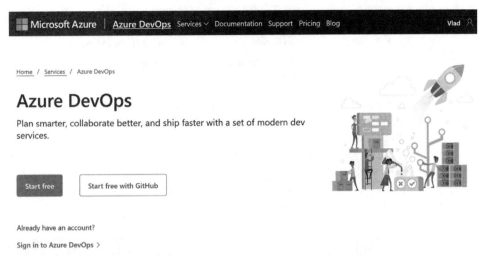

Figure 3.4   Signing up for Azure DevOps

Let's also generate a personal access token so we can log into DevOps from Azure CLI. Click the User Settings icon at the top right and select Personal Access Tokens, as figure 3.5 shows.

Generate a token with Full Access scope and save the token value. While Azure DevOps provides a great UI to create and configure everything we need, in the spirit of DevOps (and to keep things concise), we will use the command line to set things up via scripts. I encourage you to explore the UI and the DevOps documentation at https://docs.microsoft.com/en-us/azure/devops.

3.2.1   *Using the az azure-devops extension*

Most Azure services are part of the base Azure CLI installation, but some other services, like DevOps, are bundled into additional extensions. To interact with Azure DevOps from the command line, you need to install the azure-devops extension for `az` and log in. Listing 3.3

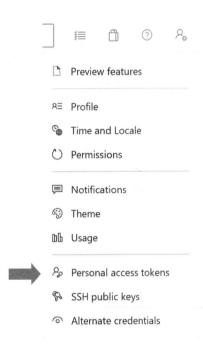

Figure 3.5   Generating a personal access token from the User Settings menu

shows how to do this. After running `az devops login`, you will be prompted for a token. Use the personal access token value you just generated.

Listing 3.3   Installing the azure-devops extension

```
az extension add --name azure-devops     ⊲——— Installs the extension

az devops login  ⊲——┤ Logs in to Azure DevOps by providing
                     │ the personal access token value
```

Alternately, instead of using az devops login and pasting the personal access token, you can put the token in the AZURE_DEVOPS_EXT_PAT environment variable. In PowerShell, that is $env:AZURE_DEVOPS_EXT_PAT = 'xxxxxxxx'.

Now, you can connect to your Azure DevOps organization. The first thing you need to do is to create a new project. A *project* is a container within an organization that includes source code repositories, pipelines, work tracking, and so on. The following listing creates a new project named DE.

Listing 3.4   Creating a new project within the organization

```
az devops project create `
--organization "https://dev.azure.com/dataengineering-$suffix" `
--name DE
```

You should see a JSON object on the console, which contains the details of the newly created organization. You can also visit the organization's URL to see the newly created project and explore the UI. Let's also save the organization and project as defaults so we don't have to repeat this in future commands. The following listing shows how to do this.

Listing 3.5   Configuring organization and project defaults

```
az devops configure `
--defaults `
organization="https://dev.azure.com/dataengineering-$suffix" `
project=DE `
```

All az devops commands need to run against an organization and project. Having defaults configured makes the extension use these if none are provided. This saves us a lot of extra typing.

Now we have a DevOps solution set up through which we can support source control and automated deployments. Throughout the rest of this chapter, we will fully implement our Azure Data Explorer infrastructure and page view count example as a DevOps-enabled solution.

3.3   *Deploying infrastructure*

First, let's make sure our infrastructure can be deployed from Git. Our Azure Data Explorer cluster was originally set up using Azure CLI. We will look at setting up an automated deployment from the Azure Resource Manager templates stored in Git, using Azure Pipelines. I'll introduce all of these in the following sections.

DEFINITION The *Azure Resource Manager (ARM)* is the deployment and management service for Azure. It provides a management layer that enables you to create, update, and delete resources in your Azure account.

As we saw in chapter 1, we have multiple ways to interact with Azure: we can use the Azure portal UI, the Azure SDKs for our language of choice, Azure CLI, and so on. All these ultimately end up calling the Azure REST API, behind which sits the Azure Resource Manager. Figure 3.6 shows the stack for interacting with Azure.

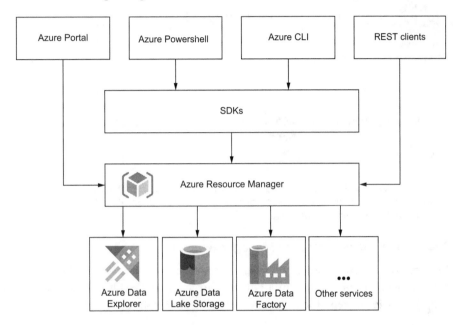

Figure 3.6 Azure Portal, Azure PowerShell, Azure CLI, all SDKs, and any other REST clients go through the Azure Resource Manager in order to provision and configure any resources. The Azure Resource Manager uses templates to declare and deploy infrastructure.

DEFINITION Azure Resource Manager *templates* are JSON files that define the infrastructure and configuration of Azure resources. The templates use a declarative syntax, where you specify the resources to deploy and the properties of those resources.

Azure Resource Manager templates can get complex, so you wouldn't usually create them "by hand." You either get them already set up by someone else, or you initially deploy your resources interactively using the Azure Portal or CLI, and then export the corresponding Azure Resource Manager template. Exporting the template for a resource means Azure generates the corresponding JSON to describe an existing deployment. Figure 3.7 shows the typical flow.

We'll do just that for our adx-rg resource group. (We already deployed it in chapter 2.) Next, we'll export the Azure Resource Manager template, store it in source control, and create a deployment pipeline.

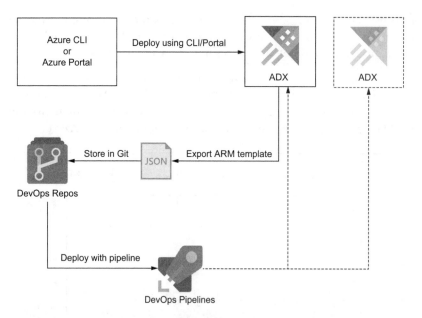

Figure 3.7 We'll create the original deployment via Azure CLI or Azure Portal. Then, we'll export the Azure Resource Manager template and store it in Git. From there, we can recreate the deployment using Azure Pipelines.

3.3.1 Exporting an Azure Resource Manager template

Let's export the Azure Resource Manager template for our Azure Data Explorer cluster deployment and store it in a Git repo in our new DevOps instance. Let's start by setting up the Git repo locally as the following listing shows.

Listing 3.6   Initializing a Git repo

```
mkdir DE       Creates a new DE folder
cd DE          and navigates to it

git init    ⟵  Initializes a Git repository in this folder
```

When we create a new Azure DevOps project like we did in section 3.2 with the DE project, it comes with a default Git repository with the same name (DE in our case). We can create any number of other repositories, but for our infrastructure deployment, we'll use the default one.

Let's create an Azure Resource Manager subfolder and use Azure CLI to export the Azure Resource Manager template and write it to a file in this subfolder. Make sure the Azure Data Explorer cluster is running when exporting the template, otherwise Azure Resource Manager won't be able to retrieve all the information. The following listing shows how to save an Azure Resource Manager template to a file.

Listing 3.7   Exporting an Azure Resource Manager template

Creates a new ARM subfolder for storing ARM templates

Exports an ARM template for a resource group

```
mkdir ARM

az group export `
--name adx-rg `
--include-parameter-default-value `
 | Out-File ./ARM/adx-rg.json
```

Names the adx-rg resource group that contains our ADX deployment

Makes the existing values of the template parameters defaults. More about this when we look at the exported ARM template.

Pipes output to a file; here we pipe it to adx-rg.json in the ARM folder.

Let's open the JSON file and look at its content. You can use your favorite text editor for this or just print the file to the terminal. The next listing shows the JSON file.

Listing 3.8   Contents of adx-rg.json

These properties show the schema of the deploymentTemplate.json file and its version.

```
{
  "$schema": "https://schema.management.azure.com/schemas/2015-01-01/
  deploymentTemplate.json#",
  "contentVersion": "1.0.0.0",
  "parameters": {
    "Clusters_adxvladris_name": {
      "defaultValue": "adxvladris",
      "type": "String"
    }
  },
  "resources": [
    {
      "apiVersion": "2020-02-15",
      "location": "Central US",
      "name":
"[parameters('Clusters_adxvladris_name')]",
      "properties": {
        "enableDiskEncryption": false,
        "enableStreamingIngest": false,
        "trustedExternalTenants": [
          {
            "value": "*"
          }
        ]
      },
      "sku": {
        "capacity": 1,
        "name": "Dev(No SLA)_Standard_D11_v2",
        "tier": "Basic"
      },
      "type": "Microsoft.Kusto/Clusters"
    },
    {
```

Defines the template parameter for the cluster name, showing my $suffix value; yours will look different. Because we opted to export defaults, the existing name is provided as a default value.

Deploys our first resource, the ADX cluster. The template specifies the name as a parameter and a set of other properties.

This is the SKU we specified when we created the cluster using Azure CLI.

The resource type; here a Kusto cluster (remember, Kusto is the code name for ADX).

```
      "apiVersion": "2020-02-15",
      "dependsOn": [
        "[resourceId('Microsoft.Kusto/Clusters',
    ➡ parameters('Clusters_adxvladris_name'))]"  ⬅
      ],
      "kind": "ReadWrite",
      "location": "Central US",
      "name": "[concat(parameters('Clusters_adxvladris_name'),
    ➡ '/telemetry')]",
      "properties": {},
      "type": "Microsoft.Kusto/Clusters/Databases"
    },
    {

      "apiVersion": "2020-02-15",
      "dependsOn": [
        "[resourceId('Microsoft.Kusto/Clusters',
    ➡ parameters('Clusters_adxvladris_name'))]"
      ],
      "name": "[concat(parameters('Clusters_adxvladris_name'),
    ➡ '/e0bd2cb3-cb3e-4942-82a3-76e67f739905')]",
      "properties": {
        "principalId": "vladris@outlook.com",
        "principalType": "User",
        "role": "AllDatabasesAdmin",
        "tenantId":
    ➡ "0b3ff2b5-20bc-4f48-9455-da8535828246"
      },
      "type": "Microsoft.Kusto/Clusters/
    ➡ PrincipalAssignments"
    },
    {
      "apiVersion": "2020-02-15",
      "dependsOn": [
        "[resourceId('Microsoft.Kusto/Clusters/Databases',
    ➡ parameters('Clusters_adxvladris_name'), 'telemetry')]",
        "[resourceId('Microsoft.Kusto/Clusters',
    ➡ parameters('Clusters_adxvladris_name'))]"
      ],
      "name": "[concat(parameters('Clusters_adxvladris_name'),
    ➡ '/telemetry/9a1512eb-8dd8-4af9-bf18-43a910bc40ab')]",
      "properties": {
        "principalId": "vladris@outlook.com",
        "principalType": "User",
        "role": "Admin",
        "tenantId": "0b3ff2b5-20bc-4f48-9455-da8535828246"
      },
      "type": "Microsoft.Kusto/Clusters/Databases/
    ➡ PrincipalAssignments"
    }
  ],
  "variables": {}
}
```

Specifies the Kusto cluster database as the resource type

This resource depends on the previous one. It tells ARM to deploy this once, when the dependency is ready.

The telemetry database, a read/write database. The name is specified in terms of the cluster name parameter by concatenating it with /telemetry.

Specifies AllDatabaseAdmin as the resource type, which we granted ourselves in the previous chapter. In your template, principalId and tenantId will be different.

Specifies the database-level principal assignment as a last resource. Because I have the cluster level AllDatabasesAdmin permission, I'm the admin for the telemetry database.

You can see why we wouldn't author such a template by hand in a text editor. That being said, it's good to understand its structure because it is the preferred method to deploy infrastructure automatically. Let's commit it to Git and push it to our DevOps remote repository. The following listing shows the steps for that.

> **Listing 3.9 Pushing adx-rg.json to the DevOps remote repository**

```
git add *                                      Adds and commits our
git commit -m "ADX ARM template"               adx-rg.json to Git

git remote add origin "https://dataengineering-$suffix
 ➡ dev.azure.com/dataengineering-$suffix/DE/_git/DE"  ◁

git push -u origin   ◁─── Pushes the changes to the remote repo
```

> Adds the origin remote for our local Git repo. Here we specify the URL of the DE Git repo in our DevOps project, and we use the $suffix variable to ensure uniqueness.

After this step, our changes will be in DevOps Git. You can use the web UI to explore your DevOps instance and check that the file shows up there.

To summarize what we have done so far, we took an existing deployment in Azure (our Azure Data Explorer cluster including its database and principal assignments), exported it as an Azure Resource Manager template, and saved it in source control. The next step is to build a pipeline to take this template from Git and deploy it to Azure. This allows us to recreate our Azure Data Explorer cluster on demand, without having to go through any manual steps. We will use Azure Pipelines to deploy the Azure Resource Manager template. Azure Pipelines is part of Azure DevOps.

> **DEFINITION** *Azure Pipelines* is a cloud service that you can use to automatically build and test code, publish it to other users, and deploy it automatically.

Pipelines are a key piece of our DevOps story. We store everything in Git, and we deploy everything through pipelines. Before jumping into authoring pipelines, there's one more step we need to take—connecting our Azure DevOps project to our Azure subscription.

3.3.2 Creating Azure DevOps service connections

We need to create a service connection from Azure DevOps, which will allow our pipelines to make changes in our Azure subscription. Service connections provide an interface between Azure DevOps Pipelines and the services they connect to, as figure 3.8 shows.

Pipelines run in the cloud as part of our Azure DevOps, so they won't be authenticating using our user accounts. And because our Azure subscriptions are secure, they won't allow pipelines to make changes unless we explicitly grant those rights. To do this, we will create a service principal in Azure Active Directory (AAD). As a reminder, a service principal is an identity meant to be used to represent applications as opposed to humans. Then we will create an Azure DevOps service connection using this principal.

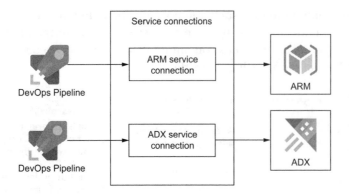

Figure 3.8   Service connections provide an interface between pipelines and the services they connect to. For example, an Azure Resource Manager service connection allows a pipeline to connect to Azure Resource Manager, while an Azure Data Explorer service connection allows a pipeline to connect to an Azure Data Explorer cluster.

The service principal has an identity in Azure Active Directory and a secret. If an external service like a pipeline claims to be the service principal, it is authorized if it can supply this secret. This way, Azure AD knows that the principal is who it claims to be because, otherwise, it wouldn't know the secret. The following listing creates a service principal in Azure Active Directory.

Listing 3.10   Creating a service principal in Azure Active Directory

```
$sp = az ad sp create-for-rbac | ConvertFrom-Json
```
Creates a service principal in AAD, which we then convert from JSON to a PowerShell object and save it in the $sp variable

If you want to see the details of the service principal, type $sp in the terminal to print the variable. You should see five fields:

- appId—A GUID (globally unique identifier) that represents the Azure Active Directory ID of the service principal.
- displayName—The display name of the principal. Because you didn't specify one, it's autogenerated.
- name—The internal name of the principal, which is autogenerated.
- password—The secret. It should look like a long string of random letters, digits, and symbols.
- tenant—The Azure Active Directory tenant corresponding to your Azure subscription.

Let's create a service connection using this principal. Service connections allow Azure DevOps to connect to various other services like Azure subscriptions, NuGet package feeds, GitHub accounts, and more. In our case, we want to connect to Azure Resource Manager for our Azure subscription. The following listing shows how to do this using Azure CLI.

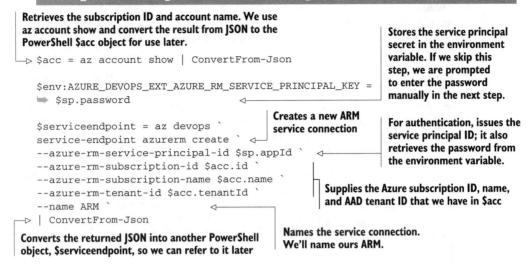

Listing 3.11 Creating an Azure Resource Manager service connection

Retrieves the subscription ID and account name. We use
az account show and convert the result from JSON to the
PowerShell $acc object for use later.

Stores the service principal
secret in the environment
variable. If we skip this
step, we are prompted
to enter the password
manually in the next step.

```
$acc = az account show | ConvertFrom-Json

$env:AZURE_DEVOPS_EXT_AZURE_RM_SERVICE_PRINCIPAL_KEY =
    $sp.password

$serviceendpoint = az devops `
service-endpoint azurerm create `
--azure-rm-service-principal-id $sp.appId `
--azure-rm-subscription-id $acc.id `
--azure-rm-subscription-name $acc.name `
--azure-rm-tenant-id $acc.tenantId `
--name ARM `
| ConvertFrom-Json
```

Creates a new ARM
service connection

For authentication, issues the
service principal ID; it also
retrieves the password from
the environment variable.

Supplies the Azure subscription ID, name,
and AAD tenant ID that we have in $acc

Converts the returned JSON into another PowerShell
object, $serviceendpoint, so we can refer to it later

Names the service connection.
We'll name ours ARM.

We have our service connection established. If you want to try out the web UI, you can navigate to the DE project in Azure DevOps, click Project Settings, and then under the Pipelines heading, you should see Service Connections. If you click it, you should see the Azure Resource Manager service connection aptly named ARM.

We need to do just one more quick step before moving on to author our pipeline: we need to authorize pipelines to use this service connection. Azure comes with secure defaults, so pipelines are not allowed by default to use a service connection unless explicitly granted access. The following listing shows how we can grant all pipelines in this Azure DevOps project access to our Azure Resource Manager service connection.

Listing 3.12 Granting access for all pipelines to the ARM service connection

```
az devops service-endpoint update `
--id $serviceendpoint.id `
--enable-for-all
```

Updates an existing service connection

Supplies the service connection ID
that's included in $serviceendpoint

Makes the service connection available to all pipelines

We are now ready to create a pipeline. This takes the Azure Resource Manager template from Git and deploys it in Azure.

3.3.3 Deploying Azure Resource Manager templates

We'll first go through the steps of setting up a pipeline to deploy an Azure Resource Manager template, and then in the next section, we'll zoom out and talk about Azure Pipelines. Don't worry if some of the steps in this section seem confusing; I'll explain everything in the following section.

Following the same theme of infrastructure as code, pipelines are also defined as code, using a subset of YAML. See the sidebar to learn more about YAML.

> ## YAML
>
> *YAML* stands for *YAML Ain't Markup Language*. It is a superset of JSON, meaning any JSON document can be translated to YAML, but some YAML documents can't be translated to JSON.
>
> The reason Azure Pipelines uses YAML as opposed to JSON is that YAML is meant to be easier to read and write by humans. Unlike Azure Resource Manager templates, which we can export and tweak without having to write manually, we need to define the steps in our pipelines manually. YAML makes it easier for us to do so. You can find a good quick reference for YAML on the Learn X in Y Minutes website at https://learnxinyminutes.com/docs/yaml/.
>
> In this book, we will go over the YAML code, but when you are authoring a pipeline yourself, you have some options to make your life easier. If you use the DevOps web UI for editing, you get IntelliSense support and templates for various tasks that you can just fill in. If you use Visual Studio Code, get the Azure Pipelines extension from the marketplace, which will help you with autocompletion.

In the same DE Git repository where we are storing our Azure Resource Manager template, let's create another subfolder, YML, and then create a deploy-adx.yml file inside it. The following listing shows the steps.

Listing 3.13   YML folder containing deploy-adx.yml

```
mkdir YML  ◁—— Creates a new subfolder called YML

New-Item -Name deploy-adx.yml `
-Path YML -ItemType File        ◁——
```

Creates a new item named deploy-adx.yml of type File under the YML path. This is the PowerShell way to create a new file.

Now, open the newly created file in your favorite text editor and paste the content of the following listing into it.

Listing 3.14   Pasting to deploy-adx.yml

```
trigger:
  branches:
    include:
    - master
  paths:
    include:
      - ./ARM

jobs:
  - job:
    displayName: Deploy ADX cluster
    steps:
      - task: AzureResourceManagerTemplateDeployment@3
        inputs:
          deploymentScope: 'Resource Group'
```

```
azureResourceManagerConnection: 'ARM'
subscriptionId: '<GUID>'                          ◁——
action: 'Create Or Update Resource Group'
resourceGroupName: 'adx-rg'
location: 'Central US'
templateLocation: 'Linked artifact'
csmFile: 'ARM/adx-rg.json'
deploymentMode: 'Incremental'
```

Replace <GUID> with your subscription ID. Because this is already stored in the $acc variable, you can find it by printing $acc.id in the terminal.

Let's go over the trigger and jobs sections of the files separately. It is important to get familiar with Azure Pipelines and YAML as these are foundational for DevOps. The following listing covers the trigger part.

Listing 3.15 Pipeline trigger

Specifies the branches that trigger the pipeline

Triggers define when to run the pipeline automatically.

```
└─▷ trigger:
  ┌──▷  branches:
         include:
         - master
  ┌──▷  paths:
         include:
           - ./ARM
```

Includes the master branch so that changes to the master trigger the pipeline. We can also exclude branches, and then all commits outside those branches trigger the pipeline. If we don't specify anything, commits on any branches trigger the pipeline.

Because we deploy the ARM template, we only want to trigger the build if there's a change in the ./ARM folder.

We can also filter which paths in our folder structure act as triggers.

With this trigger configuration, the pipeline automatically starts running when a change inside the ./ARM subfolder is committed to the master branch. Other changes will not trigger the pipeline, which is what we want. We don't want to redeploy the Azure Resource Manager template if it hasn't changed, and we don't want to redeploy if someone is committing changes to a personal branch.

Note that we can always trigger a pipeline manually, which we will do once we have everything set up. The next listing covers the jobs section of the file.

Listing 3.16 Pipeline jobs

```
jobs:
  - job:
      displayName: Deploy ADX cluster
      steps:
        - task:
          ➡ AzureResourceManagerTemplateDeployment@3
          ▷ inputs:  deploymentScope: 'Resource Group'
        ▷  azureResourceManagerConnection: 'ARM'
             subscriptionId: '<GUID>'
             action: 'Create Or Update Resource Group'  ◁——
```

A pipeline contains one or more jobs. Here we have a single job, Deploy ADX cluster.

A job contains one or more steps. Here we have a single task of type ARM deployment v3.

Deploys a resource group

Specifies the service connection

Creates or updates a resource group. Other actions are delete, start, stop, restart, etc.

Supplies the resource group and location ⊢

Specifies the ARM template adx-rg.json ⊢

```
resourceGroupName: 'adx-rg'
location: 'Central US'
        templateLocation: 'Linked artifact'  ◁─
        csmFile: 'ARM/adx-rg.json'
        deploymentMode: 'Incremental'
```

Specifies the ARM template location that can be either a linked artifact (file in source control or produced by build) or a URL (if we want to point to an external entity)

Incremental deployment means existing resources are left unchanged. In contrast, a complete deployment deletes all resources and recreates them.

We now have our pipeline definition. Let's push it to our repo and create a pipeline in Azure Pipelines based on this definition. The following listing shows how to do this.

Listing 3.17 Creating a pipeline

```
git add *
git commit -m "ADX deployment pipeline"
git push

az pipelines create `
--name 'Deploy ADX' `
--repository DE `
--repository-type tfsgit `
--yml-path YML/deploy-adx.yml `
--skip-run
```

Commits deploy-adx.yml to Git and pushes to remote repo

Creates a new pipeline

Names our pipeline (here Deploy ADX)

Points Azure Pipelines to the repository where it can find the pipeline definition (here the DE repository of type tfsgit)

Provides the path to the definition file

By default, a pipeline kicks off once created. This flag prevents the pipeline from running.

The pipeline is now ready. You can check it out in the web UI by navigating to Pipelines in the DE project. Because this is an incremental deployment, we can run it, and it shouldn't have any effect as our resources are already provisioned. We can manually kick off the pipeline from Azure CLI with the command in the following listing.

Listing 3.18 Kicking off the ADX deployment pipeline

```
az pipelines run `
--name "Deploy ADX" `
--open
```

Specifies a pipeline either by name or ID

The optional --open flag opens a browser window where we can view the progress of the pipeline.

Note that we can easily create another pipeline in a different resource group that provisions a similar cluster infrastructure. The following listing shows a second pipeline, highlighting the differences.

Listing 3.19 Deploying a second ADX cluster based on the same template

```
trigger:
  branches:
    include:
    - master
  paths:
    include:
```

```
            - ./ARM
    jobs:
      - job:
        displayName: Deploy second ADX cluster
        steps:
          - task: AzureResourceManagerTemplateDeployment@3
            inputs:
              deploymentScope: 'Resource Group'
              azureResourceManagerConnection: 'ARM'
              subscriptionId: '<GUID>'
              action: 'Create Or Update Resource Group'
              resourceGroupName: 'adx-rg2'
              location: 'Central US'
              templateLocation: 'Linked artifact'
              csmFile: 'ARM/adx-rg.json'
              overrideParameters:
                '-Clusters_adxvladris_name adx2vladris'
              deploymentMode: 'Incremental'
```

Specifies a different resource group (adx-rg2 instead of adx-rg) ┈▷ `resourceGroupName: 'adx-rg2'`

Overrides the cluster name parameter in the ARM template using the overrideParameters setting. This example contains my alias, Clusters_adx$suffix_name; your parameter name would be different.

We need a unique name across Azure for the cluster, so the exported Azure Resource Manager template conveniently makes it a parameter. If we create another pipeline with this updated definition, we can deploy two clusters with the same configuration (same SKU, same databases, same configured access privileges).

Parameters are overridden either by using a JSON file provided via the `csm-ParametersFile` attribute or in the template itself (under `overrideParameters`), passing any number of parameter names and values separated by a space as follows:

```
overrideParameters: '-param1 newValue1 -param2 newValue2'
```

We can tweak the template and, for example, parameterize the region, and then we can replicate the infrastructure in multiple regions. Alternatively, we can plug in another subscription ID and deploy in a different subscription.

3.3.4 Understanding Azure Pipelines

So far, we've implemented a pipeline definition and created a pipeline based on that. Let's now step back to better understand how Azure Pipelines work. An Azure pipeline definition consists of several sections, most of which are optional:

- A *trigger section specifies which changes trigger the pipeline to run.* As we previously saw, we can specify which Git branches to include (or exclude) from the trigger and which folders to include (or exclude).
- A *schedules section defines scheduled runs for the pipeline.* Sometimes we can forgo continuous deployment and opt, instead, to deploy on some weekly cadence. Schedules allow us to automate this.
- A *pool section specifies the virtual machine pool that executes the pipeline.* Here is where we can pick the operating system we need from the ones offered by Azure DevOps or, for more advanced uses, we can make our own custom virtual machines (VMs) available to Azure DevOps.

We won't need special VMs for the examples in this book because we won't be doing any fancy code building. We'll use the defaults, but note that pipelines are flexible enough that we can configure where to run them.

- *The jobs section defines the actual pipeline steps.* Under it, we can have one or more jobs. Each job has one or more tasks. The tasks are the units of work (for example, "deploy ARM template").

We can use pipelines to automate pretty much anything. In terms of execution, figure 3.9 shows the initial steps.

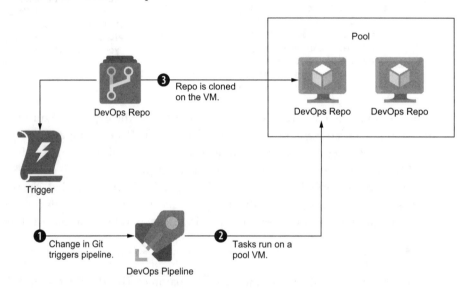

Figure 3.9   A change in Git triggers the pipeline. The pipeline is queued until a VM from the pool is available to execute it. The Git repo is cloned on the VM so source files are available in the execution environment.

Once the pipeline is triggered, usually by a change in Git (though it can be a scheduled run or started manually), it is queued until a VM from the pool is available to execute it. Once available, the VM clones the Git repo so the files are available in the execution environment. All pool VMs have a DevOps agent running, which knows how to execute pipeline tasks. The tasks can do everything: build code, run scripts, deploy resources, and so on.

Azure Pipelines can also integrate with GitHub and other services. We use Azure DevOps Repos in this book just so we have fewer services to deal with. Alternatively, we can have a setup where our repositories live in GitHub, and we use DevOps just to execute pipelines. Now that we understand Azure Pipelines and have a way to deploy our infrastructure, let's go back to Mary's total page views query to see how we can apply DevOps to Azure Data Explorer objects and analytics.

3.4 Deploying analytics

Tracking infrastructure in Git and deploying it automatically from there is a standard software engineering practice. For data engineering, the same applies to the domain-specific artifacts. In our example, this is the PageViews table and the query to count the total page views. Both are Azure Data Explorer objects.

Tables and queries exist at a higher abstraction level than the infrastructure, so ARM won't help us in this case. We need to connect to Azure Data Explorer from DevOps and execute commands as part of a pipeline. First, we'll extend our DE repository with a folder structure for tracking Azure Data Explorer objects. The following listing shows how to create the new folders.

Listing 3.20 Creating a folder structure for ADX objects

```
mkdir -p ADX\telemetry\tables
mkdir -p ADX\telemetry\functions
```

We created a base Azure Data Explorer folder, a database-specific subfolder under it (called telemetry), and then a couple of subfolders under that, one for tables and one for queries packaged as functions. We'll then add a PageViews.csl file under /tables with the content of the next listing.

Listing 3.21 Contents of ADX/telemetry/tables/PageViews.csl

```
.create-merge table PageViews (UserId: long, Page: string,
➥ Timestamp: datetime)
```

The `.create-merge table` command creates or updates a table schema. If the table schema already exists, nothing changes. This is important! Because we will run our deployment pipeline many times, we need our Azure Data Explorer commands to be idempotent.

> **DEFINITION** *Idempotence* means that whether applying an operation once or applying it multiple times, it has the same effect.

In Azure Data Explorer, we can wrap queries into functions and then store those inside a database. This lets us name and capture common queries. The following listing shows how we can package the total page views query into a function named `TotalPageViews`.

Listing 3.22 Contents of ADX/telemetry/functions/TotalPageViews.csl

```
.create-or-alter function TotalPageViews() {
    PageViews
    | where Timestamp > startofmonth(now()) and UserId != 12345
    | count
}
```

Like the idempotent `.create-merge table` command for tables, we use the `.create-or-alter` function to create a new function or to update one if it already exists. If the function already exists and has the same definition, running this command has no effect.

Let's start tracking our database objects in Git. We will commit these two new files and push them to our DevOps repository. The following listing shows the steps for that.

Listing 3.23   Pushing to Git

```
git add *
git commit -m "ADX objects"
git push
```

We now have both infrastructure and objects in Git. We still need to set up the deployment pipeline to execute the Azure Data Explorer commands against our cluster.

3.4.1   Using Azure DevOps marketplace extensions

DevOps doesn't provide an out-of-the-box way to connect to Azure Data Explorer and execute commands. Because we can (and should) use DevOps for everything, the service is extensible. There is a marketplace where Microsoft and other partners can publish extensions. The administrator of a DevOps instance can install these extensions to enhance the capabilities of the service.

In our case, we will install the Azure Data Explorer Pipeline Tools extension, which comes with an Azure Data Explorer service endpoint that enables us to set up an Azure Data Explorer connection from DevOps, and a PublishToADX deployment task, which enables us to execute commands like the ones we stored in PageViews.csl and TotalPageViews.csl. We will do all this with Azure CLI, but working with extensions is usually easier through the web UI, so feel free to experiment with that. The following listing shows how to search the marketplace and how to install an extension from the marketplace.

Listing 3.24   Installing the PublishToAdx extension

Searches the Azure DevOps marketplace

```
az devops extension search `
  --search-query "PublishToAdx" `
  --output table
```

> Our search query is PublishToAdx, but we can pass any string here.

> Formats the results as a table

```
az devops extension install `
  --extension-id PublishToAdx `
  --publisher-id Azure-Kusto
```

> The extension ID and publisher ID correspond to the extension name and publisher name returned by the search.

Installs an extension from the marketplace to our DevOps instance

We've now extended our DevOps service with Azure Data Explorer capabilities. Just like we had to set up an ARM connection to deploy our infrastructure, we'll have to set up an Azure Data Explorer connection to deploy our database objects.

The first step will be to grant the service principal we created in the previous section permissions to run commands against our Azure Data Explorer cluster. In a real-life environment, you should consider using different service principals to deploy infrastructure and to connect to Azure Data Explorer. This type of isolation is a security best practice. In case one of the principals is compromised, the attacker won't instantly gain access to everything. To keep things simple, though, we will reuse our service principal whose details are already stored in the $sp variable.

Listing 3.25 shows how to grant that principal database admin rights. This uses the Kusto Azure CLI extension, not the out-of-the-box Kusto commands. If you haven't done so already in chapter 2, run `az extension add -n kusto` first.

Listing 3.25   Granting ADX rights to the service principal

This is the same command we used to grant ourselves rights when we set up the cluster.

```
az kusto cluster-principal-assignment create `
  --cluster-name "adx$suffix" `
  --resource-group adx-rg `
  --principal-id $sp.appId `
  --principal-type App `
  --tenant-id $sp.tenant `
  --role AllDatabasesAdmin `
  --principal-assignment-name devopsadmin
```

Specifies the cluster name and resource group

Specifies the principal ID and tenant, which come from the $sp variable. The principal type is App.

Grants this principal admin rights for all databases

Names the required principal assignment devopsadmin

Now that our service principal can connect to Azure Data Explorer, let's create a service connection like the one we set up for ARM. Let's see where the UI is simpler.

The `az devops service-endpoint` command has an easy way to configure connections to Azure Resource Manager and Git, where we can pass all the required parameters on the command line. For all other service endpoints, we need to supply a JSON file with all the required parameters. Figuring out what should be in that file is not straightforward, so in most cases, you are better off using the web UI to create a new service connection. That's because the UI gives you a form to fill in with all the required parameters. The next listing shows a config.json file that we can use to create an Azure Data Explorer connection.

Listing 3.26   Contents of config.json

```
{
  "authorization": {
    "parameters": {
      "authenticationType": "spnKey",
```

Authenticates using a service principal with a key

```
     "serviceprincipalid":
  ➥  "<replace with $sp.appId>",
     "serviceprincipalkey":              Replaces these attributes
  ➥  "<replace with $sp.password>",      with the details from $sp
     "tenantid": "<replace with $sp.tenant>"
   },  "scheme": "ServicePrincipal"
 },
 "name": "ADX",
 "owner": "library",
 "serviceEndpointProjectReferences": [
   {
     "name": "ADX",
     "projectReference": {
       "name": "DE"
     }
   }
 ],
 "type": "AzureDataExplorer",              Replaces this URL with your
 "url": "https://adx<replace with $suffix>.centralus    $suffix, which should be the
  ➥  .kusto.windows.net/"       ⟵————————  URL of your ADX cluster
 }
```

The following listing shows how to create this service endpoint. It then deletes the JSON file because we don't want to keep the service principal key around for someone else to find.

Listing 3.27   Creating an ADX service endpoint

Unless we connect to ARM or Git, we need to provide
a configuration JSON-specific to the service.

```
$adxendpoint = az devops `
service-endpoint create `
--service-endpoint-configuration config.json `
| ConvertFrom-Json
                          Deletes the file so we don't persist
rm config.json     ⟵————  the service principal key

az devops service-endpoint update `
--id $adxendpoint.id  `          As with our ARM service endpoint, allows all
--enable-for-all                 pipelines to use the ADX service endpoint
```

Now that we have the Azure Data Explorer service endpoint, we can create a pipeline to deploy Azure Data Explorer objects. We could add another step to our previous pipeline, but it is likely that we will update database objects more often than we update infrastructure. We expect to add more tables and queries daily, while infrastructure changes would only happen occasionally (for example, if we need to scale or replicate our environment). Let's create a deploy-adx-objects.yml file under the YML folder as the next listing shows.

Listing 3.28 Contents of YML/deploy-adx-objects.yml

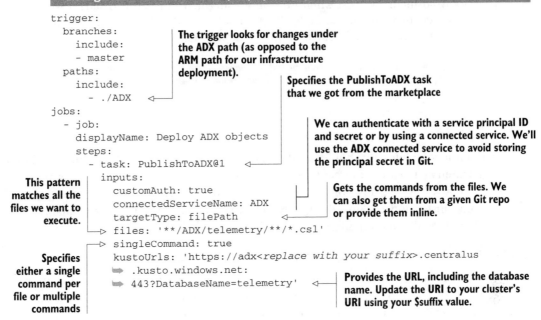

```
trigger:
  branches:
    include:
    - master
  paths:
    include:
    - ./ADX
jobs:
  - job:
    displayName: Deploy ADX objects
    steps:
    - task: PublishToADX@1
      inputs:
        customAuth: true
        connectedServiceName: ADX
        targetType: filePath
        files: '**/ADX/telemetry/**/*.csl'
        singleCommand: true
        kustoUrls: 'https://adx<replace with your suffix>.centralus
        .kusto.windows.net:
        443?DatabaseName=telemetry'
```

The trigger looks for changes under the ADX path (as opposed to the ARM path for our infrastructure deployment).

Specifies the PublishToADX task that we got from the marketplace

We can authenticate with a service principal ID and secret or by using a connected service. We'll use the ADX connected service to avoid storing the principal secret in Git.

This pattern matches all the files we want to execute.

Gets the commands from the files. We can also get them from a given Git repo or provide them inline.

Specifies either a single command per file or multiple commands

Provides the URL, including the database name. Update the URI to your cluster's URI using your $suffix value.

Note that authoring this file in the web UI gives you IntelliSense code completion. This is useful if you don't know the parameters you need to pass to a certain task.

Assuming we created the pipeline definition locally, our next step is to push the YAML file to our DevOps repository and create a new pipeline based on it. The next listing shows the steps for that.

Listing 3.29 Creating the Azure Data Explorer's objects pipeline

```
git add *
git commit -m "ADX objects pipeline"
git push

az pipelines create `
--name 'Deploy ADX objects' `
--repository DE `
--repository-type tfsgit `
--branch master `
--yml-path YML/deploy-adx-objects.yml `
--skip-run
```

Uses the same command as in listing 3.17

Names this pipeline Deploy ADX objects

Uses our new definition

Skips the automatic run to kick it off manually

We now have everything needed to deploy our Azure Data Explorer objects. Listing 3.30 shows how to invoke the pipeline.

NOTE Remember, we are keeping the Azure Data Explorer cluster stopped to avoid incurring cost when we're not using it. You'll want to start it when working through the examples in the book and stop it when not using it. Make sure it is started before running a deployment.

Listing 3.30   Running the Azure Data Explorer's objects pipeline

```
az pipelines run `
--name "Deploy ADX objects" `
--open
```

After it completes, we should see the newly deployed `TotalPageViews` function in the telemetry database. Connect to the cluster using the Azure Data Explorer web experience at https://dataexplorer.azure.com/ or from the Azure portal by navigating to your cluster and clicking the Query tab. If you expand the telemetry database, you should see the new function.

3.4.2 *Storing everything in Git; deploying everything automatically*

One of the key principles of engineering we can bring to our data is storing everything in Git and deploying everything automatically. As we learned from software engineering, source control allows us to collaborate on code; keep a history of changes that allows us to revert to a previous state if something goes wrong; and, most importantly, ensure that nothing gets lost.

Source control combined with automatic deployment allows us to reproduce an environment so that we can replicate it when needed, rebuild it in case it becomes unavailable, and automatically update it as changes come in. We're applying these software engineering lessons to data, where we treat as code both our infrastructure and our domain objects. Figure 3.10 shows our current setup.

We went from a one-off deployment of our infrastructure that we did using Azure CLI in chapter 2 to an automated deployment using ARM templates stored in Git. Now we can update our infrastructure, redeploy it, or replicate it easily. Remember the usual steps: deploy using Azure CLI or portal, export the ARM template, and store it in Git.

We also briefly looked at deploying analytics. We took our PageViews table and Mary's query, stored them in Git, and enabled a pipeline to update them. Git allows data scientists to collaborate on queries, review their code, and ensure nuances (like our test traffic gotcha) are captured for everyone. We will talk more about DevOps for analytics in chapter 6. Not only did we capture our whole environment in source control, even the pipelines we use to automate deployments are stored in Git as YAML files. This is another example of infrastructure as code.

This chapter focused on perhaps the most important engineering aspect of data engineering: DevOps. We added DevOps capabilities to our data platform, making it robust. In the next chapter, we'll add the final core infrastructure pieces: orchestration and monitoring.

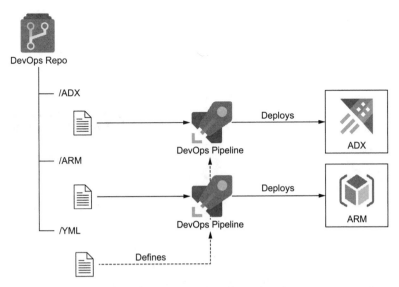

Figure 3.10   We store our Azure Data Explorer objects in Git and deploy them using a pipeline. We store our Azure infrastructure in Git and deploy it using a pipeline as well. We even store the pipelines themselves in Git.

Summary

- Our mantra is this: *everything in Git, everything deployed automatically.*
- Azure DevOps is the Microsoft solution for DevOps, including Git repositories and pipelines.
- Azure pipelines are described using YAML files and contain triggers, jobs, and more.
- The Azure Resource Manager (ARM) handles deployment and configuration of Azure resources.
- ARM templates are an infrastructure-as-code way to store and deploy Azure resources.
- Service connections allow Azure DevOps to connect to external services.
- We can also store domain objects in Git (in our case, Azure Data Explorer (ADX) tables and functions).
- We can find third-party deployment tasks in the DevOps marketplace.

Orchestration 4

This chapter covers

- Building a data ingestion pipeline
- Introducing Azure Data Factory
- DevOps for Azure Data Factory
- Monitoring with Azure Monitor

In this chapter, we'll look at the final pieces of core infrastructure for our data platform: orchestration and monitoring. DevOps is where we store all our code and configurations and from which we deploy our services. The *storage layer* is where we ingest data and on top of which we run our workloads. The *orchestration layer* handles data movement and all other automated processing. Figure 4.1 highlights the platform layer we'll focus on in this chapter.

We'll start with a real-world scenario: ingesting the Bing COVID-19 Open Research Dataset into our data platform. Microsoft provides several open datasets for everyone's use. One of these tracks COVID-19 cases. We'll use Azure Data Factory (ADF) to create a pipeline to bring this dataset into an Azure Data Explorer (ADX) cluster.

As a reminder, Azure Data Factory is Azure's cloud ETL (extract, transform, load) service for scale-out serverless data integration and data transformation.

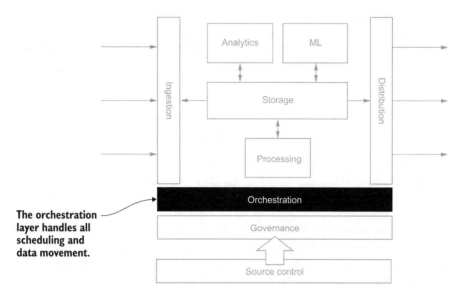

The orchestration layer handles all scheduling and data movement.

Figure 4.1 The orchestration layer handles scheduling for all tasks and data movement into and out of the data platform.

We'll spin up an Azure Data Factory instance, set up the pipeline, and get an overview of the Azure Data Factory components. After running the pipeline, we will have the data in our Azure Data Explorer cluster. Then we will set up DevOps for Azure Data Factory and talk about how we can set up continuous integration/continuous deployment (CI/CD), including both a development and a production environment. Remember, everything in Git and everything deployed automatically.

As we work through the setup, we'll keep an eye on security and make sure we use best practices in terms of access control, without risking any data leaks. For this, we'll introduce and use an Azure Key Vault to store a password.

Finally, we will enable monitoring for our data factory. We'll set up Azure Monitor to send us an email when a pipeline fails and talk about some of the other features Azure Monitor offers. Let's get started!

4.1 Ingesting the Bing COVID-19 open dataset

Azure has a catalog of open datasets that we can access at https://azure.microsoft .com/en-us/services/open-datasets/. One of these is the COVID-19 dataset, which powers the Bing COVID-19 tracker at https:// bing.com/covid/. The dataset is available in several formats: CSV, JSON, JSON-Lines, and Parquet. It has many columns, but we won't use all of them.[1] We will limit our ingestion to the columns in table 4.1.

We'll download the data in JSON format and ingest it into a table in Azure Data Explorer, where we'll perform a full load. Instead of determining what data we have

---

[1] See the Columns tab here: https://azure.microsoft.com/en-us/services/open-datasets/catalog/bing-covid-19-data/.

Table 4.1   Covid19 ingested schema

Column name	Type	Description	Sample value
id	int	Unique identifier	28325786
updated	datetime	As at date, for the record	2020-07-21
confirmed	int	Confirmed case count for the region	200
deaths	int	Death case count for the region	2
country_region	string	Country/region	Norway
load_time	datetime	The date and time the file was loaded from the Bing source on GitHub	2020-07-30 00:05:34.121000

and what data we are missing and then ingesting the delta, the pipeline will ingest the whole dataset into a temporary table, then swap that table with the Covid19 table. Remember from chapter 2, this is the pattern to perform a full load in Azure Data Explorer. Figure 4.2 shows the overall dataflow.

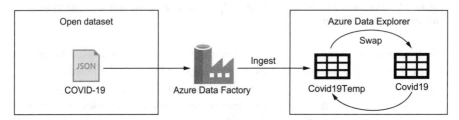

Figure 4.2   We ingest the open COVID-19 dataset using Azure Data Factory into a Covid19Temp table, then swap that table with the Covid19 table.

Our ETL pipeline has the following four steps:

1 Create a Covid19Temp table
2 Ingest the Covid19 dataset into the Covid19Temp table
3 Swap the Covid19Temp table with the Covid19 table
4 Drop the Covid19Temp table (which becomes the oldCovid19 table)

Let's start by creating a table in Azure Data Explorer to store the Covid19 data. Make sure to start the Azure Data Explorer cluster if it's stopped. We can rely on the DevOps setup from chapter 3 for this. Instead of running the command directly against the database, we can push a Covid19.csl file to Git under the /ADX/telemetry/Tables folder. The following listing shows the contents of the file.

Listing 4.1   Contents of /ADX/telemetry/Tables/Covid19.csl

```
.create-merge table Covid19 (id: int, updated: datetime, confirmed: int,
⇨ confirmed_change: int, deaths: int, deaths_change: int, country_region:
⇨ string, load_time: datetime)
```

Once we create the file, we can push it to Git. The following listing displays the commands for this.

Listing 4.2   Pushing the new file to Git

```
git add *
git commit -m "Covid19 table"
git push
```

At this point, the Azure pipeline handling Azure Data Explorer object deployment kicks off and runs the script. You can check that the Covid19 table is created by connecting to the Azure Data Explorer using the web UI. Now that we have our source (the open dataset) and our destination (our newly created Azure Data Explorer table), let's get to the orchestration part. Let's get familiar with Azure Data Factory.

4.2   Introducing Azure Data Factory

In this section, we'll spin up an Azure Data Factory instance and set up all the necessary pieces to move data daily from the Bing COVID-19 open dataset into our newly created table. If you'd rather skip a few steps, you can run the setup.ps1 script in the Chapter4 folder of this book's GitHub repository and then go to section 4.2.3.

NOTE   The COVID-19 open dataset is available at http://mng.bz/y9vy.

The script creates the Azure Data Factory instance and the prerequisites for implementing a data movement pipeline. That being said, the prerequisites introduce some important concepts, so I do recommend that you work through all of the following steps. We'll start with the infrastructure. The following listing shows how to create a new Azure Data Factory.

Listing 4.3   Creating a new data factory

```
az group create `
--location "Central US" `          Creates a new resource group
--name adf-rg          ◁───────┘    to host our data factory

                                               As we did for Azure DevOps,
                                               installs the datafactory extension
az extension add --name datafactory    ◁───

az datafactory factory create `   ◁──── Creates a new ADF
--location "Central US" `
--name "adf$suffix" `          ◁──┐  Specifies a unique name
--resource-group adf-rg           └─ using the $suffix variable
```
Provisions the data factory in the
newly created resource group

Azure Data Factory has a great visual editor for authoring ETL pipelines. You can access the editor either from the Azure Data Factory's Azure Portal page (by clicking the Author & Monitor link) or by navigating to https://adf.azure.com/ and selecting your factory.

Usually, you would set up the data movement through the visual editor. We're going to use Azure CLI because it is more concise; instead of showing a series of screenshots, we'll create a JSON file and run a command. That being said, I encourage you to use the UI to inspect the created objects and try to recreate these from there. In fact, once we set up DevOps for Azure Data Factory, we should *not* use CLI to provision objects. We'll talk about setting up our data source next.

4.2.1   *Setting up the data source*

First, we need to set up our data source: the Bing COVID-19 open dataset. We will start by creating a linked service.

> **DEFINITION**   *Linked services* are much like connection strings. They define the connection information needed for the data factory to connect to external resources.

Azure Data Factory can connect to many external resources, from Azure-native services like Azure SQL, Azure Data Explorer, and Azure Data Lake Storage to Amazon S3, SAP HANA, and to generic resources like FTP shared, HTTP servers, and so on. For our scenario, we need to connect to an HTTP server for the source and Azure Data Explorer for the destination. We can load it with a simple HTTP GET request—no authentication needed.

Listing 4.4 shows the JSON describing a linked service of type HttpServer, pointing to the Bing COVID-19 open dataset hosted by Microsoft. The remaining JSON files, similar to the one in listing 4.4, are only needed for the commands immediately following the file listings, so we don't need to store them in Git.

Listing 4.4   Contents of bingcovid19.json

```
{                                          Specifies that the linked service is for an HTTP server
    "type": "HttpServer",  ◁
                                           Type properties are different among
    "typeProperties": {    ◁               linked services, depending on the type.
                                                                          Specifies the
"url": "https://pandemicdatalake.blob.core.windows.net/",  ◁             root URL
        "enableServerCertificateValidation": true,
        "authenticationType": "Anonymous"   ◁
    }                                            We don't need to deal with
}                                                authentication in this case.
```

The next listing creates a linked service based on the JSON definition in our newly created data factory.

Listing 4.5   Creating an HttpServer linked service

```
                                                   Creates a linked service in the ADF
az datafactory linked-service create `  ◁
--factory-name "adf$suffix" `            For most ADF commands, we need to supply
--resource-group adf-rg `                the factory name and its resource group.
```

```
  --name bingcovid19 `
⌐⊳ --properties '@bingcovid19.json'        ⟵⎯┐
│                                              │  Names the linked service bingcovid19
│  The properties can be supplied as an inline
│  JSON string or as a file using the @ prefix.
```

We just configured our Azure Data Factory to connect to the open dataset via HTTP. Figure 4.3 shows this first step. Then we'll define the dataset.

DEFINITION A *dataset* is a named view of data that simply references the data you want to use in ADF.

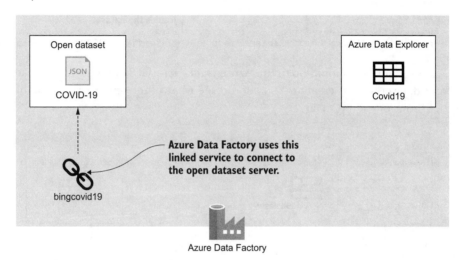

Figure 4.3 The linked service enables the data factory to connect to the open COVID-19 dataset via HTTP.

Linked services tell Azure Data Factory how to connect to an external resource. Datasets tell Azure Data Factory what to expect there. The following listing shows the JSON describing the COVID-19 dataset.

Listing 4.6 Contents of bingcovid19dataset.json

```
{
    "linkedServiceName": {
        "referenceName": "bingcovid19",    ⟵⎯┐
        "type": "LinkedServiceReference"   },
    "type": "Json",
    "typeProperties": {    ⟵⎯┤
        "location": {
            "type": "HttpServerLocation",
            "relativeUrl": "public/curated/covid-19/bing_covid-19_data/
            ➥ latest/bing_covid-19_data.json"    ⟵⎯┐
        }
    }
}
```

This dataset is available by connecting to the bingcovid19 linked service.

Defines the type (format) of this dataset as JSON

Defines the type-specific properties for a JSON object downloaded over HTTP

Defines the relative path to the linked service root URL for the GET request

We pass this JSON to the az datafactory dataset create command as shown in listing 4.7. This creates the dataset in Azure Data Factory. The command is almost identical to the one in listing 4.5 except here we call dataset create instead of linked-service create.

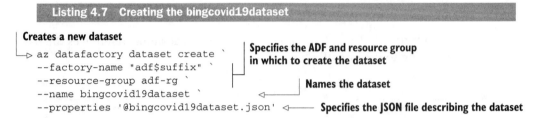

Listing 4.7 Creating the bingcovid19dataset

Creates a new dataset

```
az datafactory dataset create `
  --factory-name "adf$suffix" `
  --resource-group adf-rg `
  --name bingcovid19dataset `
  --properties '@bingcovid19dataset.json'
```

Specifies the ADF and resource group in which to create the dataset

Names the dataset

Specifies the JSON file describing the dataset

At this point, you should open the Azure Data Factory UI and check the linked service and dataset we just created. You should see what other options are available. Figure 4.4 shows our setup so far.

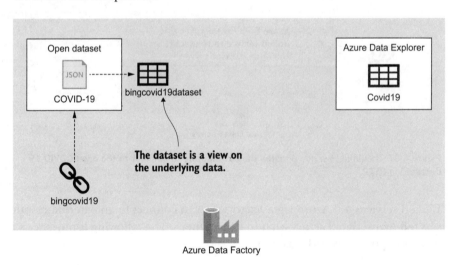

Figure 4.4 The bingcovid19dataset dataset provides a view on the underlying JSON Covid19 dataset. The Bing COVID-19 open dataset is the source for our data.

Next, we'll set up the destination linked service and dataset, which is our Azure Data Explorer cluster. In data factory terms, the destination of a data copy is called a *sink*.

4.2.2 *Setting up the data sink*

Before updating the Data Factory, we'll create a service principal that Azure Data Factory can use to connect to the Azure Data Explorer cluster. We'll need to grant that cluster principal permissions to perform all the operations required. Listing 4.8 shows how to do this. (We did something similar in chapter 3 when we used a service principal to grant Azure DevOps access.)

Listing 4.8 Creating a service principal and granting access to Azure Data Explorer

```
$sp = az ad sp create-for-rbac | ConvertFrom-Json   ←── Creates a service principal and
                                                          saves the result in a JSON object

az kusto database-principal-assignment create `   ←── Assigns database-level permissions
--cluster-name "adx$suffix" `
--database-name telemetry `        ┐  Specifies our ADX cluster
--principal-id $sp.appId `         │  and telemetry database
--principal-type App `             ┘
--role "Admin" `                      Specifies the principal's ID and type
--tenant-id $sp.tenant `
--principal-assignment-name adf `
--resource-group adx-rg
```

Grants Admin rights to the database

Before moving on, check out the sidebar for an important note on security.

> ## A note on security
>
> We already have a service principal provisioned for Azure DevOps to connect to Azure Data Explorer. The reason we are not reusing it here is that each principal (be it service or user) should have only the permissions needed to perform their task. If we use the same principal across many systems, it eventually gathers the superset of rights required by all the systems. In case it gets compromised, a breach is catastrophic—the attacker gets all those privileges!
>
> In our case, we might want to grant Azure DevOps access to other databases. But if we reuse the same service principal, Azure Data Factory also gets that extra access, even when not needed. The key takeaway is *don't reuse service principals.*
>
> You might also have noticed that we granted the Admin role to the Azure Data Factory service principal. The reason for this is the full load steps we will take. Azure Data Explorer has several security roles:
>
> - The Ingestor role ingests data without having other types of access to the data (can't read it, for example).
> - The Viewer role only reads data.
> - The User role can additionally create tables and functions.
> - The Admin role can do anything in the database.
>
> In our pipeline, we will perform four operations: create a temporary table (User can do that), ingest data into it (Ingestor can do that), swap the tables (Admin can do that), and drop the tables (Admin can do that too). Because of this, we have to give Admin rights to our service principal, but we shouldn't do this as a default. The key takeaway here is *always use the least amount of privileges required.*

We can now create a linked service for Azure Data Explorer, using our new service principal to connect to it. The next listing shows the JSON file describing the Azure Data Explorer linked service.

Listing 4.9   Contents of adx.json

```
{
    "type": "AzureDataExplorer",
    "typeProperties": {
        "endpoint": "https://adx<use $suffix>.centralus.kusto.windows.net",
        "tenant": "<use $sp.tenant>",
        "servicePrincipalId": "<use $sp.appId>",
        "servicePrincipalKey": {
            "type": "SecureString",
            "value": "<use $sp.password>"
        },
        "database": "telemetry"
    }
}
```

This is an ADX linked service. ⊳ "type": "AzureDataExplorer",

The ADX URL. Make sure to update it with your $suffix. → "endpoint"

The service principal tenant, ID, and key. Replace these with the values from $sp.

Connects to the telemetry database ← "database": "telemetry"

We pass the JSON file to the command shown in the following listing. This creates the linked service in Azure Data Factory.

Listing 4.10   Creating an Azure Data Explorer linked service

```
az datafactory linked-service create `
--factory-name "adf$suffix" `
--resource-group adf-rg `
--name adx `
--properties '@adx.json'
```

Creates a linked service ← `az datafactory linked-service create`

Defines the ADF and resource group in which to create the linked service

Names the linked service → `--name adx`

Sets the JSON file that describes the linked service

We now have another linked service; this one is for our Azure Data Explorer instance. Figure 4.5 shows the latest for our environment.

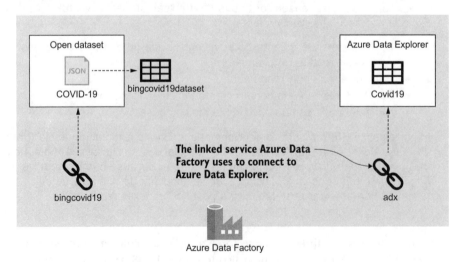

Figure 4.5   We add the ADX linked service so Azure Data Factory can use it to connect to our Azure Data Explorer cluster.

Let's go ahead and create the COVID-19 dataset for Azure Data Explorer. Because we want to do a full load of the data and swap tables, we'll use a Covid19Temp table instead of the final destination table, Covid19. The following listing shows the JSON describing this dataset.

Listing 4.11   Contents of adxtempcovid19dataset.json

```
{
    "linkedServiceName": {
        "referenceName": "adx",
        "type": "LinkedServiceReference"
    },
    "type": "AzureDataExplorerTable",     ◁── This dataset describes an ADX table.
    "typeProperties": {
        "table": "Covid19Temp"    ◁── Names the ADX table
    }
}
```

We create the dataset by passing the JSON file to the command shown in the following listing.

Listing 4.12   Creating the Azure Data Explorer Covid19 dataset (adxtempcovid19dataset)

Creates a new dataset
```
az datafactory dataset create `       Specifies the ADF and resource group
--factory-name "adf$suffix" `         in which to create the dataset
--resource-group adf-rg `
--name adxtempcovid19dataset `                   Names the dataset
--properties '@adxtempcovid19dataset.json' ◁── Sets the JSON file that describes the dataset
```

Now we have both source and destination datasets defined. You can check them out in the Azure Data Factory UI. Figure 4.6 shows our progress so far.

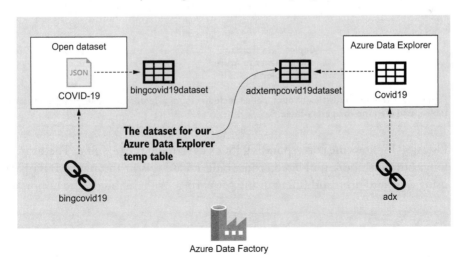

Figure 4.6   The adxtempcovid19dataset describes the Azure Data Explorer temporary table in which we will ingest our data.

With both source and sink defined, it's time to create the pipeline that will copy the data. The next section describes this process.

4.2.3 Setting up the pipeline

ETL pipelines like the one we want to build are simply called pipelines in Azure Data Factory (not to be confused with Azure DevOps Pipelines that we covered in chapter 3).

> **DEFINITION**   A *pipeline* is a logical grouping of activities that together perform a task.

We defined pipelines in terms of activities. Let's also define an activity.

> **DEFINITION**   The *activities* in a pipeline define actions to perform on your data. These represent the steps Azure Data Factory needs to execute.

In our case, the steps are these: create a temporary table, ingest data into it, swap tables, then drop the old table. For the second step, we will use a copy activity, the Azure Data Factory activity for copying data from a source into a sink. For the other steps, we will use the Azure Data Explorer command activity, which issues a command to Azure Data Explorer through the linked service. Figure 4.7 shows a visual representation of our pipeline as we will see it in the Azure Data Factory UI.

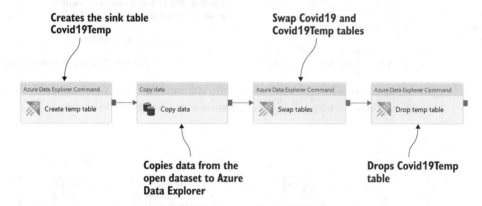

Figure 4.7   The four activities of our pipeline include create a temporary table, copy data, swap tables, and drop the temporary table.

Listing 4.13 shows the corresponding JSON describing the pipeline. The listing is quite long, but don't be intimidated. You would create this in the Azure Data Factory UI using drag-and-drop and filling in the properties. We'll highlight the important bits.

Listing 4.13   Contents of ingestcovid19data.json

```
{
    "activities": [
        {
            "name": "Create temp table",
```

```
        "type": "AzureDataExplorerCommand",
        "typeProperties": {
            "command": ".create-merge table Covid19Temp (id: int,
            ➡ updated: datetime, confirmed: int, deaths: int,
            ➡ country_region: string,
            ➡ load_time: datetime)",           ◁──┐  Creates the Covid19Temp
            "commandTimeout": "00:20:00"            │  table. This activity issues
        },                                          │  an ADX command.
        "linkedServiceName": {
            "referenceName": "adx",
            "type": "LinkedServiceReference"
        }
    },
    {
        "name": "Copy data",
        "type": "Copy",                             Copies data (the
        "dependsOn": [                              second activity) that has
            {                                        a dependency on the first
                "activity": "Create temp table",  ┐ activity and only runs if
                "dependencyConditions": [         │ the first activity succeeds
                    "Succeeded"
                ]
            }
        ],
        "typeProperties": {
            "source": {                            The JSON source has some
                "type": "JsonSource",              additional properties; this
                "storeSettings": {                 defines the request method
                    "type": "HttpReadSettings",  ┐ to use (in our case, GET).
                    "requestMethod": "GET"
                },
                "formatSettings": {
                    "type": "JsonReadSettings"
                }
            },
            "sink": {
                "type": "AzureDataExplorerSink"
            },
            "enableStaging": false
        },                                         Specifies
        "inputs": [                                bingcovid19dataset
                                                   as the input for the
    {                                              copy
                "referenceName": "bingcovid19dataset",  ◁── 
                "type": "DatasetReference"
            }
        ],                            Specifies adxtempcovid19dataset
        "outputs": [                                as the output
            {
                "referenceName": "adxtempcovid19dataset",  ◁──
                "type": "DatasetReference"
            }
        ]
    },
    {
        "name": "Swap tables",
```

```
        "type": "AzureDataExplorerCommand",
        "dependsOn": [
            {
                "activity": "Copy data",          Copies data (the third activity),
                "dependencyConditions": [          which only runs if the second
                    "Succeeded"                    activity succeeds
                ]
            }
        ],
        "typeProperties": {
            "command": ".rename tables Covid19 = Covid19Temp,
            ➥ Covid19Temp = Covid19",              ◄──┐  .rename tables swaps
            "commandTimeout": "00:20:00"              │  the two tables.
        },
        "linkedServiceName": {
            "referenceName": "adx",
            "type": "LinkedServiceReference"
        }
    },
    {
        "name": "Drop temp table",
        "type": "AzureDataExplorerCommand",
        "dependsOn": [                          Swaps the tables (the last
            {                                   activity), depending on
                "activity": "Swap tables",   ◄──┘ the previous command
                "dependencyConditions": [
                    "Succeeded"
                ]
            }
        ],                                      .drop table discards the
        "typeProperties": {                     temporary (now the old)
            "command": ".drop table Covid19Temp", ◄──┘ table.
            "commandTimeout": "00:20:00"
        },
        "linkedServiceName": {
            "referenceName": "adx",
            "type": "LinkedServiceReference"
        }
    }
   ]
}
```

We'll use Azure CLI to set up this pipeline in Azure Data Factory. The following listing shows the command. It's similar to the previous commands but uses the pipeline sub-command instead.

Listing 4.14   Creating the pipeline

```
az datafactory pipeline create `
--factory-name "adf$suffix" `
--name ingestcovid19data `
--resource-group adf-rg `
--pipeline '@ingestcovid19data.json'
```

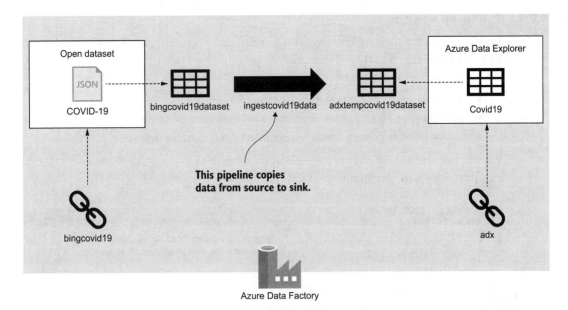

Figure 4.8 The pipeline copies data from the source (open dataset) to the sink (the Azure Data Explorer table).

We can now copy the data to our Azure Data Explorer cluster. Figure 4.8 shows our current setup.

Let's take it for a spin. We can start a run either by clicking Debug on the UI or by issuing the command shown in the next listing.

Listing 4.15 Running the pipeline

```
az datafactory pipeline create-run `          The pipeline create-run
--factory-name "adf$suffix" `                  command kicks off a pipeline.
--resource-group adf-rg `
--name ingestcovid19data                       Besides the factory name and resource group,
                                               we need to provide the pipeline name.
```

Once the pipeline finishes executing, the data should be available in Azure Data Explorer. Try running a few queries to explore the dataset.

So far, we've learned about the pieces needed to move data: linked services, which enable Azure Data Factory to connect to external resources; datasets, which describe the data; and pipelines consisting of activities, which perform the ETL steps. There's one piece missing though: automatically scheduling pipeline execution.

4.2.4 *Setting up a trigger*

In Azure Data Factory, we can schedule execution using a trigger. *Triggers* represent a unit of processing that determines when a pipeline execution needs to be kicked off. We can create several types of triggers in Azure Data Factory. Here are a few:

- Schedule triggers execute pipelines on a schedule.
- Tumbling-window triggers execute pipelines on a periodic interval.
- Event-based triggers execute a pipeline in response to an event.

We will use a schedule trigger for our pipeline. The following listing shows the JSON that describes a trigger that fires at 2 A.M. UTC every day.

Listing 4.16   Contents of dailytrigger.json

```
{
    "runtimeState": "Stopped",       ⟵──  Triggers can be enabled or disabled.
                                          We create this one in a Stopped state.
    "pipelines": [
        {
            "pipelineReference": {
                "referenceName": "ingestcovid19data",
                "type": "PipelineReference"
            }
        }
    ],
    "type": "ScheduleTrigger",       ⟵──  Defines a schedule trigger
    "typeProperties": {
        "recurrence": {
            "frequency": "Day",          Defines a by-day frequency
            "interval": 1,               with an interval of one day
            "startTime": "2020-07-28T02:00:00.000Z",   Starts at 2 A.M. UTC
            "timeZone": "UTC"                          on 28/07/2020
        }
    }
}
```

A trigger can kick off multiple pipelines.

We can create the trigger based on the JSON definition in the following listing. Figure 4.9 shows the complete picture with all objects we just created.

Listing 4.17   Creating the trigger

```
az datafactory trigger create `
--factory-name "adf$suffix" `
--resource-group adf-rg `
--name daily `
--properties '@dailytrigger.json'
```

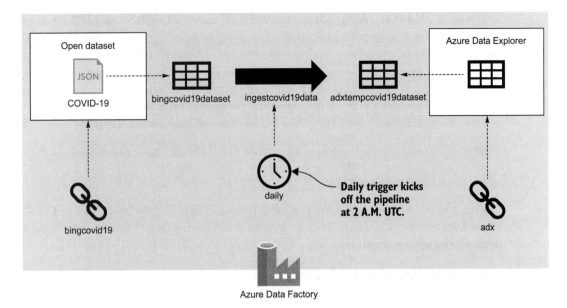

Figure 4.9 The daily trigger executes the pipeline automatically.

4.2.5 *Orchestrating with Azure Data Factory*

Before moving on to the next section, let's recap what we did so far and see why Azure Data Factory is a good option for our main orchestration service.

We created a couple of linked services, a couple of datasets, a pipeline, and a trigger. It should be obvious by now that Azure Data Factory excels at moving data around. We can connect pretty much any source with any sink, regardless of where the data comes from. Azure Data Factory has many linked service types to accommodate most scenarios. When something isn't available out of the box, we can always implement a web service to handle any custom logic and invoke it from Azure Data Factory using the Web activity.

Pipelines can range from simple to complex. We created a straightforward pipeline consisting of four activities, but Azure Data Factory capabilities go beyond that; pipelines can contain loops (using the For Each or Until activities) and conditional branching (using the If Condition and Switch activities). We specified a simple dependency chain, where each activity depended on the previous one, but an activity can depend on multiple other activities and can (conditionally) run if some previous activity succeeds, fails, or completes, regardless of the outcome.

Our simple example was hardcoded, but pipelines also support variables and dynamic content. A simple language allows you to configure various properties to be dynamic and to use variable values resolved at run time. For example, a source or a destination table can be parameterized, and a pipeline can be reused in multiple instances with different parameters.

There is a lot more to say about Azure Data Factory, though it wouldn't all fit in this book. We won't deep dive because we're trying to get a comprehensive view of all the aspects of a data platform, orchestration being just one of these aspects. But I can tell you that my team has been running this at scale: hundreds of pipelines running every day, copying data, processing it, and running machine learning (more on that in chapter 7). If you are trying to decide which orchestration solution to use, I encourage you to read more about Azure Data Factory and explore its capabilities.

> **NOTE** An orchestration solution for a data platform should scale well, excel at data movement, be flexible enough to extend and customize, and have great scheduling capabilities.

You might have noticed something missing from this section. We haven't talked at all about DevOps. Let's next see how we can sync our Azure Data Factory with Git and deploy from source control.

4.3   DevOps for Azure Data Factory

So far, we've updated our Azure Data Factory using either the CLI or the UI. Both the UI and Azure CLI connected to the Azure Data Factory service we provisioned, read its configuration, and updated it. Figure 4.10 illustrates this.

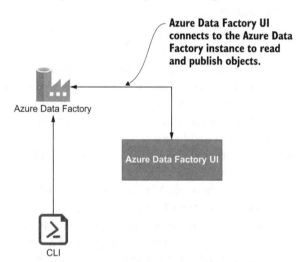

Figure 4.10   Both Azure CLI and Azure Data Factory UI connect to the data factory we provisioned.

Now let's throw DevOps Repos into the mix and see how we can persist the Azure Data Factory configuration in Git. We could have done this using Azure CLI, but at the time of writing, only the UI provides the option to import the existing configuration into Git, so we'll set it up through the UI. Figure 4.11 shows how.

From Manage, Git Configuration, fill in the form choosing Azure DevOps Git as the repository type. Use your current subscription. Pick the dataengineering-$suffix account (in my case, this is dataengineering-vladris). The project name is DE, which

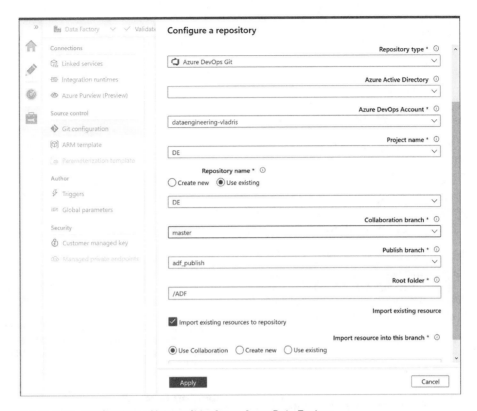

Figure 4.11 Configuring a Git repository for an Azure Data Factory

is the project we created in chapter 3. Select the Use Existing repository radio button and then pick DE from the drop-down list. We'll use the master branch for collaboration and the /ADF root folder. Check Import Existing Resources to Repository and, for branch, choose Use Collaboration.

Finally, click Apply. You should see a new ADF folder in Git, complete with the definitions of all the Azure Data Factory objects we created in the previous sections. Figure 4.12 shows the folder structure.

If you open one of the JSON files, it should look similar to the ones we created in the previous section, although not identical. We only specified the properties part of each object. Now these include name and type. In some cases, we completely omitted some properties for which Azure Data Factory created defaults. For example, if you peek into the ingestcovid19data.json pipeline definition, you will see each activity also has an execution policy including timeout, number of retries, and so on.

At this point, we should no longer use Azure CLI because the Azure Data Factory UI considers Git to be the "source of truth" for the state of Azure Data Factory. Figure 4.13 shows the new configuration.

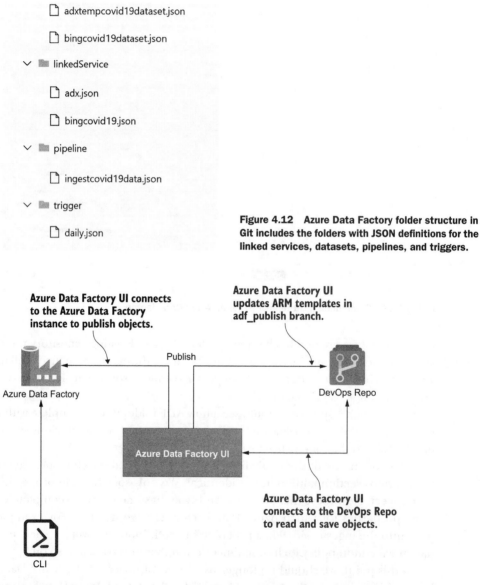

Figure 4.12   Azure Data Factory folder structure in Git includes the folders with JSON definitions for the linked services, datasets, pipelines, and triggers.

Figure 4.13   The Azure Data Factory UI now reads and saves the Azure Data Factory state to Git, while Azure CLI still connects directly to the Azure Data Factory instance.

Contrast this with figure 4.10, where both the UI and the CLI connected only to the service. Now, if we use the CLI to create a new linked service, for example, it updates the Azure Data Factory instance, but the change won't be captured in Git. The Azure Data Factory UI no longer reads the state from the Azure Data Factory instance, rather, it reads it from Git. You don't want to get the two out of sync because it will be a nightmare to figure out what is going on.

With Git enabled, when you click Save in the UI, the changes immediately get reflected in Git. The Azure Data Factory instance isn't updated, though. To publish the changes, you need to click Publish. Once you do that, not only does Azure Data Factory get updated, a special branch in Git called adf_publish is also updated. This branch contains the Azure Resource Manager template and parameter files required to set up an Azure Resource Manager deployment from Git.

4.3.1 *Deploying Azure Data Factory from Git*

Azure Data Factory DevOps integration is designed in such a way that all development happens on a development instance of the data factory, where team members author pipelines and publish to the instance. Then, from the adf_publish branch in Git, a DevOps Pipeline deploys the generated Azure Resource Manager templates to the production environment. Figure 4.14 shows the flow.

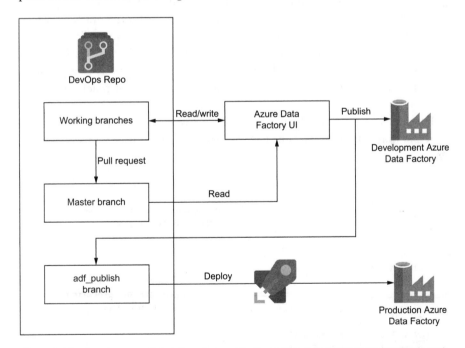

Figure 4.14   Developers collaborate using working branches. You can lock the master branch using branch policies that only accept pull requests. Publishing the master branch from the Azure Data Factory UI not only updates the development Azure Data Factory, it also updates the Azure Resource Manager templates in adf_publish. A DevOps Pipeline then deploys the Azure Resource Manager templates to the production data factory.

This is the first time we've touched on development and production environments, so let's talk about this for a bit before setting up our DevOps deployment. Environment separation is another engineering practice from the world of software, which we can bring to the realm of data. A development environment that is available to everyone on the team might sometimes break and generally is used for trying things out. Once development is complete, the artifact (code, service, Azure Data Factory pipeline, etc.) moves to the production environment. The production environment must always work and is actively monitored, and access is restricted to fewer team members to prevent accidental breakage.

4.3.2   *Setting up access control*

Why is access control a good thing for Azure Data Factory? Remember how we had to grant administrator-level permissions to the service principal Azure Data Factory uses to connect to Azure Data Explorer? That means that anyone on the team can issue an admin-level command to the Azure Data Explorer telemetry database via an Azure Data Factory activity, even if their personal accounts don't have that level of access. This is a potential security leak! What if we have sensitive data in the database that, for compliance reasons, only a small number of people should be able to see?

Environment separation helps with this. The linked services are parameters of the Azure Resource Manager template, so we can use different endpoints for development and production. That means that in our development environment, everyone gets access to a development database that doesn't contain any sensitive data. In production, we can swap the linked service with one that connects to a production database that includes sensitive data and, at this point, is out of reach of the developers. We'll do that now.

First, let's create a production database in Azure Data Explorer and a new service principal that gets administrator-level access to it. The following listing sets this up.

> **Listing 4.18   A production database and a new service principal**

```
az kusto database create `            The same command we used in chapter 2,
--cluster-name "adx$suffix" `         just a different database name
--database-name production `
--resource-group adx-rg `
--read-write-database `
location="Central US"

                                              Creates a new service
                                              principal, our production
$prodsp = az ad sp `                          service principal
create-for-rbac | ConvertFrom-Json    <—┘

az kusto database-principal-assignment create `
--cluster-name "adx$suffix" `
--database-name production `          Grants Admin rights to the production
--principal-id $prodsp.appId `        service principal for the production database
--principal-type App `
--role "Admin" `
```

```
--tenant-id $prodsp.tenant `
--principal-assignment-name adf `
--resource-group adx-rg
```

We're almost ready to set up our deployment, there's just one more prerequisite: we need to provide the service principal key to the DevOps Pipeline so it can fill in the Azure Resource Manager template parameter. It's not a good idea to store this key in the pipeline YAML. That makes it visible to anyone with access to the Git repo, which is a big security hole. Instead, we will store the key in the Azure Key Vault.

Azure Key Vault is a secrets storage solution. We can save secrets in the vault and control who has access to them. Let's create an Azure Key Vault and store the `$prodsp.password` there. The following listing shows how to do that.

Listing 4.19 Creating an Azure Key Vault and storing a secret

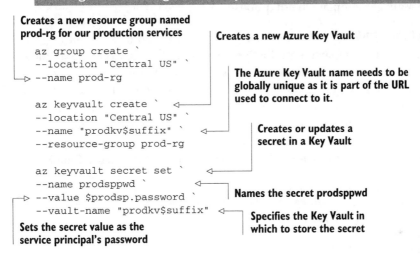

Creates a new resource group named prod-rg for our production services

Creates a new Azure Key Vault

```
az group create `
--location "Central US" `
--name prod-rg
```

```
az keyvault create `
--location "Central US" `
--name "prodkv$suffix" `
--resource-group prod-rg
```

The Azure Key Vault name needs to be globally unique as it is part of the URL used to connect to it.

Creates or updates a secret in a Key Vault

```
az keyvault secret set `
--name prodsppwd `
--value $prodsp.password `
--vault-name "prodkv$suffix"
```

Names the secret prodsppwd

Specifies the Key Vault in which to store the secret

Sets the secret value as the service principal's password

Our service principal is now safe. In fact, it is so safe, nobody can read it! We'll need to add an access policy to allow our Azure DevOps to read the secret. That enables the pipeline to use it when running, without us having to store it anywhere in Git. Azure DevOps registers an application with the following naming schema.

```
<organization name>-<project name>-<subscription id>
```

This is the app we need to grant access to. Next, we'll query Azure Active Directory for an app whose name starts with `dataengineering-$suffix` (as we named our organization). As a reminder, Azure Active Directory is the identity management solution offered by Azure. Each Azure account has its own Azure Active Directory instance managing the users and applications within that tenant. We'll get the ID of this app and grant it permissions to read secrets. The following listing shows how we can do this.

Listing 4.20   Granting Azure DevOps access to read from the key vault

**Queries the Azure AD directory
and stores the result in $adoid**

**Looks for an app whose display name starts with
the name of our Azure DevOps organization**

```
$adoid = az ad app list `
--filter "startswith(displayName, 'dataengineering-$suffix')" `
--query "[0].appId" `
```
Extracts the appId part from the result

```
az keyvault set-policy `       ←—— Sets a key vault access policy
--secret-permissions get list `    ←—
--name "prodkv$suffix" `           Gets and lists permissions to secrets
--spn $adoid    ←—— Names the service principal for Azure DevOps
```

We can also use the Azure portal UI to grant this access from the Access Policies tab of the Key Vault. Now that we know that we are securely storing the secret, let's set up a pipeline to deploy our production Azure Data Factory that's based on the Azure Resource Manager template in adf_publish.

4.3.3   *Deploying the production data factory*

We'll create another deployment pipeline definition file under our /YML folder. This pipeline has two steps: get the service principal from the Azure Key Vault and deploy the Azure Resource Manager template, filling in some parameters. These parameters differentiate the production Azure Data Factory from the original one used for development.

   We'll call the production Azure Data Factory prodadf$suffix and place it in the prod-rg resource group. Let's create this Azure Data Factory, leave it empty, then update it through a deployment pipeline. The following listing creates Azure Data Factory.

Listing 4.21   Creating the production ADF

```
az datafactory factory create `
--location "Central US" `
--name "prodadf$suffix" `
--resource-group prod-rg
```

When we deploy the Azure Resource Manager template from the development Azure Data Factory, we'll change the name and also update the Azure Data Explorer linked service so that it connects to the production database using the production service principal. The following listing shows our new deploy-adf.yml file.

Listing 4.22   Contents of deploy-adf.yml

```
trigger:
  - adf_publish    ←—
jobs:                  Triggers the pipeline when a change
                       is pushed to the adf_publish branch
  - job:
    displayName: Deploy ADF
    steps:                          The first task, AzureKeyVault,
      - task: AzureKeyVault@1   ←—  enables the pipeline to read secrets.
```

We use the ARM service connection we created in chapter 3.

Replace this with the name of your Azure Key Vault, prodkv$suffix.

The second task deploys an ARM template.

Replaces subscription Id with your subscription GUID

Specifies the path to ARMTemplateForFactory.json. The folder name is the name of the development ADF adf$suffix.

Overrides the template parameters factoryName and the ADX linked service configuration

Specifies the path to ARMTemplateParametersForFactory.json. The folder name is adf$suffix.

```
  inputs:
    azureSubscription: 'ARM'
    KeyVaultName: '<use AKV name>'
    SecretsFilter: '*'
    RunAsPreJob: false
- task: AzureResourceManagerTemplateDeployment@3
  inputs:
    deploymentScope: 'Resource Group'
    azureResourceManagerConnection: 'ARM'
    subscriptionId: '<use subscription ID>'
    action: 'Create Or Update Resource Group'
    resourceGroupName: 'prod-rg'
    location: 'Central US'
    templateLocation: 'Linked artifact'
    csmFile: '<use adf$suffix>/ARMTemplateForFactory.json'
    csmParametersFile: '<use adf$suffix>/
    ➥ ARMTemplateParametersForFactory.json'
    overrideParameters: '-
    ➥ factoryName <use prodadf$suffix> -
    ➥ adx_servicePrincipalKey $(prodsppwd) -
    ➥ adx_properties_typeProperties_servicePrincipalId
    ➥ <use $prodsp.appId> -
    ➥ adx_properties_typeProperties_database
    ➥ production'
    deploymentMode: 'Incremental'
```

Because we're deploying the adf_publish branch, we need to commit deploy-adf.yml in that branch. The following listing shows how to do this.

Listing 4.23 Pushing the YML file to the adf_publish branch

```
git pull
git checkout -b adf_publish

... create the YML folder and place the file inside it

git add *
git commit -m "ADF deployment pipeline"
git push -set-upstream origin adf_publish
```

We'll create a pipeline based on this definition, like we did in chapter 3 for the Azure Data Explorer and Azure Data Explorer's objects pipelines. The following listing shows how to do that.

Listing 4.24 Creating the Azure Data Factory deployment pipeline

```
az pipelines create `
--name 'Deploy ADF' `
--repository DE `
--branch adf_publish `
--repository-type tfsgit `
--yml-path YML/deploy-adf.yml `
--skip-run
```

The only difference from the previous pipelines we created is that here we specify a branch.

The pipeline kicks off when we click Publish in the Azure Data Factory UI on the development Azure Data Factory and applies the updates to the production Azure Data Factory. Start the pipeline and, after it runs, log into the Azure Data Factory UI and check out the production Azure Data Factory. It should have the same linked services, datasets, and pipeline as the development one, except the Azure Data Explorer linked service is connected to the production database with the production service principal.

One final note: in a real-world production environment, we need a couple more steps in our pipeline. First, we need to pause triggers in the production Azure Data Factory before deployment if we want to update them. Azure Data Factory doesn't allow updating active triggers, which might cause the deployment to fail. Next, we need to unpause the triggers once deployment completes. That is because active triggers cannot be updated. The Azure Data Factory team provides PowerShell scripts for this. You'll find them here: http://mng.bz/Mg5o. We would update our deployment pipeline so that it runs the pause script before the Azure Resource Manager deployment, then runs the unpause script.

4.3.4   *DevOps for the Azure Data Factory recap*

We did quite a lot in this section. Let's stop and review where we started and what we ended with. Initially, we had an Azure Data Factory, our development data factory, for which we wanted to implement DevOps. We set things up using the Azure recommended settings for Azure Data Factory. We connected our development Azure Data Factory to Git, then set up a deployment pipeline to move changes to the production Data Factory. We saw how the Azure Resource Manager template deployment supports parameters that we can override. Everything is in Git, and everything is deployed automatically.

We also learned a bit about access control and secrets management. Azure Key Vault is the Azure service for storing secrets. Until now, we didn't need to use it; the principal password in our development Azure Data Factory is encrypted by Azure Data Factory, so it is safe. In general, Azure services that accept secrets are good about keeping them safe. The problem came up when we needed a way to pass a secret to a pipeline that is itself stored in Git. In this case, we couldn't save the password in clear text in Git, so we used the Azure Key Vault.

> **TIP**   Always keep secrets safe, never store them in source control! Azure, AWS, GCP, or any decent cloud provider has a secrets management solution exactly for this reason.

We talked a bit about our development and production environments. We'll touch on them again in part 2, when we look at how we can support various workloads. In general, a development environment is open to anyone, is not monitored 24/7, and also doesn't contain or allow access to sensitive data. The production environment, on the other hand, is open to far fewer people (on-call persons or site reliability engineers, etc.), is actively monitored, and can contain sensitive data as long as it is properly secured.

We're almost done. The last piece we'll touch on in this chapter before moving on to part 2 is monitoring. Let's see how we can use Azure Monitor to set up an alert that emails us when an Azure Data Factory pipeline fails.

4.4 Monitoring with Azure Monitor

Azure Monitor is the centralized monitoring solution offered by Azure. It collects telemetry from other Azure services running in our subscription and enables us to query logs, keep an eye on the resources, and configure alerts.

We'll not walk through all the Azure Monitor capabilities, rather, we'll use it as we examine various components of our data platform. Right now, we want to get notified when a pipeline fails in our production data factory. Figure 4.15 shows an overview of the workflow.

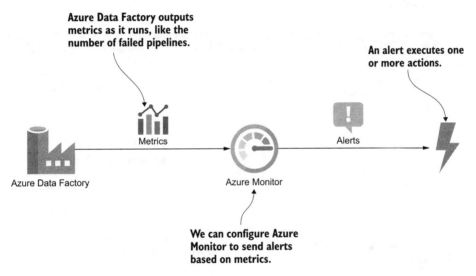

Figure 4.15   Azure Data Factory (and other services) output metrics. We can define Azure Monitor alerts based on these metrics. An alert executes one or more actions.

Let's start with the actions. *Actions* notify users that something happened. Azure Monitor provides multiple actions: send email, send SMS, invoke an Azure Function, start an Azure Logic App, invoke a webhook, and so forth. Actions are defined in action groups. An *action group* is a collection of notification actions that Azure Monitor uses to notify users that an alert has been triggered. Let's create an action group to trigger an email notification. The next listing shows how to set this up.

Listing 4.25   Creating an action group

```
az monitor action-group create `        ⟵  Creates a new action group
--name notify `
--resource-group prod-rg `
--action email "<use a name>" "<use your email address>"        ⟵  This group contains a single email action. Make sure to use a name and a real email address.
```

Services like Azure Data Factory output metrics. *Metrics* are numerical values that describe some aspect of a system at a particular time. Metrics are collected at regular intervals and are useful for alerts because they can be sampled frequently, and an alert can be fired as soon as an issue is detected. One metric that Azure Data Factory outputs is `PipelineFailedRuns`, which refers to failed pipelines during a specific time window. We will set up an alert around this metric.

> **DEFINITION**   *Metric alerts* in Azure Monitor work on top of multidimensional metrics. Metric alerts are evaluated regularly to check if conditions on one or more metric time series are true and notify us when the evaluations are met.

We will set up an alert that runs every 5 minutes and triggers the action group we just created if the total number of failed pipelines is greater than 0. The following listing shows this setup.

Listing 4.26   Creating a metric alert

```
$adf = az datafactory factory show `          ◁─────  Retrieves an object corresponding
--name "prodadf$suffix" --resource-group prod-rg `       to our production ADF
| ConvertFrom-Json

                                   Creates an Azure Monitor metric alert
az monitor metrics alert create `   ◁────┘
--name pipelinefailure `
--resource-group prod-rg `      │  Specifies a name and a resource group
--scopes $adf.id `                   ◁──────  The scope is the ID of our ADF.
--condition "total PipelineFailedRuns > 0" `   ◁──
--window-size 5m `                                      The condition to trigger the
--evaluation-frequency 5m `                            alert; total count of the failed
--description "Pipeline failure" `                     pipeline runs greater than 0.
--action notify          ◁──────
```
Azure Monitor evaluates the condition every 5 min, looking back at the previous 5 min.   **Specifies the notify action group we created in listing 4.24**

It's as easy as that. Give it a try. Stop the Azure Data Explorer cluster and run the Covid19 data ingestion pipeline. This should fail (because the destination is unavailable), and you should receive an email that something went wrong within 5 minutes.

We just stood up a major piece of our infrastructure: development and production Data Factories, backed by DevOps, and monitored with Azure Monitor. Now we have everything in place to coordinate data movement and processing. We'll move on to part 2 and talk about workloads to run on top of this infrastructure. These include data processing, analytics, and machine learning.

Summary

- Azure Data Factory is the Azure service for data movement and orchestration.
- Linked services enable connections to external resources. Datasets are views on external data, and pipelines define sequences of actions. Triggers kick off pipelines.

- A development data factory backed by Git is used for development, then, from Git, we can deploy the Azure Data Factory objects to a production Data Factory.
- Use Azure Key Vault for secrets storage and never store secrets in source control.
- The production Azure Data Factory can use different linked services to connect to a production environment.
- Azure services output metrics that Azure Monitor can query and notify you when some condition is met.

Part 2

Workloads

Part 2 covers the three main workloads a data platform needs to support: processing data, running analytics, and machine learning (ML).

- Chapter 5 discusses processing raw input data into something that better suits our analytical needs. We'll cover common schemas and see how an identity keyring helps tie the various identities throughout our system together and how a timeline view brings different events together.
- Chapter 6 is all about analytics. It also covers how data engineering can support data science by setting up an environment in which anyone can prototype and deploy analytics to production, while keeping the production environment in good shape.
- Chapter 7 covers machine learning. We'll see what we need to do to take an ML model that can run consistently and reliably from a Python script to a production pipeline backed by DevOps. Here we'll introduce Azure Machine Learning and see how it helps us automate these steps.

Processing

This chapter covers

- Processing data and common schemas
- Tying datasets together through an identity keyring
- Building a timeline view of events
- Operating continuous data processing

This chapter is all about data processing. In part 1, we looked at various infrastructure pieces for our data platform. With those in place, we'll shift our focus to supporting common workloads: data processing, analytics, and machine learning. The focus of this chapter is data processing, reshaping the raw data we ingest into our platform to better suit our analytical needs. Figure 5.1 highlights this chapter's focus on our orientation map.

First, we'll talk about some common data modeling concepts such as normalizing data to reduce duplication and ensure integrity and denormalizing data to improve query performance. We'll learn about fact tables and dimension tables and the commonly used star and snowflake schemas. Next, we'll build an identity keyring and see how it helps us connect all the different identities managed by different groups across

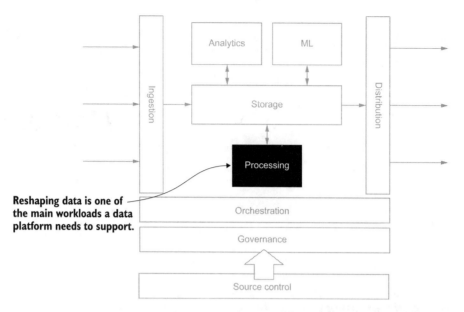

Figure 5.1   Data processing, specifically, reshaping the ingested raw data to facilitate analytics, is a common workload that we need to support.

an enterprise. This is a data model built on top of the raw data ingested in our platform, giving it a better structure, which also facilitates analytics.

Another common data model that aggregates datapoints from different teams into a common schema is a timeline view. We'll see how we can build a timeline view and how, in conjunction with a keyring, we can provide a broad view of what happens across all our systems.

Finally, we'll see how we can do this on an ongoing basis by applying DevOps practices. We'll leverage the infrastructure we stood up in the previous chapters to track everything in Git and continuously run processing. Let's start with the basic data processing and build up from there.

5.1   Data modeling techniques

As we ingest datasets into our platform, we can reshape them to better fit our needs. In this section, we'll talk about various ways in which we can lay out the data. The first trade-off we'll look at is keeping redundant data around to avoid performing joins versus using multiple tables and joining them together as needed.

5.1.1   Normalization and denormalization

Let's assume we have a dataset of user profiles consisting of name, credit card, and billing address. We also have a dataset of orders placed by the users. One option is to store these in two separate tables as shown in figure 5.2.

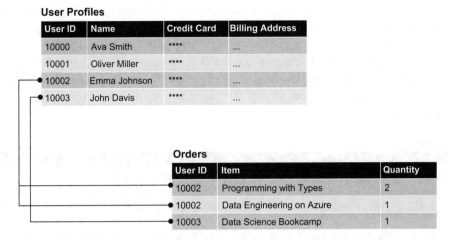

Figure 5.2 We store user profiles in one table and orders in another table. If needed, we can join the two tables on user ID.

Let's create these tables in Azure Data Explorer (ADX). Start the Azure Data Explorer cluster and run the commands in the following listing in the telemetry database context.

Listing 5.1   Creating the User Profiles and Orders tables

**Ingests the result of the
query after <| into a table**

```
.set UserProfiles <|
datatable (UserId: int, Name: string, CreditCard: string,
   BillingAddress: string) [
      10000, 'Ava Smith', '***', '...',
      10001, 'Oliver Miller', '***', '...',
      10002, 'Emma Johnson', '***', '...',
      10003, 'John Davis', '***', '...'
]
```

The datatable command specifies a set of rows inline, simulating data for the User Profiles table.

```
.set Orders <|
datatable (UserId: int, Item: string, Quantity: int) [
      10002, 'Programming with Types', 2,
      10002, 'Data Engineering on Azure', 1,
      10003, 'Data Science Bookcamp', 1
]
```

Simulates data for the Orders table using .set and datatable commands

If we want to retrieve user details from an order, we'll need to join the two tables. The following listing shows this step.

Listing 5.2   Joining the Orders table with User Profiles

```
Orders
| join kind=inner UserProfiles on UserId
| project Item, Name
```

A quick side note on Azure Data Explorer joins: by default, joins are inner unique, which means only one row from the table on the right side of the join is picked. If we want to join with all matching rows, we need to specify the join as inner.

One thing to consider is that as the data volume grows, joining becomes more and more expensive. The database engine needs to match rows from different tables, and finding these matches is not cheap. An alternative is to keep everything in a single table as figure 5.3 shows.

Orders

User ID	Name	Credit Card	Billing Address	Item	Quantity
10002	Emma Johnson	****	...	Programming with Types	2
10002	Emma Johnson	****	...	Data Engineering on Azure	1
10003	John Davis	****	...	Data Science Bookcamp	1

Figure 5.3   **We store both user profiles and orders in the same table. This introduces some redundancy; for example, the billing details of user 10002 is repeated with each order.**

This layout has redundant data because we must repeat the user profiles with each order. On the other hand, querying this table doesn't involve any joins; if we need the user profile data for an order, we have it available right there. Let's set this up in Azure Data Explorer. The following listing creates this extended table.

Listing 5.3   Creating the User Orders table

```
.set UserOrders <|
datatable (UserId: int, Name: string, CreditCard: string,
➥ BillingAddress: string, Item: string, Quantity: int) [
    10002, 'Emma Johnson', '***', '...', 'Programming with Types', 2,
    10002, 'Emma Johnson', '***', '...', 'Data Engineering on Azure', 1,
    10003, 'John Davis', '***', '...', 'Data Science Bookcamp', 1
]
```

Now if we want to retrieve the names associated with each order, we don't need to do any joining. The next listing shows the corresponding query.

Listing 5.4   Querying the User Orders table

```
UserOrders
| project Item, Name
```

One drawback of this approach is that if a user profile changes, we can't make the change in one place because this profile is replicated multiple times. We need to be careful to maintain the integrity of our data in such cases. Eliminating redundancy in a database by storing data in multiple tables and joining these is called normalization.

> **DEFINITION** *Normalization* is the process of structuring a relational database in such a way as to reduce data redundancy and improve integrity.

This is what we did with our first version of user profiles and orders, where we joined the User Profiles table with the Orders table. Alternately, inlining the data to avoid joins is called denormalization.

> **DEFINITION** *Denormalization* is the process of improving performance on a previously normalized database by adding redundant data.

The second version we looked at, where user profiles and orders are stored in the same table, is the denormalized form of our data. We won't cover all the different levels of normalization, but be aware there is solid theory behind this. Depending on how the data is laid out, it can be in one of several normal forms, and there are specific steps we can take to move from one form to another.[1] Let's clean up the tables as in the following listing, then go over a couple of data warehousing concepts.

Listing 5.5 Cleaning up the tables

```
.drop tables (UserProfiles, Orders, UserOrders)    ⟵── Drops multiple tables
```

5.1.2 Data warehousing

Data warehousing deals with integrating data from multiple sources and storing it for reporting and analysis. Expanding on the normalization concept, a common data modeling practice in data warehousing is to split datasets into dimension tables and fact tables.

> **DEFINITION** A *dimension table* consists of a primary key and a set of attributes tied to the key. A *fact table* consists of business facts and foreign keys linking into the dimension table.

In our previous normalized example, the User Profiles table is a dimension table, where we attach several attributes (name, credit card, address, etc.) to a user ID. In contrast, our Orders table is a fact table; it captures order details and links into the User Profiles table using the User ID column.

In practice, we usually have one central fact table and several dimension tables around it to represent some aspect of the business. For example, we could model a more complex order consisting of a timestamp (when the order was placed), a user ID, an item ID, and a quantity. The user ID links to the User Profiles dimension table. The item ID links to an Items dimension table that captures details about the item (for our example, details are title, author, ISBN number, etc., because we are selling books). We usually end up with a schema like figure 5.4.

---

[1] For more on normal forms, see https://en.wikipedia.org/wiki/Database_normalization#Normal_forms.

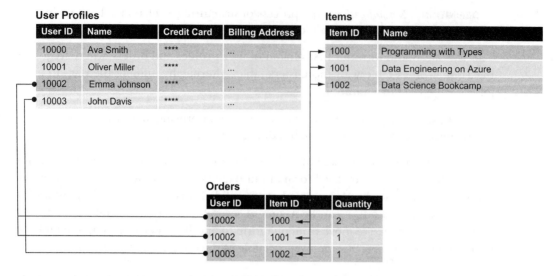

Figure 5.4   Star schema with an Orders fact table and with User Profiles and Items dimension tables.

This is known as a star schema because multiple dimension tables link to a central fact table. This gives the layout the shape of a star.

> **DEFINITION**   A *star schema* consists of one (or more) fact tables that reference any number of dimension tables. This is a widely used approach for storing business data.

In some cases, we might have dimension tables that further reference other dimension tables. As an example, our Items dimension table might have an Author ID column that links to an Authors dimension table containing information about authors. Having multiple levels of linkage makes this layout look less like a star and more like a snowflake. Thus, we call this a snowflake schema.

> **DEFINITION**   A *snowflake schema* is represented by centralized fact tables that are connected to multiple dimension tables, which in turn can be connected to other dimension tables.

Figure 5.5 shows a zoomed-out view of a star schema and a snowflake schema.

Looking at this in terms of normalized and denormalized data, in a star schema, all dimension tables are denormalized so we only connect the central fact table(s) to the dimension tables. If we further normalize the dimension tables, we end up with multiple tables and connections, which gives us a snowflake schema.

These types of schemas are commonly encountered, so it's good to know about them. In many cases, upstream data is laid out like this. In other cases, we might want to reshape data inside our data platform into, for example, a star schema. Finally, let's see what we can do when data doesn't fit a rigid structure.

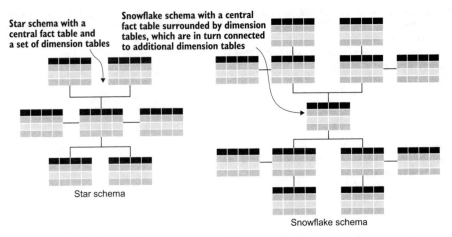

Figure 5.5   A star schema consisting of a fact table surrounded by dimension tables, and a snowflake schema consisting of a fact table surrounded by dimension tables, which are in turn connected to other dimension tables.

5.1.3   Semistructured data

In some situations, we need to deal with data that doesn't directly map to a fixed set of columns. For example, let's assume we accept orders from both individuals and companies. For individuals, we store their profile as name, credit card, and billing address. For companies, we have the company name, HQ address, and an account number. We can represent this in a couple of ways.

One option is to have separate tables for user profiles and company profiles and distinguish between the two using a Profile Type column in our Orders table. Figure 5.6 shows this layout. Then we'll recreate this in Azure Data Explorer in listing 5.6.

User Profiles

User ID	Name	Credit Card	Billing Address
10002	Emma Johnson	****	...
10003	John Davis	****	...

Company Profiles

Company ID	Name	Account Number	HQ Address
10004	Contoso	****	...
10005	Northwind	****	...

Orders

ID	Profile Type	Item	Quantity
10002	User	Programming with Types	2
10002	User	Data Engineering on Azure	1
10004	Company	Data Science Bookcamp	10

Figure 5.6   The Orders table links to both User Profiles and Company Profiles tables. The Profile Type column tells us which table to join with.

Listing 5.6   Recreating the User Profiles, Company Profiles, and Orders tables

```
.set UserProfiles <|
datatable (UserId: int, Name: string, CreditCard: string,
➥ BillingAddress: string) [
    10002, 'Emma Johnson', '***', '...',
    10003, 'John Davis', '***', '...'
]

.set CompanyProfiles <|
datatable (CompanyId: int, Name: string,
➥ AccountNumber: string, HQAddress: string) [
    10004, 'Contoso', '***', '...',
    10005, 'Northwind', '***', '...'
]

.set Orders <|
datatable (Id: int, ProfileType: string, Item: string, Quantity: int) [
    10002, 'User', 'Programming with Types', 2,
    10002, 'User', 'Data Engineering on Azure', 1,
    10004, 'Company', 'Data Science Bookcamp', 10
]
```

We have enough information to query either the User Profiles or the Company Profiles table as needed. For example, the following listing shows how we can retrieve the HQ address of companies that have placed orders.

Listing 5.7   Retrieving HQ addresses

```
Orders
| where ProfileType == 'Company'
| join kind=inner CompanyProfiles on $left.Id == $right.CompanyId
| project Item, HQAddress
```

Another option is to keep all profiles in a single table, keeping an ID column and a Profile Type column, then putting the rest of the data in a column that stores arbitrary data. In Azure Data Explorer, the dynamic data type allows us to do just that.

A *dynamic column* can store multiple key-value pairs, arrays, and nested data. Much like JSON objects, dynamic values can store complex, arbitrary data. We can "unpack" this data at query time as needed. Figure 5.7 shows how we can store profiles in a semi-structured fashion using a dynamic column.

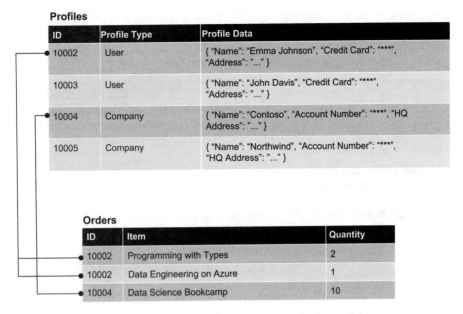

Figure 5.7 Semistructured profile data using a dynamic Profile Data column

Let's clean up the previous tables and create the Profiles table with a dynamic column as in the following listing.

Listing 5.8 Cleaning up the Profiles and Orders tables

```
.drop tables (UserProfiles, CompanyProfiles, Orders)

.set Profiles <|
datatable (Id: int, ProfileType: string, ProfileData: dynamic) [
    10002, 'User', dynamic({"Name": "Emma Johnson",
        "CreditCard": "***", "Address": "..."}),        ◁——  Passes a dynamic set
    10003, 'User', dynamic({"Name": "John Davis",             of properties as a JSON
        "CreditCard": "***", "Address": "..."}),             object to dynamic()
    10004, 'Company', dynamic({"Name": "Contoso",
        "AccountNumber": "***", "HQAddress": "..."}),
    10005, 'Company', dynamic({"Name": "Northwind",
        "AccountNumber": "***", "HQAddress": "..."}),
]

.set Orders <|
datatable (Id: int, Item: string, Quantity: int) [
    10002, 'Programming with Types', 2,
    10002, 'Data Engineering on Azure', 1,
    10004, 'Data Science Bookcamp', 10
]
```

The user-specific and company-specific data is now packed in the dynamic column, but we can extract it as needed. For example, if we want to retrieve the HQ address of companies that placed orders, we can run the query in the next listing.

Listing 5.9   Retrieving HQ addresses

```
Orders                                          Ensures we only have company
  | join kind=inner Profiles on Id              profiles where we can expect an
  | where ProfileType == 'Company'          ◁──┘ HQAddress property
  | project Item, ProfileData['HQAddress']
```
Gets the Item and the HQAddress
property from the dynamic column

Let's clean things up with the following listing. Then we'll quickly recap the data processing points we've touched on.

Listing 5.10   Cleaning up

```
.drop tables (Profiles, Orders)
```

5.1.4   Data modeling recap

We started by talking about normalized and denormalized data. A normalized dataset is modeled as multiple tables, which we can join when we need to query across them. A denormalized dataset keeps everything in a single table at the risk of storing redundant data (for example, repeating the user profile information for each order the user places). Normalized data is easier to maintain and keep consistent (a user profile change should impact only a single row in the User Profiles table). Denormalized data is easier to query at scale (no extra joins are needed).

A fact table contains some business fact (for example, a placed order) and links to dimension tables that contain various attributes (for example, user profiles for the users placing orders). This type of schema (a fact table connected to multiple dimension tables) is called a star schema. If the dimension tables are further normalized such that these also link to other tables, we have a snowflake schema. These schemas are commonly used in data modeling.

Lastly, sometimes we'll have data that doesn't fit into a rigid set of columns. In this case, one option is to rely on multiple tables (for example, one for user profiles and one for company profiles) and a type column that tells us which table we should join with. Another option is to use semistructured data, packing different attributes into a column and unpacking them as needed. In Azure Data Explorer, we can achieve this with the dynamic data type. Now that we have covered some of the basics of data modeling, let's look at another common concept for stitching together different datasets: an identity keyring.

5.2 *Identity keyrings*

In a large enough enterprise, getting a broad view of how the systems are used is not an easy task. What usually happens is that different parts of the business generate and master their own identities.

For example, the website team uses cookie IDs to identify users that aren't signed in and profile IDs for users that are signed in. The payments team uses customer IDs to identify customers and subscription IDs to keep track of which subscriptions customers buy. The customer success team uses a customer support ID to identify customers in their support tools. They also store email addresses of customers. An identity keyring pulls together all these identities across the different systems and allows us to quickly find all the connections. Figure 5.8 shows the various identities used by the different teams and how a keyring groups them together.

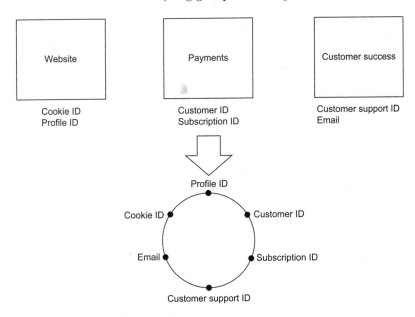

Figure 5.8 The website, payments, and customer success teams all master their own identities. A keyring groups these identities together.

The larger the business, the more identities we have and the harder it is to get the broader view of how users interact. Having a keyring allows us to correlate activity across the various systems; we can see, for example, how the time it takes to resolve a customer issue in the customer success team impacts user retention, which is tracked by the payments team. Or we can see how an A/B test run on the website impacts the subscriptions a user signs up for.

5.2.1   *Building an identity keyring*

Various systems have some connections between identities. For example, the website team might have a table that matches cookie IDs to profiles once users log in, and the user profile includes an email address. The payments team keeps a mapping of customers to subscriptions and also has the profile ID for a given customer ID. The customer success team connects each of their own IDs to an email address. Figure 5.9 shows these connections and how bringing them together lets us group all identities in the system.

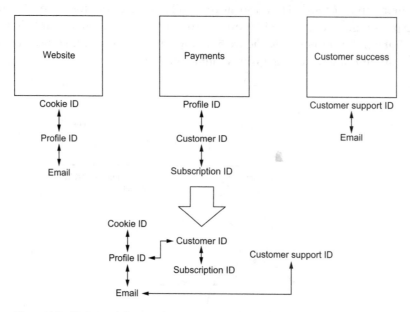

Figure 5.9   Various systems maintain various connections. Bringing these together allows us to group all identities in the system.

Let's create the Azure Data Explorer tables containing these identities as listing 5.11 shows. We'll create a Profiles table with a couple of profile IDs, emails, and cookie IDs; a Customers table that links customer IDs to profile IDs; a Subscriptions table that links customer IDs to subscription IDs; and a Customers Support table with a couple of customer support IDs and emails.

Listing 5.11   Tables containing IDs and connections

```
.set Profiles <|
datatable (ProfileId: int, Email: string, CookieId: guid) [
    10002, 'emma@hotmail.com', '657d31b9-0614-4df7-8be6-d576738a9661',
    10003, 'oliver@hotmail.com', '0864c60d-cc36-4384-81a3-e4c1eee14fe7'
]

.set Customers <
```

```
|datatable (CustomerId: int, ProfileId: int) [
    1001, 10002,
    1005, 10003
]

.set Subscriptions <|
datatable (CustomerId: int, SubscriptionId: guid) [
    1001, 'fd10b613-8378-4d37-b8e7-bb665999d122',
    1005, '55979377-ed34-4911-badf-05e07755334c'
]

.set SupportCustomers <|
datatable (SupportCustomerId: int, Email: string) [
    21, 'emma@hotmail.com',
    22, 'oliver@hotmail.com'
]
```

These tables come from different systems, but these end up ingested into our data platform. Once we have this raw data, we can build a keyring by grouping all related IDs.

The schema for our Keyring table consists of a group ID that uniquely identifies a group of related identities, a key type that specifies which identity we are capturing in each row, and a key value that is the value of the identity. We'll start by ingesting the profiles data.

We first generate new GUIDs and set the key type to `ProfileId` and the key value to the profile ID from the Profiles table. Next, we join the Profiles table with the Keyring table on `ProfileId`, which gives us the group ID, and then we add the email addresses. Finally, we join the Profiles table with the Keyring table on `ProfileId` and add the cookie ID values. The following listing shows the first batch of ingestions.

Listing 5.12 Ingesting profiles into the keyring

```
.create table Keyring(GroupId: guid, KeyType: string, KeyValue: string)

.append Keyring <| Profiles                         ←——    .append is similar to .set, but
| project GroupId=new_guid(), KeyType='ProfileId',          while .set creates a new table,
  ➡ KeyValue=tostring(ProfileId)                            .append expects an existing
                                                            table.

.append Keyring <| Profiles
| join (Keyring | where KeyType == 'ProfileId'              Joins Profiles with
    | project GroupId,                                      the ProfileId rows in the
       ProfileId=toint(KeyValue)) on ProfileId     ←——┘    keyring to get GroupIds
| project GroupId, KeyType='Email', Email   ←——
                                                    Adds Email to the keyring

.append Keyring <| Profiles
| join (Keyring | where KeyType == 'ProfileId'
    | project GroupId, ProfileId=toint(KeyValue)) on ProfileId
| project GroupId, KeyType='CookieId',
  tostring(CookieId)                      ←——|  Adds CookieId to the keyring
```

At this point, we "unrolled" the Profiles table into the keyring schema. Let's add the customers and subscriptions IDs to it as well. The following listing shows this ingestion.

Listing 5.13　Ingesting customers and subscription IDs

```
.append Keyring <| Customers
| join (Keyring | where KeyType == 'ProfileId'
    | project GroupId, ProfileId=toint(KeyValue)) on ProfileId
| project GroupId, KeyType='CustomerId', tostring(CustomerId)

.append Keyring <| Subscriptions
| join (Keyring | where KeyType == 'CustomerId'
    | project GroupId, CustomerId=toint(KeyValue)) on CustomerId
| project GroupId, KeyType='SubscriptionId', tostring(SubscriptionId)
```

This is similar to what we did before except when we bring in `SubscriptionId`, we need to join on `CustomerId` instead of `ProfileId`. That's not a problem. We can join on any identity that we already have in the keyring to find the group ID and extend the group with other identities. Finally, let's also add the customer support IDs, joining on `Email` as the following listing shows.

Listing 5.14　Ingesting customer support IDs

```
.append Keyring <| SupportCustomers
| join (Keyring | where KeyType == 'Email'
    | project GroupId, Email = KeyValue) on Email
| project GroupId, KeyType='SupportCustomerId', tostring(SupportCustomerId)
```

> We can join with any key already available in the keyring. Here we use Email instead of ProfileId.

5.2.2　Understanding keyrings

So far, we have pulled together the IDs from all these different tables into one and grouped them together. Now if we query the Keyring table, we will see something like table 5.1.

Table 5.1　Keyring table contents

Group ID	Key Type	Key Value
f03c9e90-5d97-4a11-82aa-480f74325a2c	CookieId	657d31b9-0614-4df7-8be6-d576738a9661
62159798-2447-41e3-b0ef-f1a239d55978	CookieId	0864c60d-cc36-4384-81a3-e4c1eee14fe7
f03c9e90-5d97-4a11-82aa-480f74325a2c	ProfileId	10002
62159798-2447-41e3-b0ef-f1a239d55978	ProfileId	10003
f03c9e90-5d97-4a11-82aa-480f74325a2c	Email	emma@hotmail.com

Table 5.1 Keyring table contents *(continued)*

Group ID	Key Type	Key Value
62159798-2447-41e3-b0ef-f1a239d55978	Email	oliver@hotmail.com
f03c9e90-5d97-4a11-82aa-480f74325a2c	SupportCustomerId	21
62159798-2447-41e3-b0ef-f1a239d55978	SupportCustomerId	22
f03c9e90-5d97-4a11-82aa-480f74325a2c	CustomerId	1001
62159798-2447-41e3-b0ef-f1a239d55978	CustomerId	1005
f03c9e90-5d97-4a11-82aa-480f74325a2c	SubscriptionId	fd10b613-8378-4d37-b8e7-bb665999d122
62159798-2447-41e3-b0ef-f1a239d55978	SubscriptionId	55979377-ed34-4911-badf-05e07755334c

Now, given any ID in the system, we can easily retrieve all connected IDs. For example, the following listing shows how, given `SupportCustomerId` (21), we can retrieve all related keys.

Listing 5.15 Retrieving all IDs related to a `SupportCustomerId`

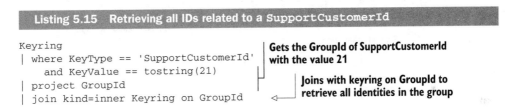

```
Keyring
| where KeyType == 'SupportCustomerId'
    and KeyValue == tostring(21)
| project GroupId
| join kind=inner Keyring on GroupId
```

Gets the GroupId of SupportCustomerId with the value 21

Joins with keyring on GroupId to retrieve all identities in the group

A keyring enables us to correlate different datasets and get a holistic view of how our systems are used. We used a schema in which we can plug as many types of IDs as needed with a Key Type column that gives us the type of ID and a Key Value column that stores the actual ID value.

The steps to build a keyring follow. For a graph-oriented view on how to build a keyring, see the following sidebar.

1 Generate a group ID and ingest one identity (`ProfileId` in our example).
2 For each new identity type, join with the keyring on a known connection to get the group ID.
3 Add the new identities to their respective groups.

Keyrings give us a unified view over all identities in our systems. Another useful view is one that shows all events that occur across our systems—a timeline.

Identity keyring as a graph

Another way to think about an identity keyring is as a graph problem. Each identity in the system represents a node in the graph, and each known connection represents an edge. For example, `ProfileId` and `Email` are nodes, and because they are connected (in the Profiles table), we have edges between pairs of these nodes.

Building a keyring means identifying all groups of connected identities. In graph terms, this means identifying all connected components of the graph and assigning a group ID to each connected component. As a reminder, a *connected component* in a graph is a subgraph in which there is a path between any pair of nodes, and there are no other connections to the supergraph.

An alternative way to build a keyring is to leverage a graph database. We load all nodes and edges, then we traverse to find connected components.

5.3   *Timelines*

A common timeline view helps us understand the various interactions users have with our systems. Let's say we're trying to understand how customer support issues are correlated with user retention. To do this, we need to see when support tickets are opened and closed, and when users cancelled their subscriptions. These datapoints again come from different teams: the customer success team handles support tickets, and the payments team knows when users cancel their subscriptions. Figure 5.10 shows how this can be plotted on a timeline.

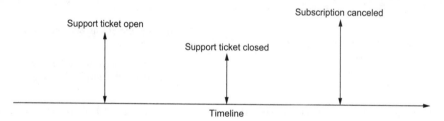

Figure 5.10   Timeline view of multiple events: when the support ticket opens and closes and when the subscription is cancelled.

5.3.1   *Building a timeline view*

We can define a common schema for these events with a Timestamp column to capture when an event occurs, Key Type and Key Value columns to capture the type and value of the identity tied to the event, an Event Type column, and a dynamic Event Properties column to capture event-specific properties. We'll again leverage semi-structured data to package different types of properties because various event types have their own associated properties. The next listing creates this table.

Listing 5.16 Timeline table

```
.create table Timeline (Timestamp: datetime,
    KeyType: string, KeyValue: string, EventType: string,
    EvenProperties: dynamic)
```

Now let's assume we want to ingest a Support Tickets table from the customer success team and a Subscription Orders table from our payments team that captures new and cancelled subscriptions. The following listing populates these tables with some sample data.

Listing 5.17 Populating `SupportTickets` and `SubscriptionOrders`

```
.set SupportTickets <|
datatable (Timestamp: datetime, SupportCustomerId: int,
  TicketId: int, Status: string, Message: string) [
    datetime(2020-07-01), 21, 5001, 'Opened', '...',
    datetime(2020-07-03), 21, 5002, 'Opened', '...',
    datetime(2020-07-04), 21, 5001, 'Updated', '...',
    datetime(2020-07-05), 21, 5001, 'Closed', '...',
    datetime(2020-07-19), 21, 5002, 'Closed', '...',
]

.set SubscriptionOrders <|
datatable (Timestamp: datetime, CustomerId: int,
  SubscriptionId: guid, Order: string) [
    datetime(2020-06-01), 1001,
        'fd10b613-8378-4d37-b8e7-bb665999d122', 'Create',
    datetime(2020-07-19), 1001,
        'fd10b613-8378-4d37-b8e7-bb665999d122', 'Cancel'
]
```

The following listing shows how we can ingest these tables into our Timeline table.

Listing 5.18 Ingesting into Timeline

```
.append Timeline <| SupportTickets
| where Status == 'Opened'
| project Timestamp, KeyType='SupportCustomerId',
    KeyValue=tostring(SupportCustomerId),
    EventType='SupportTicketOpened',
    EventProperties=pack("Message", Message)   <──┐ pack() creates a dynamic value from
                                                   │ a set of property names and values.
.append Timeline <| SupportTickets
| where Status == 'Closed'
| project Timestamp, KeyType='SupportCustomerId',
    KeyValue=tostring(SupportCustomerId),
    EventType='SupportTicketClosed',
    EventProperties=pack("Message", Message)

.append Timeline <| SubscriptionOrders
| where Order == 'Create'
| project Timestamp, KeyType='CustomerId',
```

```
    KeyValue=tostring(CustomerId),
    EventType='SubscriptionCreate',
    EventProperties=pack("SubscriptionId", SubscriptionId)

.append Timeline <| SubscriptionOrders
| where Order == 'Cancel'
| project Timestamp, KeyType='CustomerId',
    KeyValue=tostring(CustomerId),
    EventType='SubscriptionClose',
    EventProperties=pack("SubscriptionId", SubscriptionId)
```

5.3.2 *Using timelines*

If we query the Timeline table, we get something like table 5.2.

Table 5.2   Timeline table contents

Timestamp	Key Type	Key Value	Event Type	Event Properties
2020-06-01T00:00:00Z	CustomerId	1001	Subscription-Create	{"SubscriptionId": "fd10b613-8378-4d37-b8e7-bb665999d122"}
2020-07-01T00:00:00Z	Support-CustomerId	21	SupportTicket-Opened	{"Message":"..."}
2020-07-03T00:00:00Z	Support-CustomerId	21	SupportTicket-Opened	{"Message":"..."}
2020-07-05T00:00:00Z	Support-CustomerId	21	SupportTicket-Closed	{"Message":"..."}
2020-07-19T00:00:00Z	Support-CustomerId	21	SupportTicket-Closed	{"Message":"..."}
2020-07-19T00:00:00Z	CustomerId	1001	Subscription-Close	{"SubscriptionId": "fd10b613-8378-4d37-b8e7-bb665999d122"}

We have the various events on a timeline with their specific properties captured in the Event Properties column. Combining this with the keyring gives us a great perspective on how our systems are used.

Let's go back to our example where we want to correlate support tickets with subscription cancellations. The query in the following listing retrieves all support tickets opened within 30 days of a subscription being cancelled.

Listing 5.19   Support tickets opened before a subscription cancellation

```
Timeline                                          Gets all SubscriptionClose events
| where EventType == 'SubscriptionClose'  ←
| join kind=inner (Keyring                        Joins with Keyring on
    | where KeyType == 'CustomerId') on KeyValue  ←  CustomerId to get GroupId
```

```
| join kind=inner (Keyring
    | where KeyType == 'SupportCustomerId') on GroupId
| join kind=inner (Timeline
    | where EventType == 'SupportTicketOpened') on
    $left.KeyValue2 == $right.KeyValue
| project Delta=(Timestamp - Timestamp1), CustomerId=KeyValue,
    SupportCustomerId=KeyValue2
| where Delta < timespan(30d)
```

Joins again with Keyring on GroupId to get the associated SupportCustomerId

Subtracts the ticket open timestamp from the subscription close timestamp

Looks for SupportTicketOpened events for SupportCustomerId

Filters the rows where the ticket was opened 30 days or fewer before the subscription closed

The key takeaway here is that these datapoints (support tickets opened/closed, subscriptions cancelled) come from different systems of our enterprise and are identified using different IDs. Using an identity keyring and a timeline, we aggregate these into a common schema from which we can produce our business reports.

To recap, both keyrings and timelines are generalized data models we can build on top of the raw data available in our system. These help connect the dots and bring together otherwise disjoint datasets into a unified view of how users interact with our system. It falls to the data engineers to build and maintain such models. Of course, data processing also needs to run reliably on a schedule. Next, let's apply DevOps to our keyring and timeline ingestion.

5.4   Continuous data processing

Let's make our data processing workflows production ready. We'll do this for a subset of our keyring, so we can get the hang of how things work. The same pattern can be applied for all the keyring build steps and for building the timeline. As we saw in chapter 3 when we discussed DevOps, we want all of the steps captured in Git. We already have an Azure DevOps pipeline set up to deploy Azure Data Explorer objects, so we only need to wrap each build step in a function and store them in Git.

5.4.1   Tracking processing functions in Git

Listing 5.20 shows the `ProfileId` ingestion step as a function. Functions in Azure Data Explorer are a convenient way to save queries and rerun them without having to retype them. We name this KeyringIngestProfileId.csl and push it to our Git repo under the ADX/telemetry/functions path.

> **NOTE**   Make sure you are on the master branch before working through these examples (the previous code listings took us to another branch). You can do this by running `git checkout master`, then `git pull` to get the latest changes. Once on the master branch, add the file in the next listing and continue with the following listings.

Listing 5.20   Creating ADX/telemetry/functions/KeyringIngestProfileId.csl

```
.create-or-alter function
  KeyringIngestProfileIds() {
    Profiles
    | project GroupId=new_guid(),
      KeyType='ProfileId', KeyValue=tostring(ProfileId)
}
```

> Wraps the ProfileId ingestion into a function with no arguments

The following listing shows the email ingestion step.

Listing 5.21   Creating ADX/telemetry/functions/KeyringIngestEmail.csl

```
.create-or-alter function KeyringIngestEmails() {
    Profiles
    | join (Keyring | where KeyType == 'ProfileId'
        | project GroupId, ProfileId=toint(KeyValue)) on ProfileId
    | project GroupId, KeyType='Email', Email
}
```

> Wraps the email ingestion into a function with no arguments

We won't create functions for the other IDs because the process should be evident: take each individual query and wrap it in an Azure Data Explorer function. We'll also create a metadata function to list all the functions we need to call when building the keyring. We'll call it KeyringIngestionSteps.csl. The following listing shows its implementation.

Listing 5.22   Creating ADX/telemetry/functions/KeyringIngestionSteps.csl

```
.create-or-alter function KeyringIngestionSteps() {
    datatable (FunctionName: string) [
        'KeyringIngestProfileIds',
        'KeyringIngestEmails'
    ]
}
```

Once we add these files to Git and push them to our repo, the DevOps Pipeline we set up should kick off and apply them to our Azure Data Explorer cluster. The following listing shows this step.

Listing 5.23   Pushing to Git

```
git add *
git commit -m "Keyring functions"
git push
```

When we want to add another ID to our keyring, we can create another ingestion function and update the Keyring Ingestion Steps table by adding the new function to it. Having wrapped all these steps into functions, the only remaining step is to create an Azure Data Factory (ADF) pipeline that calls all of them, in turn, in order to rebuild the keyring.

5.4.2 Keyring building in Azure Data Factory

Let's first take a look at the high-level pipeline workflow, then quickly review the JSON describing the pipeline. We'll use our `KeyringIngestionSteps` function to drive this pipeline. The first step is to define a dataset based on this function. The following listing shows the JSON describing this new dataset.

Listing 5.24 Content of ADF/dataset/KeyringIngestionSteps.json

```
{
    "name": "KeyringIngestionSteps",
    "properties": {
        "linkedServiceName": {
            "referenceName": "adx",
            "type": "LinkedServiceReference"
        },
        "annotations": [],
        "type": "AzureDataExplorerTable",
        "schema": [],
        "typeProperties": {
            "table": "KeyringIngestionSteps"       ◁─── We can reference a function as if it
        }                                                were a table as long as it doesn't
    }                                                    need any arguments.
}
```

You would create this dataset using the Azure Data Factory UI, defining a Keyring-IngestionSteps dataset as an Azure Data Explorer dataset using the Azure Data Explorer linked service, telemetry database, and the `KeyringIngestionSteps` function as the table. (Fortunately, we can use functions as tables in Azure Data Factory.) After you click the Save button on the UI, the JSON file in listing 5.23 should show up in Git. Our pipeline will then look like figure 5.11.

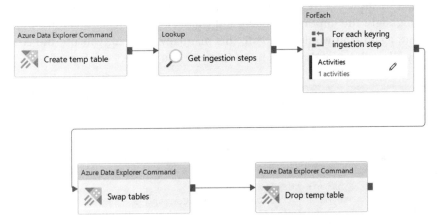

Figure 5.11 Keyring build pipeline, where we create a temporary table, get the ingestion steps, execute each ingestion step, swap the tables, and then drop the temporary table

Let's go over this pipeline before viewing the JSON. The first step is to create a staging table in which we ingest an updated keyring. The command is

```
.create table Staging_Keyring(GroupId: guid, KeyType: string, KeyValue: string)
```

Next, we read the KeyringIngestionSteps dataset we just defined. Then, we loop each row returned from the KeyringIngestionSteps dataset and ingest it. The loop contains a single activity, another Azure Data Explorer command, that references the keyring ingestion step:

```
append Staging_Keyring <| @{item().FunctionName}
```

Azure Data Factory pipelines support dynamic content, an expression language through which we can reference parameters and variables.[2] In our case, the ForEach loop iterates over the rows of the dataset, and in each iteration, the current row can be referenced as item(). The column is Function Name, so we call item().FunctionName.

The @{...} syntax inserts the result of the expression into the command. Note that this is a great feature of Azure Data Factory, which makes pipelines very flexible—we are not limited to hardcoded values. In our case, we drive the ingestion using steps stored in Azure Data Explorer. Once we have ingested everything in the staging table, we can swap it with the old Keyring table. The command for this Azure Data Explorer activity is

```
.rename tables Staging_Keyring=Keyring, Keyring=Staging_Keyring
```

Finally, we drop the staging table (now the old Keyring table):

```
.drop table Staging_Keyring
```

Listing 5.25 show the JSON that should show up in Git once you save the pipeline. We'll highlight the important details and you can cross-check with your implementation but, again, you wouldn't create this manually. Instead, you use the Azure Data Factory UI, and the JSON shows up in Git once you save it.

Listing 5.25   Content of ADF/pipeline/buildkeyring.json

```json
{
    "name": "buildkeyring",
    "properties": {
        "activities": [
            {
                "name": "Create temp table",
                "type": "AzureDataExplorerCommand",
                "dependsOn": [],
                "policy": {
```

[2] See http://mng.bz/gxR8 for more on expressions and functions in Azure Data Factory.

```
                        "timeout": "7.00:00:00",
                        "retry": 0,
                        "retryIntervalInSeconds": 30,
                        "secureOutput": false,
                        "secureInput": false
                    },
                    "userProperties": [],
                    "typeProperties": {
                        "command": ".create table Staging_Keyring(
                    ➥ GroupId: guid,KeyType: string,
                    ➥ KeyValue: string)",
                        "commandTimeout": "00:20:00"
                    },
                    "linkedServiceName": {
                        "referenceName": "adx",
                        "type": "LinkedServiceReference"
                    }
                },
                {
                    "name": "Get ingestion steps",
                    "type": "Lookup",
                    "dependsOn": [
                        {
                            "activity": "Create temp table",
                            "dependencyConditions": [
                                "Succeeded"
                            ]
                        }
                    ],
                    "policy": {
                        "timeout": "7.00:00:00",
                        "retry": 0,
                        "retryIntervalInSeconds": 30,
                        "secureOutput": false,
                        "secureInput": false
                    },
                    "userProperties": [],
                    "typeProperties": {
                        "source": {
                            "type": "AzureDataExplorerSource",
                            "query":
                        ➥ "KeyringIngestionSteps",
                            "queryTimeout": "00:10:00"
                        },
                        "dataset": {
                            "referenceName":
                        ➥ "KeyringIngestionSteps",
                            "type": "DatasetReference"
                        },
                        "firstRowOnly": false
                    }
                },
                {
                    "name": "For each keyring ingestion step",
                    "type": "ForEach",
```

Creates the staging table

References the dataset. We can tweak the query if needed by editing the query property.

We kept defaults throughout the pipeline, except for this property, which returns all the rows from the dataset, not just the first one.

```
        "dependsOn": [
            {
                "activity": "Get ingestion steps",
                "dependencyConditions": [
                    "Succeeded"
                ]
            }
        ],
        "userProperties": [],
        "typeProperties": {
            "items": {
                "value": "@activity('Get ingestion steps')
                    .output.value",
                "type": "Expression"
            },
            "activities": [
                {
                    "name": "Ingest Id",
                    "type": "AzureDataExplorerCommand",
                    "dependsOn": [],
                    "policy": {
                        "timeout": "7.00:00:00",
                        "retry": 0,
                        "retryIntervalInSeconds": 30,
                        "secureOutput": false,
                        "secureInput": false
                    },
                    "userProperties": [],
                    "typeProperties": {
                        "command": {
                            "value": ".append Staging_Keyring <|
                            @{item().FunctionName}",
                            "type": "Expression"
                        },
                        "commandTimeout": "00:20:00"
                    },
                    "linkedServiceName": {
                        "referenceName": "adx",
                        "type": "LinkedServiceReference"
                    }
                }
            ]
        }
    },
    {
        "name": "Swap tables",
        "type": "AzureDataExplorerCommand",
        "dependsOn": [
            {
                "activity": "For each keyring ingestion step",
                "dependencyConditions": [
                    "Succeeded"
                ]
            }
        ],
```

Sets item() for the loop as the output value of the previous activity ⇨

Calls the function corresponding to the current iteration and ingests the result into the staging table ⇨

```
        "policy": {
            "timeout": "7.00:00:00",
            "retry": 0,
            "retryIntervalInSeconds": 30,
            "secureOutput": false,
            "secureInput": false
        },
        "userProperties": [],
        "typeProperties": {
            "command": ".rename tables Staging_Keyring=Keyring,
                Keyring=Staging_Keyring",
            "commandTimeout": "00:20:00"
        },
        "linkedServiceName": {
            "referenceName": "adx",
            "type": "LinkedServiceReference"
        }
    },
    {
        "name": "Drop temp table",
        "type": "AzureDataExplorerCommand",
        "dependsOn": [
            {
                "activity": "Swap tables",
                "dependencyConditions": [
                    "Succeeded"
                ]
            }
        ],
        "policy": {
            "timeout": "7.00:00:00",
            "retry": 0,
            "retryIntervalInSeconds": 30,
            "secureOutput": false,
            "secureInput": false
        },
        "userProperties": [],
        "typeProperties": {
            "command":
                ".drop table Staging_Keyring",
            "commandTimeout": "00:20:00"
        },
        "linkedServiceName": {
            "referenceName": "adx",
            "type": "LinkedServiceReference"
        }
    }
],
"annotations": []
    }
}
```

Swaps the staging table with the Keyring table →

Drops the staging table (now the old Keyring table) ←

Adding new IDs to our keyring doesn't require any pipeline updates; we simply create new ingestion functions and add them to the Keyring Ingestion Steps data table. The steps for building a timeline are similar, so we won't cover the whole implementation but rather summarize what needs to happen:

1 Wrap each event ingestion into its own function.
2 List all the functions in a Timeline Ingestion Steps data table.
3 Build an Azure Data Factory pipeline that iterates over the ingestion steps.

Now we have everything in Git and we can run this on a scheduled trigger. We already set up monitoring in chapter 4, so if anything goes wrong, we'll get a notification. This setup allows us to run our data processing continuously.

5.4.3   *Scaling out*

One quick note on scaling out. As we briefly saw in chapter 2 (section 2.2.3), Azure Data Explorer has certain query limits that we might run into if we process large data-sets. As a reminder, a query can return, at most, 500,000 rows and 64 MB of data. Especially for our keyring and timeline scenarios, we might hit those limits.

We can work around this by partitioning our ingestion. That means that instead of ingesting the whole dataset in one go, we can split it up in multiple batches to keep the data volume below Azure Data Explorer's limits. Let's update our ingestion functions accordingly. The following listing shows the partitioned version of the Keyring Ingest Profile Ids table.

Listing 5.26   Content of ADX/telemetry/functions/KeyringIngestProfileId.csl

```
.create-or-alter function KeyringIngestProfileIds(          Adds the currentPartition and
    currentPartition: int, partitionCount: int) {            partitionCount arguments
    Profiles
    | where hash(ProfileId,                           Uses hash() modulo partitionCount;
        partitionCount) == currentPartition           only keeps profile IDs that hash to
    | project GroupId=new_guid(),                     the current partition
        KeyType='ProfileId', KeyValue=tostring(ProfileId)
}
```

We can call this updated function with, for example, a `partitionCount` of 10 and a `currentPartition` between 0 and 9, and it would return only 1/10 of the profile IDs. We can similarly update our `KeyringIngestEmail` function as the next listing shows.

Listing 5.27   Updating ADX/telemetry/functions/KeyringIngestEmail.csl

```
.create-or-alter function KeyringIngestEmails(currentPartition: int,
    partitionCount: int) {
    Profiles
    | where hash(Email, partitionCount) == currentPartition
    | join (Keyring | where KeyType == 'ProfileId'
        | project GroupId, ProfileId=toint(KeyValue)) on ProfileId
    | project GroupId, KeyType='Email', Email
}
```

We can apply the same pattern to all ingestion functions. In Azure Data Factory, we can replace the single ingestion activity inside our `ForEach` loop with a pipeline, as figure 5.12 shows.

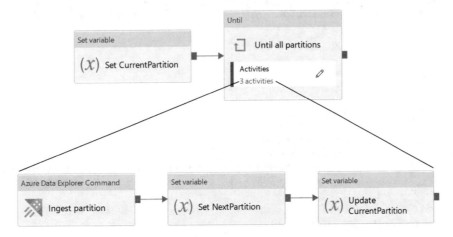

Figure 5.12 Pipeline for ingesting partitions

This pipeline has a parameter and two variables. The parameter is `FunctionName`, the Azure Data Explorer function to be called for ingesting. The two variables are `CurrentPartition` and `NextPartition`. The pipeline works as follows:

1 Set `CurrentPartition` to 0.
2 Repeat until `CurrentPartition` equals 10, our partition count.
3 Inside the loop, we ingest one partition by calling

```
.append Staging_Keyring
➥ <| @{pipeline().parameters.FunctionName}
➥ (int(variables('CurrentPartition')), 10)}
```

Let's unpack this. First, we get the function name from the pipeline parameter using `pipeline().parameters.FunctionName`. Then we pass it the value of `CurrentPartition` as an int and the partition count, which is 10.

4 Increment `CurrentPartition`.

At the time of writing, Azure Data Factory has a limitation so that a Set Variable activity cannot reference the variable itself when updating the value. That means we can't increment `CurrentPartition` in place. We can, however, work around that by first updating `NextPartition` to `CurrentPartition + 1`, then setting `CurrentPartition` to `NextPartition`.

Let's take a quick look at the JSON for this pipeline. We'll highlight the important bits in the following listing.

Listing 5.28   Contents of ADF/pipeline/keyringingestionstep.json

```
{
    "name": "keyringingestionstep",
    "properties": {
        "activities": [
            {
                "name": "Set CurrentPartition",
                "type": "SetVariable",
                "dependsOn": [],
                "userProperties": [],
                "typeProperties": {
                    "variableName": "CurrentPartition",      Sets the CurrentPartition
                    "value": "0"                              variable to 10
                }
            },
            {
                "name": "Until all partitions",
                "type": "Until",
                "dependsOn": [
                    {
                        "activity": "Set CurrentPartition",
                        "dependencyConditions": [
                            "Succeeded"
                        ]
                    }
                ],
                "userProperties": [],
                "typeProperties": {
                    "expression": {
                        "value": "@equals(int(variables(    Loops until
                   ➡    'CurrentPartition')), 10)",  ⟵─  CurrentPartition equals 10
                        "type": "Expression"
                    },
                    "activities": [
                        {
                            "name": "Ingest partition",
                            "type": "AzureDataExplorerCommand",
                            "dependsOn": [],
                            "policy": {
                                "timeout": "7.00:00:00",
                                "retry": 0,
                                "retryIntervalInSeconds": 30,
                                "secureOutput": false,
                                "secureInput": false
                            },
                            "userProperties": [],
                            "typeProperties": {
                                "command": {
                                    "value": ".append Staging_Keyring \
➡ <| @{pipeline().parameters.FunctionName}
```

```
  ⟶  ⇒  (int(variables('CurrentPartition')), 10)}",
                                  "type": "Expression"
                          },
                          "commandTimeout": "00:20:00"
                  },
                  "linkedServiceName": {
                      "referenceName": "adx",
                      "type": "LinkedServiceReference"
                  }
          },
          {
              "name": "Set NextPartition",
              "type": "SetVariable",
              "dependsOn": [
                  {
                      "activity": "Ingest partition",
                      "dependencyConditions": [
                          "Succeeded"
                      ]
                  }
              ],
              "userProperties": [],
              "typeProperties": {
                  "variableName": "NextPartition",
                  "value": {
                      "value":
  ⇒  "@{add(int(variables('CurrentPartition')), 1)}",
                      "type": "Expression"
                  }
              }
          },
          {
              "name": "Update CurrentPartition",
              "type": "SetVariable",
              "dependsOn": [
                  {
                      "activity": "Set NextPartition",
                      "dependencyConditions": [
                          "Succeeded"
                      ]
                  }
              ],
              "userProperties": [],
              "typeProperties": {
                  "variableName":
  ⇒  "CurrentPartition",
                  "value": {
                      "value":
  ⇒  "@variables('NextPartition')",
                      "type": "Expression"
                  }
              }
          }
      ],
      "timeout": "7.00:00:00"
```

Ingests data into the keyring by calling the function with the current partition and partition count

Sets NextPartition to CurrentPartition + 1

Sets CurrentPartition to NextPartition

```
            }
        }
    ],
    "parameters": {
        "FunctionName": {
            "type": "string",
            "defaultValue": " "
        }
    },
    "variables": {
        "CurrentPartition": {
            "type": "String",
            "defaultValue": "0"
        },
        "NextPartition": {
            "type": "String",
            "defaultValue": "0"
        }
    },
    "annotations": []
    }
}
```

This pipeline has a parameter, **FunctionName**, provided by the caller of the pipeline.

This pipeline also has a couple of variables, **CurrentPartition** and **NextPartition**.

The original pipeline replaces the ingestion step in the ForEach loop with a call to this pipeline, supplying it the FunctionName. Note that we can make things a bit more flexible by also making the PartitionCount a parameter and updating our Keyring-IngestionSteps to not only track which functions we need to call, but also how many partitions we want for each function based on the data volume. That way, we can split IDs that come in large numbers into many partitions, and IDs with smaller row counts into fewer partitions. We won't walk through the code here, but try making these updates yourself as an exercise.

In general, we can use this technique to move around large datasets that exceed the limits of our storage solution. The exact number of partitions depends on the dataset. When you run a query in the Azure Data Explorer UI, the engine returns not only the results of your query but also the query stats. These include the number of rows and size of the returned dataset. These are good datapoints for determining the partition size, considering the limits of at most 500,000 rows and 64 MB per query.

As a quick recap, this chapter was all about data processing and how we can reshape the data ingested into our platform to better support our workloads. We saw how we can build a keyring using our DevOps setup and Azure Data Factory. We built a pipeline that uses KeyringIngestionSteps to determine the steps it needs to run. To scale this for large datasets, we saw how we can partition our ingestion functions and create a pipeline that handles partitioned ingestion. We can use the same pattern to build timeline ingestion pipelines. This automates our data processing.

In this chapter, we focused on raw data and how to reshape it. The next chapter focuses on analytics—the workloads our data science team will run on our data platform and curated data model.

Summary

- Normalize data to reduce duplication and improve consistency; denormalize data to improve performance.
- Fact tables contain business facts and link to dimension tables.
- Dimension tables capture additional properties of various objects.
- A star schema has one or more fact tables at the center and multiple dimension tables.
- A snowflake schema is a more complex model, where the dimension tables of a star schema are further normalized into multiple other dimension tables.
- Sometimes we need to store semistructured data, when the various datapoints don't fit a rigid common schema.
- An identity keyring helps us connect identities created and mastered by various systems.
- A timeline view creates a holistic view of relevant events across the systems of an enterprise, enabling us to correlate otherwise disjointed events.
- We use DevOps for data processing, tracking everything in Git, and automatically running to periodically update.

Analytics

6

This chapter covers

- Separating development and production environments
- Creating an analytics workflow
- Supporting self-serve data movement

This chapter focuses on analytics, one of the major workloads a data platform needs to support. We briefly touched on the topic in chapter 3 when we took a query from our data scientist, Mary, and implemented DevOps for it, including tracking it in source control and deploying it using an Azure Pipeline. We'll expand on that topic in this chapter. Figure 6.1 highlights our current focus.

Our approach here will be quite different than the previous chapter. In the previous chapter, we focused on how we would implement various aspects of data processing, but when it comes to analytics, we should empower data scientists to do their work. That means enabling an infrastructure that allows them to self-serve their needs and putting good guardrails in place to keep things running smoothly.

In this chapter, instead of focusing on the actual analytics, we will focus on how we can best design our system to require minimum engineering involvement for data movement and data processing, while maintaining a high quality bar. First, we'll look

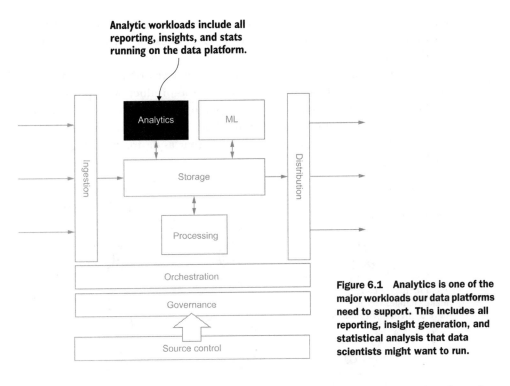

Analytic workloads include all reporting, insights, and stats running on the data platform.

Figure 6.1 Analytics is one of the major workloads our data platforms need to support. This includes all reporting, insight generation, and statistical analysis that data scientists might want to run.

at structuring storage to provide a development environment and an isolated production environment, and at the various options and trade-offs for this. Next, we'll implement a workflow that encourages moving analytics through a number of stages: prototyping, acceptance testing, and, finally, production. We'll see how we can enforce this using retention policies and access control. All production is backed by DevOps.

We will also see how we can open Azure Data Factory (ADF) for self-service, so data scientists can build their own ETL pipelines (ETL is short for extract, transform, load). We'll operate these in production, so we'll see how we can add some guardrails using annotations and build-time validation. The data engineers are responsible for the production environment, overall operations, and platform health. They shouldn't be a bottleneck for supporting analytics. That means designing an environment where data scientists can meet their own needs without jeopardizing the production scenarios. Let's start with structuring storage to enable this.

6.1 Structuring storage

In chapter 4, we briefly touched on having separate development and production environments. We created a separate production database and two Azure Data Factories, one for development and one for production. Let's expand on that now to see how we can best structure our storage and what trade-offs we should consider.

We know from the world of software engineering that the production environment should be locked down and always functioning. Only on-call SREs (site reliability engineers) can make changes to the production environment. But the development environment is more open and can sometimes be broken without impacting production workloads.

All team members can make changes to the development environment. For example, a website has at least two deployments: the production deployment, serving live traffic from its customers, and a development deployment, used by the engineering team for trying out new features. Sometimes, there is also a preproduction environment used for integration, but we'll leave that aside for now. Figure 6.2 shows the common setup.

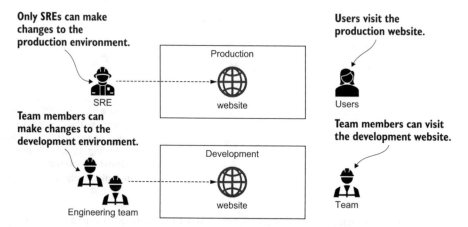

Figure 6.2 Managing production and development environments. Only SREs can make changes to the production environment, including deploying new features. Anyone on the team can make changes to the development environment. Users visit the production website. The team working on the website can visit the development version.

We can also do something similar with the data platform. We can have a production environment, against which all automation runs, and a development environment, where our data scientists can experiment. If a prototype in development is deemed valuable, it graduates to the production environment (deployed by an SRE). Figure 6.3 shows what this looks like for a data platform.

In the data platform case, we probably won't have company-external users connecting to the data directly, but we will have various processes (like data modeling, training machine learning models, publishing data to downstream consumers or serving it through an API, etc.). These processes need to run reliably, so it makes sense to provide a separate production environment: we don't want a junior data scientist accidentally running an expensive query that hogs up all compute resources and have our API fail. There are several ways to support a development environment for analytics:

- Provide development data.
- Replicate the production data.
- Provide read-only access to the production data.

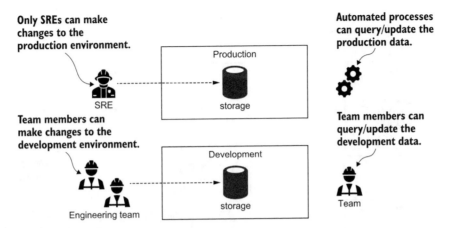

Figure 6.3 Only SREs can make changes to the production environment, but anyone on the team can make changes to the development environment. Automated processes connect to the production storage. Team members connect to the development storage.

We'll cover each of these and discuss the trade-offs. Note that we are talking about "access" in broad terms here—who gets access to the production environment data and who doesn't. In practice, we will need an additional, more granular layer of access control to properly secure data. Someone might be allowed access to only certain datasets, while more sensitive data would be protected and restricted to fewer viewers. We'll cover this in chapter 10, when we discuss compliance and proper data handling. For now, we're talking about the outer layer of access control—who would get access to at least some data in the environment.

6.1.1 Providing development data

The first option is to maintain a separate development environment with its own datasets. We would maintain ingestion pipelines that move data to that environment. This development data is usually a subset of the whole set of production data. Having ETL dedicated to supporting a development environment also gives us a chance to filter sensitive information, which otherwise would be available in a production environment.

As an example, say we want to run a sentiment analysis on the support ticket messages. While we can feed these messages to Azure Cognitive Services, we might not want to expose all these messages to the whole data science team due to privacy implications. Figure 6.4 shows how this setup looks.

The main drawback of this approach is that we must maintain a whole set of pipelines just for development. This introduces more failure points. We'd rather focus on keeping the production pipelines running smoothly without having to worry about development-only ETL failing. There's also an extra tax on keeping these development pipelines up to date. For example, if a schema changes in production, we need to make sure the change is also reflected in the development environment. In general, I would not recommend this approach due to its high maintenance cost. We have other alternatives, like replicating the production data or providing read-only access to it.

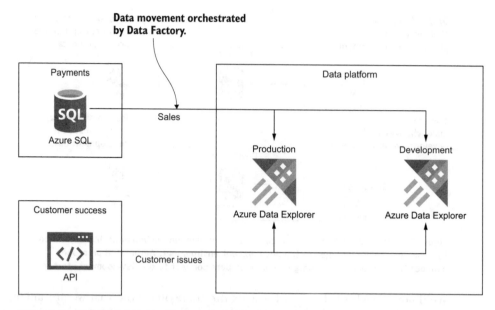

Figure 6.4   We ingest data from the payments team and customer success team into both production storage and development storage. Data movement is orchestrated by Azure Data Factory, and data ingested into development storage can be further filtered if needed.

6.1.2   *Replicating production data*

Replicating the production data in the development environment is usually more economical because we're not adding any development-specific logic. We simply ensure that everything that is available in the production environment is also replicated in the development environment. Figure 6.5 shows how this would look.

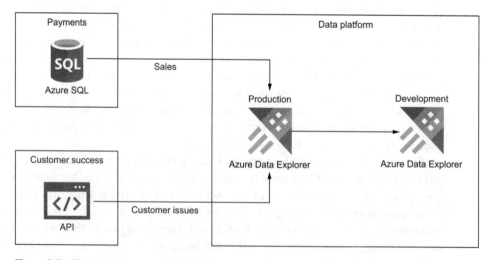

Figure 6.5   The development environment is a full replica of the production environment.

This type of replication means we still copy data, so we do have to maintain ETL pipelines to build the development environment, but we don't do much extra work besides fully mirroring the data. There's an even better option available though: read-only access with the storage services themselves handling data replication. Then we don't have to maintain ETL pipelines.

6.1.3 *Providing read-only access to the production data*

When possible, the best approach is to provide a read-only view of the production data in the development environment. The key difference between the previous options and this one is that here we don't do any additional data movement. Depending on the storage solution, we have different ways to set up read-only access.

If data resides in a storage service that doesn't come with its own compute (for example, Azure Data Lake Storage or ADLS), we can simply grant read-only access to it in the development environment. Minus some high scale limits (see http://mng .bz/eMpG), reading from an Azure Data Lake Storage account shouldn't negatively impact other workloads that are reading from or writing to it.

If the service also owns compute, like Azure SQL or Azure Data Explorer (ADX), we need to be more careful. We run the risk of an expensive development query impacting the overall performance of the service and affecting production workloads. Fortunately, these types of services provide ways to replicate data automatically.

With Azure SQL, automatic replication of databases is sometimes used for API backends to provide multiple read replicas in different regions for faster geo-availability. We can leverage the same feature to create read-only replicas of databases for our team to use in their development environment. For Azure Data Explorer, we can use a leader/follower setup, where a database from one cluster (the leader) is attached as a read-only replica to another cluster (the follower). This feature of Azure Data Explorer replicates data within minutes of ingestion from the leader to the follower without us having to do any extra work.

While the data is the same, production workloads run against the production Azure Data Explorer cluster, using its dedicated compute; development then happens in the development cluster, using that cluster's compute. This effectively isolates compute as figure 6.6 shows and ensures that inefficient queries running in the development Azure Data Explorer do not impact queries running in the production Azure Data Explorer.

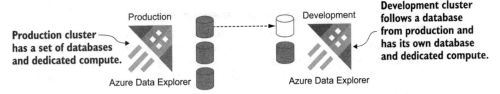

Figure 6.6 The production Azure Data Explorer cluster has a set of databases and dedicated compute nodes. The development cluster has its own database and dedicated compute. In addition, the cluster follows a database from the production Azure Data Explorer.

Let's create this setup in our environment. We already have an adx$suffix cluster with a telemetry database. Let's consider this our production cluster and stand up an adxdev$suffix to follow that database. Listing 6.1 shows how to set up a follower database. Remember to start the adx$suffix cluster using this command:

```
az kusto cluster start --cluster-name "adx$suffix" --resource-group adx-rg
```

Listing 6.1   Setting up a dev Azure Data Explorer cluster and follower database

```
az kusto cluster create `
--location "Central US" `
--cluster-name "adxdev$suffix" `          ◁── We used this command in chapter 2
--resource-group adx-rg `                      to create the adx$suffix cluster. Here
--sku name='Dev(No SLA)_Standard_D11_v2' capacity=1 tier='Basic'    we use a different name.

$leader = az kusto cluster show `          Retrieves the leader's
--resource-group adx-rg --cluster-          adx$suffix info as an object
name "adx$suffix" | ConvertFrom-Json ◁──

                                           Creates a follower
az kusto attached-database-configuration create `  ◁── database
--attached-database-configuration-
name telemetryConfiguration `  ◁──── Names the configuration, which can be anything
--cluster-name "adxdev$suffix" ` ◁──── Names the follower cluster
--location "Central US" `
--cluster-resource-id $leader.id `
--database-name telemetry `  ◁──── Names the follower database
--default-principals-modification-kind Union `  ◁── See the following sidebar for details
--resource-group adx-rg  ◁──                          on access control overrides.
```

The resource ID of the leader. We
get this from the $leader object.

Resource group in which to store the
configuration. We keep this in adx-rg.

Location for both clusters (see the following sidebar)

You should now be able to connect to the newly created cluster, adxdev$suffix, using the web UI at https://dataexplorer.azure.com/. Here the telemetry database is replicated as a read-only follower. You can issue queries against the data (which run on the follower's computer). Because this is a follower, the database is read-only; you can only create new objects or ingest data in the leader. See the following sidebar for more on Azure Data Explorer leader/follower setup.

> ### Notes on Azure Data Explorer leaders/followers
> The clusters must reside in the same Azure region (Central US in our code examples), and you cannot follow a database from a cluster provisioned in a different region. Following happens at a database level. It is possible for cluster A to follow databases from cluster B, while at the same time, cluster B can follow other databases from cluster A.

There are three ways to configure access control override on the followed database: none (use leader permissions), union (use leader permissions and any additional permissions configured on the follower), replace (use only permissions configured on the follower). This override allows us, for example, to grant data scientists access to the follower development cluster without granting access to the production cluster.

We can also override the caching policy. Caching makes Azure Data Explorer queries extremely fast but impacts cost. The more we cache, the more expensive cluster SKU we need. Sometimes the leader (production) might need a larger cache than the follower (development), in which case, we can override the caching policy. The commands to do this are documented here: http://mng.bz/pJ6R.

6.1.4 *Storage structure recap*

In this section, we'll look at the various ways in which we can structure our storage solutions to provide a controlled production environment and an open development environment. One option is to provide a separate ETL for the development environment. This gives us a chance to filter the data before landing it in the development environment, but it is extremely costly. We'll have to maintain and operate pretty much double the number of ETL pipelines.

Another option is to completely mirror the production data into the development environment. This option is slightly cheaper than the previous one, but it is still fairly costly maintenance-wise. The third and *recommended* option is to provide a read-only view of the production data in the development environment. Implementing this depends on the storage solution we use:

- For storage that doesn't come with its own compute (like Azure Data Lake Storage), we can simply grant read-only access.
- For integrated storage and compute (like Azure SQL, Azure Data Explorer, etc.), our solutions usually provide some replication mechanism. For Azure Data Explorer, we can leverage the leader/follower setup.

In general, we want to provide a locked down production environment that can't be impacted by what happens in the development environment, and at the same time, enable a larger part of the team to access the data we are processing in production and in the development environment. Next, let's see how analytics can move from development to production.

6.2 *Analytics workflow*

In this section, we'll focus on designing a workflow for analytics, where a data scientist can build their queries and reports in a development environment with access to the production data where appropriate. Once tested and validated, these queries and reports graduate to the locked-down production environment. Conceptually, analytics flow from prototyping to development/user acceptance, then to production as figure 6.7 illustrates.

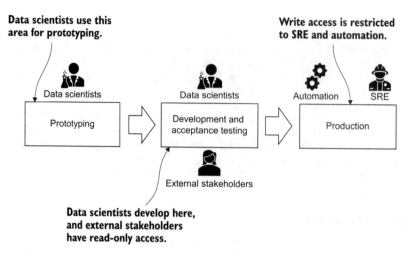

Figure 6.7   Data scientists prototype in the prototyping area. Then they develop in the development and acceptance testing area, where external stakeholders have read-only access for validation. Production is locked down so only automation and SREs have write access.

It is critically important that dependencies never flow backward: production should never take dependency on a dataset that has not itself graduated to production. That's because we can't provide any guarantees for something outside of production (the data might get deleted, might not get updated, etc.). Production is where we apply rigorous engineering and also where we provide various guarantees.

We'll use Azure Data Explorer again for this scenario, although we can apply the same patterns to other storage solutions with specific implementations. For now, let's create the databases mapping to this environment in our `adxdev$suffix` cluster. The following listing shows how we can achieve that.

Listing 6.2   Creating the prototyping and development databases

```
az kusto database create `              Creates the databases in the
--cluster-name "adxdev$suffix" `        development ADX cluster
--database-name prototyping `
--resource-group adx-rg `               Identifies our prototyping area
--read-write-database location="Central US"

az kusto database create `
--cluster-name "adxdev$suffix" `        Identifies our development
--database-name development `           (and acceptance testing) area
--resource-group adx-rg `
--read-write-database location="Central US"
```

We'll consider the telemetry database as our production area. That database is already hooked up to Azure DevOps (ADO), as we set this up in chapter 3. Now, let's implement our access model.

We will create a security group for our data science team and a security group for external users who need access for acceptance testing. These will be Azure Active Directory (AAD) security groups. We can then add users to the groups. The following listing creates the security groups.

Listing 6.3 Creating security groups

Creates an AAD security group

```
az ad group create `
--display-name "Data Science Team" `
--mail-nickname dsteam
```
Names the security group for members of our data science team

```
az ad group create `
--display-name "External Stakeholders" `
--mail-nickname external
```
Names the security group for external stakeholders

Let's map these security groups to our environment:

- *Prototyping*—Only the Dsteam security group gets read/write permissions to the database.
- *Development*—The Dsteam security group gets read/write access; the External security group gets read access.
- *Production*—Both Dsteam and External security groups get read-only access.

Now we'll get the Azure AD object IDs for the two groups. We can do this by running `az ad group list` to get a list of all the security groups. All of them should have an `objectId` property. The following listing shows the Azure Data Explorer commands we would run in the Azure Data Explorer UI to set this up.

Listing 6.4 Assigning permissions with Azure Data Explorer

```
.add database prototyping users
    ('aadgroup=<dsteam objectId>')
```
Grants dsteam read/write access to the prototyping database

```
.add database development users
    ('aadgroup=<dsteam objectId>')
```
Grants dsteam read/write access to the development database

```
.add database development viewers
    ('aadgroup=<external objectId>')
```
Grants external read access to the development database

```
.add follower database telemetry viewers
    ('aadgroup=<dsteam objectId>',
     'aadgroup=<external objectId>')
```
Grants both dsteam and external read access to the follower database

Note the general shape of the command in Azure Data Explorer: `.add <objectType> <objectName> <role> (<list of IDs>)`. The Users role grants read/write access, and the Viewers role grants read-only access.

For the follower database, note the command is `.add follower database`. Access is granted only on the follower database, not on the leader. This means that the data science team members and external stakeholders can query the telemetry database in the `adxdev$suffix` cluster but not in the `adx$suffix` leader. Our production environment is protected from runaway queries and such. Now that we have our databases created and access granted, let's talk more about each area, starting with the prototyping area.

6.2.1   *Prototyping*

We can think of prototyping as an analytics playground where data scientists can explore data and bring in various datasets or samples of data to see what is possible. With a large data science team, this quickly becomes unwieldy: abandoned prototypes live next to critical insights the business depends on; there is no way to enforce code review; documentation is scarce, etc. This is expected of a prototyping area, and it's not something we necessarily want data engineers to manage. That said, there are two things we need to ensure:

- The prototyping area is secured.
- There's an incentive to graduate from this prototyping area.

Once it is clear a prototype is something that the business can rely on, we want to move it out of this area and apply all engineering best practices (like source control ensuring the code is reviewed, access is restricted so it is not as easy to accidentally make breaking changes, etc.).

Because we are operating a data platform, we usually work with multiple external stakeholders who need to consume our analytics. We'll talk about patterns of distributing data in chapter 11. For now, one thing we should ensure is that access to the prototyping area is restricted to only our data science team. We need to do this because someone on the team might incorporate sensitive data into this area, while another team member might want to share their nonsensitive work with an external stakeholder. Opening the prototyping area to the external person might accidentally leak the collocated sensitive data. Figure 6.8 shows how this can happen.

The first key thing we need to guarantee is that *access to the prototyping area is always restricted to team members only, with no exceptions.* This avoids situations like the one in figure 6.8, where sensitive information can potentially leak. The second thing we want to do is to *ensure there is an incentive to eventually graduate from this area into the next step of our workflow.* That means, once it is clear a prototype has value, engineering rigor is applied so the business can rely on it in the long run. One way to incentivize this is to add a retention policy.

> **DEFINITION**   A *retention policy* is a key part of the life cycle of a record. It describes how long we need to keep the record and ensures the record is disposed of when it is time.

For example, we can configure a retention policy such that everything in the prototyping area is only kept for 30 days. This policy should provide enough time for our data

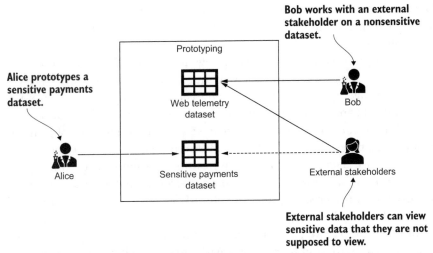

Figure 6.8 Alice brings in a sensitive dataset she uses for prototyping. Bob works with an external stakeholder on some nonsensitive data. The external stakeholders can peek at the sensitive dataset, even though they are not supposed to.

scientists to wrap up the exploratory work and move on to the next stage. In our case, Azure Data Explore allows this out of the box. The following listing shows how we configure a 30-day retention policy on our prototyping database.

Listing 6.5 Applying a retention policy

```
.alter database prototyping policy retention '{
  "SoftDeletePeriod": "30.00:00:00", "Recoverability": "Disabled" }'
```

The retention policy is represented by a JSON object with two properties: `Soft-DeletePeriod` determines when the data gets deleted, and `Recoverability` determines whether deleted data can be recoverable. This establishes that any data imported or produced in this area is removed (after 30 days in our case), so there is a strong incentive to progress to the next stage: the development/user acceptance area.

6.2.2 Development and user acceptance testing

The main difference between development and prototyping is who gets access to this data. At some point in the development cycle, data scientists need to show their work to external stakeholders for acceptance testing. That means we need to be careful to avoid the sensitive data-leak scenario we showed in figure 6.8, while allowing access to some people outside the team. We also still need to provide an incentive to graduate this work to production.

The best way to think about the development and user acceptance testing area is to not treat it as development from a DevOps perspective, but as production from a governance perspective. From a DevOps perspective, this is still an area where the data science team has write access. We don't necessarily need deployment automation, and we definitely don't want automated monitoring. This is still an area of active development.

From a governance perspective, things look a bit different. We can potentially store sensitive data, and, by design, we want to grant access to external stakeholders to some of the data in this area, but we need to enforce compliance and avoid data leaks.

We will talk about more granular access control in chapter 10. For now, one implementation we can look at based on what we've done so far is to split this area across multiple databases. Let's say we have nonsensitive data (website traffic) but also a couple of sensitive datasets based on data from our payments team, which contain customer shipping addresses. The shipping addresses that include names and street addresses is considered user-identifiable information, which is more sensitive and requires different handling.

In our example, we partner with two different teams. The marketing team cares about website traffic and how various marketing campaigns impact user engagement. The logistics team cares about customer addresses so they can optimize delivery routes. Figure 6.9 shows our datasets and how they align with our partners.

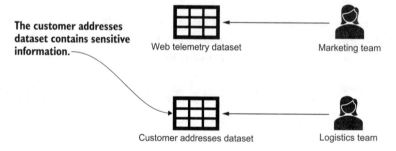

The customer addresses dataset contains sensitive information.

Web telemetry dataset   Marketing team

Customer addresses dataset   Logistics team

Figure 6.9   The marketing team cares about our web telemetry dataset. The logistics team cares about our customer addresses dataset. Customer addresses are considered sensitive information.

When we produce new data or a report that requires acceptance testing, we need to bring in someone from the marketing or the logistics team to our environment so they can validate our output. In this case, we can split our development/user acceptance environment across two databases, as figure 6.10 shows.

We would only grant access to the Development_General database to the marketing team and, more importantly, only grant access to the Development_Sensitive database to the logistics team. Now we can safely share our work around website traffic analytics without risking leaking customer addresses to people who shouldn't see them. We can share datasets in the Development_Sensitive database with our logistics team because they are already cleared to view customer addresses. We'll not recreate the setup in Azure Data Explorer because it's not much different than what we set up before—just an extra database and extra security group.

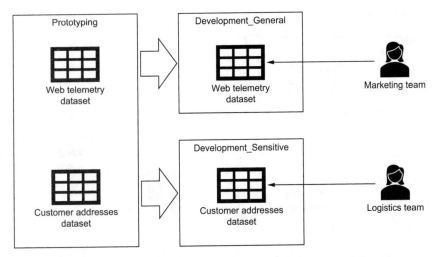

Figure 6.10 The prototyping area is restricted to our team so we can colocate all datasets. Moving to development/acceptance testing, we provision a Development_General area and a Development_Sensitive area. We grant different security groups access to these areas to ensure only people who are supposed to view sensitive data get access to it.

One key point that shows up again multiple times in the third part of the book centers around education: *make sure the whole team understands proper data handling and which datasets belong in which database.* Especially here, where everyone on the team has write access, it is critical to ensure our setup is not bypassed by a data scientist who mistakenly places logistics data into the website traffic data.

Another best practice to encourage adoption of our workflow is to have a retention policy on the read-only security groups themselves. That means if someone from the website team gets read-only access to the Development_General database to validate some analytics, they should only get that access for a short period of time. This should discourage them from taking any production dependency on something that is still in development stage. Once development is done, analytics should be published in the production environment.

6.2.3 Production

The production environment is where everything needs to run automatically and reliably. In chapter 3, we saw how Mary, a data scientist on the team, owns a report on the website's page views. In this chapter, we'll look at scaling this out to all analytics produced by our data science team.

Access to the production environment should be limited to SREs. We already saw in chapter 3 how we can set up an Azure DevOps pipeline to deploy Azure Data Explorer objects from Git and how we can package our analytics into Azure Data Explorer functions. As a reminder, figure 6.11 shows the general flow.

Because we already have this pipeline in place, we won't rebuild it. Instead, we'll look at some of the process aspects. Once an artifact graduates to production, the

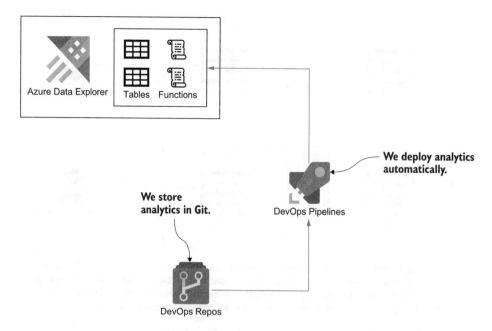

Figure 6.11   We store analytics in Git and deploy them automatically using Azure DevOps Pipelines.

SREs/data engineering teams takes responsibility for ensuring its reliability. Of course, SREs won't always have the business context, so if something if fundamentally broken, the data scientist should be looped in to help with the fix. But because an SRE is responsible for ongoing support, we need to implement a good handoff process.

One of the key elements of this is *code review.* Usually, the data scientist has a good understanding of the business context and query logic, while the data engineer knows more about query optimizations, storage efficiency, and so on. Code review allows the data engineer to sign off on the artifacts before they move to production. Let's see how we can enforce this using branch policies, an important part of the Git workflow.

> **DEFINITION**   *Branch policies* enable isolating work in progress from completed work in the master branch that automatically includes the right code reviewers for every change and enforcing best practices.

Let's create a reviewers team in Azure DevOps to handle code reviews. We'll add the engineering team members to this team. The following listing shows how to do this using the Azure CLI.

Listing 6.6   Creating a data engineering ADO team

```
az devops team create  `        ⟵——— Creates an Azure DevOps team
--name "Data Engineering"
```

Azure DevOps teams can contain users or security groups. These provide a DevOps equivalent of Active Directory security groups, which allows us to grant various rights to sets of users.

Next, let's set up our branch policies such that changes under the /ADX path in the DE Git repo need to be submitted via a pull request. This cannot happen directly on the master branch, and sign-off needs to be required from at least one member of the reviewers team. The following listing sets this up.

Listing 6.7 Applying branch policies

Means pull requests can't be merged unless the policy is satisfied.

```
$repo = az repos show `
--repository DE | ConvertFrom-Json
```
Stores the details of the DE repo into the $repo variable

```
az repos policy required-reviewer create `
```
Creates a new branch policy

```
--blocking true `
--branch master `
```
Applies the policy to the master branch

```
--enabled true `
```
Enables the policy

```
--message "A data engineering team member needs to
  review this change" `
```
Displays a message

```
--repository-id $repo.id `
--required-reviewer-id "Data Engineering" `
```
This is the DevOps group we just created.

```
--path-filter "/ADX/*"
```
Defines the repo ID; we get this from the $repo variable

Ensures this policy only applies for changes under the /ADX/ path

---

Now, all changes and additions under the /ADX path require a code review. We can ensure that the engineering team is the gatekeeper for production Azure Data Explorer objects.

6.2.4 Analytics workflow recap

In this section, we looked at a pattern to implement a workflow for analytics as figure 6.7 showed. This is repeated as figure 6.12 for reference and highlights the best practices data engineering can bring at each step.

First, we have a prototyping area that is limited to the data science team, where "everything goes." That's where the exploratory work happens. Access is strictly limited, and a retention policy encourages moving on to the next step. Next, the development/user acceptance area is where external stakeholders can validate analytics before moving on to production. Here we need to be careful about data leaks and secure datasets based on who is allowed to view what. Finally, the production area is locked down, and only an SRE and automation can make changes here. We can deploy to this area from Git using Azure DevOps Pipelines.

Graduating from development to production is where artifacts are handed off from the data scientists to the engineers/SREs. We need a process to facilitate this

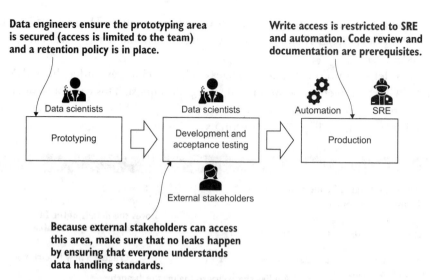

Figure 6.12   The prototyping area is secured and access restricted to the team. Acceptance testing is done by external stakeholders, so everyone needs to understand proper data handling to ensure that no leaks occur. Production is locked down so only automation and SREs have write access. Getting artifacts to production requires code review, documentation, and so forth.

hand-off, which consists of enforcing code review. We saw how to implement this using branch policies. But this workflow can be implemented on any data fabric, be it Azure SQL, Azure Databricks, or any other service. The concept of a prototyping area, a development area, and a production area, including who gets access to what, is independent of the actual storage.

The automation we put in place guides data scientists towards graduating their work through the staging areas and requires just the right amount of involvement from data engineering: reviewing code before it gets into production. Let's see how we can extend this to data movement by enabling data scientists to create their own data movement flows and then get these flows under SRE supervision.

6.3   *Self-serve data movement*

A common scenario is for data scientists to be tasked with answering some business question. For example, how does a customer support issue turnaround time impact customer retention? Sometimes, not all the data needed to answer this question is available in our data platform. We need to ingest it from an upstream source.

Let's say we have the customer subscription data from our payments team readily available as we used it for some other scenarios, but the support ticket data from the customer success team is not currently available. We have two processes we can use to get this missing dataset:

- The data scientists can ask the data engineers to stand up the pipeline that ingests this data.
- The data scientists stand up the ingestion pipeline themselves and then hand it off for the data engineers or an SRE to operate.

The first approach works but doesn't scale as well; the data engineering team becomes a bottleneck for all data ingestions. We already covered ETL using Azure Data Factory, so if this is the approach we want to take, we should be ready to go. Figure 6.13 shows this approach.

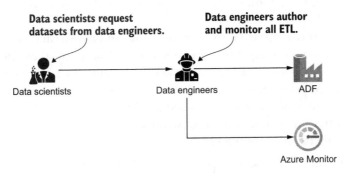

Figure 6.13 Data scientists request new datasets. Data engineers author the ETL pipelines and monitor them.

The alternative is to empower data scientists to create their own ETL pipelines, deploy them to the production environment, and have the data engineers (or SRE) monitor them. Figure 6.14 shows the alternative approach.

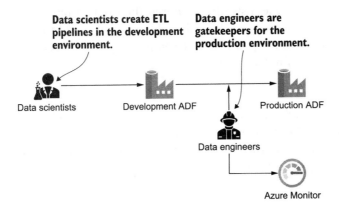

Figure 6.14 Data scientists can develop their own ETL in the development environment. Data engineers are the gatekeepers of what goes to production. They own production and monitoring of production workloads.

Much like with the analytics workflow, this section is about putting the right guardrails and processes in place to support self-serve data ingestion while ensuring quality and maintainability. First, let's review the support model.

6.3.1   *Support model*

We first need to clearly define responsibilities. We have a development Azure Data Factory where data scientists can develop pipelines that bring data into the system. This is synced with Git. We use Azure DevOps Pipelines to deploy a production Azure Data Factory. We already went over this setup in chapter 4, where we covered orchestration through Azure Data Factory and monitoring using Azure Monitor.

Our proposed self-serve setup has data scientists developing in the development Data Factory, submitting pull requests with their changes, then those changes get applied to the production environment. By design, the production environment is locked down and only SREs have access to it.

Our main goal with this approach is to scale things out and have a small number of SREs support a large number of pipelines developed by all data scientists on the team. We need to clarify that this does not mean that once a pipeline makes it to production, an SRE is solely responsible for it. That's because this doesn't scale. If we have one or two engineers maintaining a few hundred pipelines, we can't expect them to have all context to fix any of the pipelines. A workable support model is an SRE responds as a front line to production incidents:

- For transient issues (for example, an upstream data source times out due to a heavy load), an SRE can attempt to mitigate by rerunning a pipeline manually.
- For minor issues (for example, a column renamed upstream that broke the pipeline), the same approach can be taken.
- For anything more involved, an SRE would loop in the original pipeline developer.

To resolve an issue, the data scientists who authored the original pipeline will have more context on both the dataset and the stakeholders. We'll spend the rest of this chapter talking about some of the guardrails we can put in place to keep this process running smoothly, starting with data contracts.

6.3.2   *Data contracts*

We can see which source and destination tables an Azure Data Factory pipeline uses by inspecting the pipeline JSON or opening it up in the Azure Data Factory UI. This doesn't show us some other important datapoints though, for example:

- Who are the right people to contact if something goes wrong?
- What scenarios are enabled by this?

We can capture this additional information in a data contract. Listing 6.8 shows a lightweight Markdown template for such a contract.

> **DEFINITION**   A *data contract* is a document that accompanies data movement and captures relevant information (like upstream contacts, service-level agreement, scenarios enabled, etc.).

Listing 6.8 A data contract template

```
# Dataset source

Document source location and contacts.

# SLA

Service level agreement with upstream (e.g. how often is the data going to be
➥ refreshed).

# Dataset destination

Document destination location and contacts.

# Supported scenario

What scenario is this data enabling.

# Stakeholders

Who are the stakeholders for the scenario.
```

A data contract is something we can refer to. It allows us to answer these important questions:

- Which members of our team should be contacted in case this pipeline hits a nontransient issue that requires a more involved fix?
- Which members of the upstream team should be contacted in case upstream breaks without notification?
- Who are the stakeholders we should notify in case there is a data issue with this dataset?
- Which scenarios are enabled by this dataset?

As time goes by, the last question is especially important. That's because many times scenarios are no longer relevant. For example, our data scientists identified the correlation between customer support issue turnaround and customer retention, a detailed report was produced, and nobody is looking at this data anymore. Having a data contract that captures the scenario allows us to clean up our environment and remove pipelines that are no longer needed. We will talk more about the metadata we want to capture around our datasets in chapter 8. For now, data contracts are sufficient to implement our support model.

Additionally, it is important to get developers (including data scientists) to write documentation, as this tends to be overlooked. One incentive for this is to set up a validation build that rejects pull requests that don't come with the expected documentation. Let's see how we can implement this build-time validation.

6.3.3   *Pipeline validation*

In this section, we will implement our guardrails in Azure DevOps. First, let's create a branch policy for Azure Data Factory like we did for our Azure Data Explorer objects. The following listing shows how to create this policy.

Listing 6.9   Applying branch policies for Azure Data Factory

```
$repo = az repos show --repository DE | ConvertFrom-Json

az repos policy required-reviewer create `
--blocking true `
--branch master `
--enabled true `
--message "A data engineering team member needs to review this change" `
--repository-id $repo.id `
--required-reviewer-id "Data Engineering" `
--path-filter "/ADF/*"
```

The only difference between this policy and the policy in listing 6.7 is the path filter.

If needed, we can use a different required reviewer group. Suppose we have Azure Data Explorer experts on point to review changes to be deployed to Azure Data Explorer and Azure Data Factory experts on point to review changes to Azure Data Factory. For our examples, we'll use the data engineering Azure DevOps team for both.

Any Azure Data Factory changes that would be merged to the master branch now have to be reviewed by a member of the data engineering team. We can supplement this with some additional automation. Azure Data Factory pipelines have an option to add annotations, which are arbitrary values. Figure 6.15 shows where to find this in the Azure Data Factory UI.

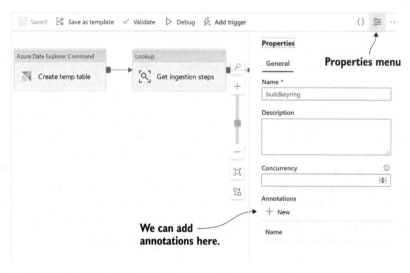

Figure 6.15   To create annotations in the Azure Data Factory UI editor, click the Properties menu. At the bottom of the pane, there is a New button to add annotations.

We can create a process around this, requiring all pipelines to have an associated data contract and an annotation that links to this contract. If our Azure Data Factory is stored under the /ADF folder in Git, we can ask all pipelines to link to a data contract under a new /Docs folder. For this we can use an annotation like `DataContract: /MyContract.md`.

When a pull request is created, we can run a validation built to read the annotations from all pipeline JSON files, ensure all pipelines have a `DataContract:...` annotation, and the Markdown document pointed at actually exists in the repo. If any pipeline is missing the annotation or is linking to a file that doesn't exist, the build fails, and the pull request can't be merged.

Let's see how we can implement this build. First, we'll write a small Python script to ensure that all Azure Data Factory pipelines have the required annotation and the associated documentation file exists. The following listing shows the Python script.

Listing 6.10 Python pipeline validation script

```
import json
from os import listdir, path            Sets the relative path
                                         to the ADF pipelines
dir = path.join('ADF', 'pipeline')       Lists all files in the
for file in listdir(dir):                pipeline folder
    with open(path.join(dir, file)) as f:
        pipeline = json.load(f)          Loads the JSON pipeline
        has_doc = False
        for annotation in pipeline['properties']['annotations']:
            if annotation.startswith(
                'DataContract:'):        Splits on the colon, getting the part
                has_doc = True           after, which is the document name
                doc = path.join('Docs',  expected under /Docs
                    annotation.split(':')[1])
                if not path.exists(doc): Fails if the document doesn't exist
                    raise Exception('Data contract not found: ' + doc)
        if not has_doc:
            raise Exception('Pipeline ' + file + ' has no data contract')
```

Searches for the annotation that starts with DataContract: and sets has_doc to True if found

If has_doc remains False, the data contract isn't found and it fails.

The script goes over each pipeline under /ADF/pipeline/ and searches for an annotation starting with `'DataContract:'`. If no annotation is found or the associated document doesn't exist, the script exits with a non-zero exit code, signifying failure. Let's save this script as /Scripts/validate_adf.py in our DE repo. We'll push it to Git using the commands in the next listing.

Listing 6.11 Pushing validate_adf.py to Git

```
git checkout -b validation_script
git add *
git commit -m "ADF validation script"
git push --set-upstream origin validation_script
```

Because we have a branch policy in place now, even though it is only requiring reviewers for changes under the /ADX path, we have to push changes to a development branch and submit a pull request to get them merged. Listing 6.11 pushes the new changes to the validation_script branch. We can submit a pull request using the Azure DevOps UI and then complete it to get the changes into the master branch. With this done, we can now create a validation build that runs this script for each pull request. First, let's switch back to the master branch and pull the changes with the commands in the following listing.

Listing 6.12   Pull changes

```
git checkout master
git pull
```

Now, let's create the validation build. The following listing shows the YAML for this build. We'll save this as /YML/validate-adf.yml.

Listing 6.13   Contents of YML/validate-adf.yml

```
trigger:
  branches:
    include:
    - master
  paths:
    include:
      - ./ADF/*

jobs:
  - job:
      displayName: Validate ADF pipeline
      steps:                                      Uses the UsePythonVersion task
        - task: UsePythonVersion@0      ◁──────┘  to ensure that we run Python 3
          inputs:
            versionSpec: '3.x'
        - task: PythonScript@0   ◁────── Executes the adf_validate.py script
          inputs:
            workingDirectory: $(Build.SourcesDirectory)
            scriptPath: $(Build.SourcesDirectory)/Scripts/adf_validate.py
```

Let's push this file to Git.

Listing 6.14   Pushing validate-adf.yml to Git

```
git checkout -b validation_build
git add *
git commit -m "ADF validation build"
git push --set-upstream origin validation_build
```

Again, we'll merge the changes to the master using a pull request. Next, we'll create a validation build pipeline using the Azure CLI command in the following listing.

Listing 6.15 Creating the Azure Data Factory validation pipeline

```
az pipelines create `          ◁──── Creates an ADO pipeline (as before)
--name 'Validate ADF pipelines' ` ◁──┐
--repository DE `                     │ Names the pipeline Validate ADF pipelines
--repository-type tfsgit `
--yml-path YML/validate-adf.yml ` ◁──── Points it to the YML we just created
--skip-run
```

Next, we can create a new branch policy that only allows pull requests when the build is successful. The following listing shows the commands to do that.

Listing 6.16 Validation build branch policy

```
$repo = az repos show `                        ┐ Stores the details of the
--repository DE | ConvertFrom-Json  ◁──┘ DE repo into $repo

$pipeline = az pipelines show -                 ┐ Stores the details of the ADF
name "Validate ADF pipelines" | ConvertFrom-Json  ◁──┘ validation pipeline in $pipeline

az repos policy build create `  ◁──── Creates a new build policy
--blocking true `                  ◁──┐
--branch master `                     │ Rejects pull requests if the build fails
--build-definition-id $pipeline.id `   ┐ Uses the repo and pipeline
--repository-id $repo.id `             │ IDs retrieved previously
--enabled true `
--manual-queue-only false `
--queue-on-source-update-only false `
--display-name "ADF validation" `
--valid-duration 0
```
Sends pull requests to the master branch

Now we can't merge any incoming pull requests unless the build succeeds. The build succeeds only if all Azure Data Factory pipelines are pointing to data contracts under /Docs.

Note that as of now, the build fails. We already created a few pipelines in the previous chapters without bothering to specify data contracts. You can update them by creating a /Docs/DE.md file and, for each JSON file under /ADF/pipeline, update the JSON so the annotations property changes from annotations: [] to annotations: [DataContract:DE.md]. As an exercise, do this on a branch and submit a pull request. The build should pass and you should be allowed to merge.

Now that we have an automated way to enforce documentation, let's look at one final best practice: learning from incidents to improve the overall health of data movement. All these practices aim to increase the overall reliability of our platform.

6.3.4   *Postmortems*

Because we are talking about data movement at scale, it is likely that multiple pipelines will fail during any period of time due to transient issues, upstream issues, scaling issues, etc. The recommendation is to *periodically look at the top offenders*: ETL pipelines generating the most incidents, even if transient. Aim to understand what is causing the issues and fix them as needed to keep the overall Azure Data Factory healthy.

For example, our pipeline ingesting website telemetry might start perfectly fine, but as traffic to the website increases and logs grow in size, the pipeline might start glitching. First, we start getting a few timeouts. Over time, the pipeline more often than not times out. While still somewhat workable, each run now requires multiple retries and sometimes manual intervention. This would be a clear sign that the original implementation no longer scales, and the pipeline needs to be optimized. A core practice for an SRE is a process for incident postmortems.

> **DEFINITION**   An *incident postmortem* brings teams together to take a deep look at an incident to understand what happened, why it happened, and how the issue can be prevented in the future.

We won't talk too much about how to run postmortems. You'll find many other resources focused on operational best practices. The only thing we want to highlight is that SRE teams usually have a recurring meeting where they do postmortems for major incidents. Rolling up top offenders into the postmortem process ensures that these issues become visible and that these don't keep adding up until our whole ETL becomes unmanageable.

6.3.5   *Self-serve data movement recap*

In this section, we looked at enabling self-serve data movement. While we already went over most of the infrastructure in chapter 4, where we covered the technologies for Azure Data Factory with Azure DevOps integration and Azure Monitor, here we focused on the processes and guardrails we need to put in place to allow anyone on the team to create ETL pipelines.

Developing Azure Data Factory pipelines is the easy part. The Azure Data Factory UI allows us to create ETL pipelines with drag and drop. We need to focus on maintainability over time. For that, we first looked at data contracts, which captured all the information an SRE needs to escalate an issue and handle communications. Next, we saw how we can ensure all pipelines are documented by ensuring that all changes to Azure Data Factory are submitted via a pull request and by running a validation build against these requests. Branch policies and Azure DevOps Pipelines allow us to set this up. Finally, we talked about postmortems and how you need to periodically review and update Azure Data Factory pipelines that cause a lot of incidents. Without this, support costs for data movement will keep growing.

The benefit of implementing all these processes is it enables everyone on the team to bring data into the platform and push ETL to the production environment. Data engineers are no longer the bottleneck for data ingestions, and as long as we ensure production stays healthy, we can scale our ingestion much more effectively.

The final major workload of a data platform we haven't covered yet is machine learning. That is the focus of the next chapter, where we'll take the knowledge from this chapter, including development and production environments, workflow to promote artifacts from development to production, and self-serve data movement, and apply it to machine learning.

Summary

- The production environment can't be impacted by what happens in the development environment.
- We want to enable a larger part of the team to access the data from the production environment in the development environment.
- For storage without compute, we can simply grant read-only access to the production environment for development; for example, for Azure Data Lake Storage (ADLS).
- For solutions that comprise both storage and compute (like Azure Data Explorer and Azure SQL), we can use a replica for development.
- Replication supported by the underlying solution saves us the trouble of maintaining a separate ETL just to support development.
- An analytics workflow moves analytics from prototyping to development to production.
- The prototyping area is strictly limited to the team and has a short retention policy to encourage moving from prototypes to development.
- The development area is considered non-production from a DevOps perspective but as production from a governance perspective. It doesn't require automatic deployment, validation, etc., but does require strict access control.
- If stakeholders from multiple external teams need access to the development area (for acceptance testing, for example), we need to split it up to avoid data leaks.
- The production area is restricted to SRE/data engineers and locked down for modifications.
- Self-serve data movement allows us to scale the ETL beyond the engineering team with proper guardrails.
- A data contract is a document that captures stakeholders, scenarios, and other metadata for an ETL pipeline.
- We can enforce that all ETL pipelines have an associated data contract using a validation build.

Machine learning 7

This chapter covers

- Training a machine learning model
- Using Azure Machine Learning
- DevOps for machine learning
- Orchestrating machine learning pipelines

This chapter focuses on the final major workload of a data platform: machine learning (ML). ML is becoming increasingly important as more and more scenarios are supported by artificial intelligence. In this chapter, we will talk about running ML in production, reliably, and at scale. Figure 7.1 highlights our current focus area.

We'll start with an ML model that a data scientist might develop on their laptop. This is a model that predicts whether a user is going to be a high spender or not, based on their web telemetry. The model is simple as the main focus is not its implementation, rather, how we can take it and run it in the cloud.

The next section introduces Azure Machine Learning (AML), an Azure service for running ML workloads. We'll spin up an instance, configure it, then take our model and run it in this environment. We'll talk about the benefits of using Azure Machine Learning for training models.

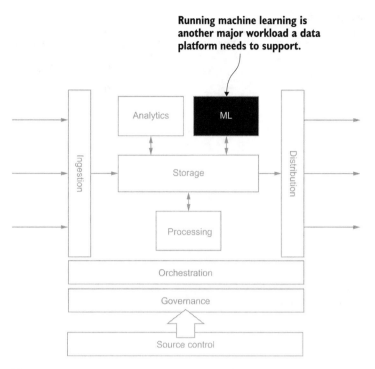

Figure 7.1 Running ML at scale is another major workload any data platform needs to support, along with data processing and analytics.

Next, we'll implement DevOps for this workload, like we did for all other components of our platform. We'll see how we can track everything in Git and deploy our model using Azure DevOps Pipelines. Machine learning combined with DevOps is also known as MLOps.

Finally, we'll touch on how we can orchestrate ML runs using our existing orchestration solution, Azure Data Factory (ADF). We'll build a pipeline that covers three main steps: copy input data, run an Azure Machine Learning workload, then copy the output data. Let's get started with our high spender model.

7.1 Training a machine learning model

This model predicts whether a user is likely to be a high spender, based on the number of sessions and page views on our website. A *session* is a website visit in which the user views one or more pages. Let's assume that the amount of money a user spends on our products is correlated to the number of sessions and page views. We'll consider a user a high spender if they spend $30 or more.

Table 7.1 shows our input data: the user's ID, the number of sessions, the number of page views, the amount of dollars spent, and whether we consider the user a high spender. Listing 7.1 shows the input CSV file corresponding to the table that we'll use for training.

Table 7.1   High spender data

User ID	Sessions	Page Views	Total Spent	High Spender
1	10	45	100	Yes
2	5	10	30	Yes
3	1	5	10	No
4	2	2	0	No
5	9	33	95	Yes
6	7	5	5	No
7	19	31	95	Yes
8	1	20	0	No
9	2	17	0	No
10	8	25	40	Yes

Listing 7.1   Content of input.csv

```
UserId,Sessions,PageViews,TotalSpend,HighSpender
1,10,45,100,Yes
2,5,10,30,Yes
3,1,5,10,No
4,2,2,0,No
5,9,33,95,Yes
6,7,5,5,No
7,19,31,95,Yes
8,1,20,0,No
9,2,17,0,No
10,8,25,40,Yes
```

You need to create this file on your machine as input.csv (or grab it from the book's Git repository). We are working with simple input and a simple model because our focus is taking a model and putting it into production, not building the model itself. There are plenty of great books covering model development and ML if you are interested in the topic.

Assuming you already have Python on your machine, let's start by installing the two packages we need for our model: pandas and scikit-learn (also known as sklearn). Listing 7.2 shows the command to install these packages using the Python package manager, pip. If you don't have Python, you can install it from https://www.python.org/downloads/.

Listing 7.2   Installing pandas and sklearn

```
pip install pandas sklearn
```

Now that we have our input file and packages, let's look at the high spender model itself. Don't worry if you haven't implemented an ML model before; our model has only a few lines of code and is very basic. We'll walk through the steps that should give you at least a high-level understanding. If you have experience with ML, feel free to skip to the implementation in section 7.1.2.

7.1.1 Training a model using scikit-learn

Our model takes an `--input <file>` argument, representing the input CSV. It reads this file into a Pandas DataFrame.

> **DEFINITION** A *DataFrame* is a fancy table data structure offered by the Pandas library. It provides various useful ways to slice and dice the data.

We'll split the data into the features used to train the model (X) and what we are trying to predict (y). In our case, we will take the Sessions and Page Views columns from the input as X, and the High Spender column as y. This model doesn't care about user ID and the exact amount spent, so we can ignore those columns.

We will split our input data so that we take 80% of it to train the model and use the remaining 20% to test our model. For the 20%, we will use the model to predict whether the user is a high spender and see how our prediction compares with the actual data. This is a common practice for measuring model prediction accuracy.

We will use `KNeighborsClassifier` from scikit-learn. This implements a well-known classification algorithm, the k-nearest neighbors vote. We use a classification algorithm because we want to classify our users into high spenders and non-high spenders. We won't cover the details of the algorithm here, but the good news is that this is fully encapsulated in the scikit-learn library, so we can create it with one line of code and train it with a second line of code. We will use the training data to train the model, then try to predict on the test data and print the predictions. Figure 7.2 shows these steps.

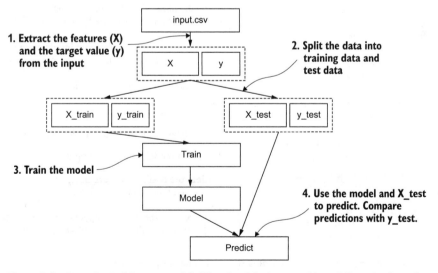

Figure 7.2 Steps for training our model. (1) extract features and target the value from the input; (2) split the dataset into train and test data; (3) train the model on the training data; (4) use the model to predict on the test data, comparing predictions with actual data.

Finally, we will save the model on disk as outputs/highspender.pkl. The idea is that once we have a trained model, another system picks it up and uses it to predict new data. For example, as users visit our website, we can use the model to predict who is likely to be a high spender and maybe offer them a discount. Or maybe we want to encourage non-high spenders to spend more time on the website, hoping it converts them into high spenders. Either way, some other service has to load this model and feed it never-before-seen data, and the model will predict if the user is likely to be a high spender or not.

7.1.2   *High spender model implementation*

Training a model might sound like a lot, but it is only 25 lines of Python code, as the following listing shows.

Listing 7.3   Contents of highspenders.py

Splits the input data into training data and data reserved for testing using a 0.2 ratio

```python
import argparse
from joblib import dump
import os
import pandas as pd
from sklearn.neighbors import KNeighborsClassifier
from sklearn.model_selection import train_test_split

parser = argparse.ArgumentParser()
parser.add_argument(
    '--input', type=str, dest='model_input')
```
Sets up argument parsing to expect an --input argument

```python
args = parser.parse_args()
model_input = args.model_input
df = pd.read_csv(model_input)
```
Grabs the input file path from the command-line argument and loads it into a Pandas DataFrame

```python
X = df[["Sessions", "PageViews"]]
y = df["HighSpender"]
```
Defines the model inputs as the Sessions and PageViews columns

Predicts the HighSpender value

```python
X_train, X_test, y_train, y_test = train_test_split(
    X, y, test_size=0.2, random_state=1)
```

Uses a KNeighborsClassifier with default settings
```python
knn = KNeighborsClassifier()
knn.fit(X_train, y_train)
```
Trains the model on the training data

```python
score = knn.predict(X_test)
```
Sets the prediction score using the trained model on the test data

```python
predictions = X_test.copy(deep=True)
predictions["Prediction"] = score
predictions["Actual"] = y_test
```
Formats the output, copying it into a new DataFrame and adding Prediction and Actual columns

```python
print(predictions)
```
Prints the predictions to the console

```python
if not os.path.isdir('outputs'):
    os.mkdir('outputs')
```
Ensures we have an outputs/ directory

```
model_path = os.path.join(
➡ 'outputs', 'highspender.pkl')    | Saves the model as
dump(knn, model_path)              | outputs/highspender.pkl
```

Let's run the script and check the output. The following listing shows the console command for running the model.

Listing 7.4 Running the high spender model script

```
python highspenders.py --input input.csv
```

You should see the test predictions and actual data printed to the console. You should also now see the outputs/highspender.pkl model file.

Strictly speaking, we don't need the prediction and printing part, but it should help if we want to play with the model. Here, we're using a small input size. The larger the input dataset, the better the accuracy. But again, our focus is taking this Python script and running it in the cloud using DevOps. The good news is that our approach to DevOps (or MLOps) scales to more complex models and larger inputs. Let's start by introducing Azure Machine Learning, the Azure PaaS (platform as a service) offering for running ML in the cloud.

7.2 Introducing Azure Machine Learning

Azure Machine Learning is Microsoft's Azure offering for creating and managing ML solutions in the cloud. An instance of Azure Machine Learning is called a workspace.

> **DEFINITION** A *workspace* is the top-level resource for Azure Machine Learning, providing a centralized place to work with all the artifacts you create.

In this section, we'll create and configure a workspace, then we'll look at everything needed for taking our high spender model from our local machine and running it on Azure. We will also learn about the Azure Machine Learning SDK. Azure Machine Learning provides an SDK for setting up various resources within a workspace. Because the main languages used in ML are Python and R, Azure Machine Learning offers rich Python and R SDKs for better integration with solutions written in those languages.

7.2.1 Creating a workspace

We'll start by using Azure CLI to create a workspace. First, we install the azure-cli-ml extension, then we create a new resource group called aml-rg to host our ML workloads, and finally, we create a workspace in the new resource group. The following listing shows the steps.

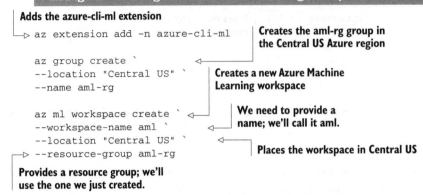

Listing 7.5   Creating an Azure Machine Learning workspace

Adds the azure-cli-ml extension

```
az extension add -n azure-cli-ml
```
Creates the aml-rg group in the Central US Azure region

```
az group create `
--location "Central US" `
--name aml-rg
```
Creates a new Azure Machine Learning workspace

```
az ml workspace create `
--workspace-name aml `
--location "Central US" `
--resource-group aml-rg
```
We need to provide a name; we'll call it aml.

Places the workspace in Central US

Provides a resource group; we'll use the one we just created.

The same way Azure Data Explorer (ADX) has a web UI accessible at https://dataexplorer.azure.com/ (as we saw in chapter 2) and Azure Data Factory has a web UI accessible at https://adf.azure.com/ (as we saw in chapter 4), Azure Machine Learning also has a web UI that you can find at https://ml.azure.com/. We will stick to the Azure CLI and the Python SDK to provision resources, but I encourage you to try the web UI. As we create more artifacts in this section, you can use the web UI to see how they are represented there. If you visit the web UI, you will see a navigation bar on the right with three sections: Author, Assets, and Manage. Figure 7.3 shows the navigation bar.

The Author section contains Notebooks, Automated ML, and Designer. We won't focus on these but here is a quick walkthrough: Notebooks enables users to store Jupyter notebooks and other files directly in the workspace; Automated ML is a codeless solution for implementing ML; and the Designer is a visual drag-and-drop editor for ML. We won't focus on these features because they facilitate model development. We'll look at the DevOps aspects of ML, using our existing Python model as an example, so this is less relevant for us. Of course, we could've built our model in Azure Machine Learning directly, but this way, we learn how we can onboard a model that wasn't created specifically to run on Azure Machine Learning.

We will, however, touch on most of the items in the Assets and Manage sections. Assets are some of the concepts Azure Machine Learning deals with, such as Experiments and Models. We'll cover these soon. The Manage section deals with the compute and storage resources for AML. Let's zoom in on these.

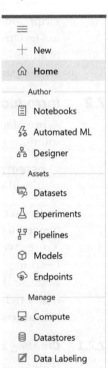

Figure 7.3   The Azure Machine Learning UI navigation bar has three sections: Author, Assets, and Manage.

7.2.2   *Creating an Azure Machine Learning compute target*

One of the great features of Azure Machine Learning is that it can automatically scale compute resources to train models. Remember, compute in the cloud refers to CPU and RAM resources. A virtual machine (VM) in the cloud provides CPU and RAM, but it incurs costs as long as it runs. This is especially relevant for ML workloads, which might need a lot of resources during training, and training might not happen continuously.

For example, maybe our high spender model needs to be trained every month to predict next month's marketing campaign targets. It would be wasteful to keep a VM running all the time if we only need it one day of the month. Of course, we could manually turn it on or off, but Azure Machine Learning gives us an even better option—compute targets.

> **DEFINITION**   A *compute target* specifies a compute resource on which we want to run our ML. This includes the maximum number of nodes and the VM size.

As a reminder, Azure has a set of defined VM sizes, each with different performance characteristics and associated costs.[1] A compute target specifies which VM type and how many instances we'll need, but it won't provision the resources until we run a model and request this target. Once the model run finishes, the resources are deprovisioned. This makes Azure Machine Learning compute elastic: resources are allocated when needed, then freed up automatically. We only pay for what we use, and the service takes care of all the underlying infrastructure.

Let's specify a compute target for our example. We'll request, at most, one node, use the economical STANDARD_D1_V2 VM size (1 CPU, 3.5 GiB memory), and name it d1compute. The following listing shows the corresponding Azure CLI command.

Listing 7.6   Creating a compute target

Creates an AML compute target

Specifies the workspace (in our case, amlcompute)

```
az ml computetarget create `
  amlcompute `
  --max-nodes 1 `
  --name "d1compute" `
  --vm-size STANDARD_D1_V2 `
  --workspace-name aml `
  --resource-group aml-rg
```

Sets the maximum number of nodes

Names the target

Targets the workspace name and resource group

Sets the VM size (in our case, STANDARD_D1_V2)

This won't cost us anything until we actually run an ML workload. If you click through the UI to the Compute section and navigate to Compute Clusters, you should see the new definition. Other compute options in Azure Machine Learning instead of AML are compute instances that include

---

[1] For more on VM sizes and costs, see https://docs.microsoft.com/en-us/azure/virtual-machines/sizes.

- VMs preimaged with common ML tools and libraries
- Inference clusters, where we can package and deploy models on Kubernetes and expose them as REST endpoints
- Attached compute that enables us to target compute resources like Azure Databricks not managed by Azure Machine Learning

Let's move on to storage now. We'll see how we can make our input available to Azure Machine Learning.

7.2.3 Setting up Azure Machine Learning storage

We'll start by uploading our input.csv file from the previous section to our Azure Data Lake Storage (ADLS) that we provisioned in chapter 2. We created an `adls$suffix` data lake, where `$suffix` is your unique ID, containing one filesystem named `fs1`. For this, we'll use the Azure CLI upload command to upload our input file under the models/highspenders/input.csv path. The next listing shows the commands.

Listing 7.7 Uploading input.csv to Azure

```
az storage fs file upload `
--file-system fs1 `
--path "models/highspenders/input.csv" `
--source input.csv `
--account-name "adls$suffix"
```

In practice, we would have various Azure Data Factory pipelines copying datasets to our storage layers. From there, we would need to make these datasets available to Azure Machine Learning. We'll do this by attaching a datastore.

> **DEFINITION** An Azure Machine Learning *datastore* enables us to connect to an external storage account like Azure's Blob Storage, Data Lake, SQL, Databricks, etc., making it available to our ML models.

First, we need to provision a service principal that Azure Machine Learning can use to authenticate. We will create a new service principal in Azure Active Directory (AAD) and grant it Storage Blob Data Contributor rights on the data lake. This allows the service principal to read and write data in the data lake. The following listing shows the steps.

Listing 7.8 Creating a service principal for ADLS

Allows read/write access on a storage account for this role

Creates a principal stored in $sp for role-base access control (RBAC)

Retrieves the details of the ADLS storage account that's stored in $acc

```
$sp = az ad sp create-for-rbac | ConvertFrom-Json
$acc = az storage account show -
name "adls$suffix" | ConvertFrom-Json

az role assignment create `
--role "Storage Blob Data Contributor" `
```

Creates a new role assignment, granting rights to the service principal

```
    --assignee $sp.appId `
  ┌─▷ --scope $acc.id
  │
  │ Sets the scope as the ID of our storage account
```

Sets the assignee as the app
ID of our service principal

The service principal can now access data in the storage account. The next step is to attach the account to Azure Machine Learning, giving it the service principal ID and secret so it can use them to connect to the account. The following listing shows how to do this.

Listing 7.9   Attaching a datastore to Azure Machine Learning

```
az ml datastore attach-adls-gen2 `       ◁────── Attaches an ADLS Gen2 datastore to AML
--account-name "adls$suffix" `           ◁────── Names the ADLS account
--client-id $sp.appId `
--client-secret $sp.password `           Specifies the service principal ID, secret,
--tenant-id $sp.tenant `                 and tenant to use to authenticate
┌─▷ --file-system fs1 `
│   --name MLData           ◁────────    Names the attached datastore
│   --workspace-name aml `               Sets the target workspace
│   --resource-group aml-rg              name and resource group
│
│ Identifies the filesystem we want to attach
```

Now if you navigate to the Storage section in the UI, you should see the newly created MLData data store. In fact, you should see a couple more data stores that are created by default and used within the workspace. In practice, we need to connect to external storage, and data stores are the way to do that.

Our workspace is now configured with both a compute target and an attached data store. Let's grant our service principal Contributor rights to the Azure Machine Learning workspace too, so we can use it for deployment. Note, in a production environment, we would have separate service principals for better security. Then if one of the principals gets compromised, it has access to fewer resources. We'll reuse our $sp service principal, though, to keep things brief. The following listing shows how to grant the rights.

Listing 7.10   Granting Contributor rights on Azure Machine Learning

Converts JSON to a PowerShell
object and stores it in $aml

Gets the details of an AML workspace

```
$aml = az ml workspace show `    ◁──┐   Defines the workspace
--workspace-name aml `              │   name and resource group
--resource-group aml-rg `        ───┘
┌─▷ | ConvertFrom-Json
│                                Creates a role assignment, granting
│                                rights to the service principal
│
az role assignment create `  ◁──┐
--role "Contributor" `           │  The Contributor role allows modifying the
--assignee $sp.appId `       ◁───┘  resource, which we need for deployment.
--scope $aml.id          ◁──────  The assignee is the app ID of our service principal.
                         │
                         The scope is the ID of our AML workspace.
```

We'll also store the service principal's password in an environment variable so that we can read it without having to embed it into the code. Listing 7.11 shows how to set an environment variable in a PowerShell session. This won't get persisted across sessions, so make a note of $sp.password.

Listing 7.11   Storing a password in an environment variable

```
$env:SP_PASSWORD = $sp.password
```

The name *password* is a bit misleading. This is an autogenerated client secret that was created when we ran az ad sp create-for-rbac (which stands for "Azure Active Directory service principal create for role-based access control"). We are all set. The next step is to publish our Python code and run it in the cloud.

7.2.4   *Running ML in the cloud*

We use the Python Azure Machine Learning SDK for this, so the first step is to install it using the Python package manager (pip). First, make sure pip is up to date. (If there is a newer pip version, you should see a message printed to the console suggesting you upgrade when you run a pip command.) You can update pip by running python -m pip install --upgrade pip as an administrator. Once pip is up to date, install the Azure Machine Learning SDK with the command in the following listing.

Listing 7.12   Installing the AML Python SDK

```
pip install azureml-sdk
```

Let's now write a Python script to publish our original ML model to the cloud, with all the required configuration. We'll call this pipeline.py. Instead of showing the whole script, we'll do it step by step in the following listings, explaining things as we go. Keep in mind that the following listings (listings 7.13–7.18) would all appear one after the other in pipeline.py. First, the following listing shows the imports and the additional parameters we need.

Listing 7.13   Imports and parameters

```
from azureml.core import Workspace, Datastore, Dataset, Model
from azureml.core.authentication import ServicePrincipalAuthentication
from azureml.core.compute import AmlCompute
from azureml.core.conda_dependencies import CondaDependencies          Imports all
from azureml.core.runconfig import RunConfiguration           ◁         packages from
from azureml.pipeline.core import Pipeline                              the azureml-sdk
from azureml.pipeline.steps.python_script_step import PythonScriptStep
⇒ import os
                                              Replace this with the ID of your tenant.
                                              You can find this in $sp.tenant.
tenant_id = '<your tenant ID>'   ◁
subscription_id = '<your Azure subscription GUID>'   ◁     Replace this with the GUID
                                                          of your Azure subscription.
```

```
service_principal_id = '<your service principal ID>'
resource_group = 'aml-rg'
workspace_name = 'aml'
```

Replace this with the ID of your service principal. You can find this in $sp.appId.

Names the Azure resource group

Names the AML workspace

Next, we connect to the workspace using the service principal and get the data store (MLData) and compute target (d1compute) needed by our model. The following listing shows the steps.

Listing 7.14 Connecting to the workspace to get the data store and compute target

```
...

# Auth
auth = ServicePrincipalAuthentication(
    tenant_id,
    service_principal_id,
    os.environ.get('SP_PASSWORD'))

# Workspace
workspace = Workspace(
    subscription_id = subscription_id,
    resource_group = resource_group,
    workspace_name = workspace_name,
    auth=auth)

# Datastore
datastore = Datastore.get(workspace, 'MLData')

# Compute target
compute_target = AmlCompute(workspace, 'd1compute')
```

Defines a service principal authentication

Gets the value of the environment variable SP_PASSWORD

Connects to the workspace with the given subscription ID, resource group, name, and auth

Gets the MLData data store from the workspace

Gets the d1compute target from the workspace

We need these to set up our deployment: the data store is where we have our input, while the compute target is where the model trains. The following listing shows how we can specify the model input.

Listing 7.15 Specifying model input

```
...

# Input
model_input = Dataset.File.from_files(
    [(datastore, '/models/highspenders/input.csv')]).as_mount()
```

Input is in our Azure data lake at /model/highspenders/input.csv.

The `from_files()` method takes a list of files. Each element of the list is a tuple consisting of a data store and a path. The `as_mount()` method ensures the file is mounted and made available to the compute that trains the model.

DEFINITION Azure Machine Learning instead of AML *datasets* reference a data source location, along with a copy of their metadata. This allows models to seamlessly access data during training.

Next, we'll specify the Python packages required by our model, from which we can initialize a run configuration. If you remember from the previous section, we used pandas and sklearn. We'll also need the azureml-core and azureml-dataprep packages required by the runtime. The next listing shows how to create the run configuration.

Listing 7.16   Creating the run configuration

```
. . .
                                                  Lists the packages we need
                                                 using CondaDependencies
# Python package configuration
conda_deps = CondaDependencies.create(pip_packages= ['pandas', 'sklearn',
    'azureml-core', 'azureml-dataprep'])
run_config = RunConfiguration(            The only configuration we need for
    conda_dependencies=conda_deps)        our model is the dependencies.
```

Conda stands for Anaconda, a Python and R open source distribution of common data science packages. Anaconda simplifies package management and dependencies and is commonly used in data science projects because it provides a stable environment for this type of workload. Azure Machine Learning also uses it under the hood.

Next, let's create a step for training our model. In our case, this is a PythonScript-Step, a step that executes Python code. We'll provide the name of the script (from our previous section), the command-line arguments, the inputs, run configuration, and compute target. The following listing shows the details.

Listing 7.17   Defining a model training step

```
. . .
                              Specifies the script
                               to upload/run       Arguments to pass to the script (here
# Train step                                       model_input resolves to the path where
trainStep = PythonScriptStep(                      the data is mounted on the node running
    script_name='highspenders.py',                 the script).
    arguments=['--input', model_input],
    inputs=[model_input],
    runconfig=run_config,          Sets the available inputs
    compute_target=compute_target)
                                    Sets the compute
Runs the configuration, specifying  target to run on
package dependencies
```

We can chain multiple steps together, but we only need one in our case. One or more steps form an ML pipeline.

> **DEFINITION** An Azure Machine Learning *pipeline* simplifies building ML workflows, including data preparation, training, validation, scoring, and deployment.

Pipelines are an important concept in Azure Machine Learning. They capture all the information needed to run an ML workflow. The following listing shows how we can create and submit a pipeline to our workspace.

Listing 7.18 Creating and submitting a pipeline

```
...

# Submit pipeline
pipeline = Pipeline(workspace=workspace,
    steps=[trainStep])                          ◄──   Creates a pipeline with a
published_pipeline = pipeline.publish(                single step, trainStep, in
    name='HighSpenders',                             our workspace
    description='High spenders model',    ◄──  Defines the pipeline
    continue_on_step_failure=False)       ◄──  name and descriptions

    open('highspenders.id', 'w').write(        Sets whether to continue
        published_pipeline.id)                 if one of the steps fails
```

Publishes the pipeline

Published pipelines have an ID that we use
to kick off the pipeline and save it to a file.

We'll save the GUID of the published pipeline into the highspenders.id file. Our pipeline automation is almost complete. But before calling this script to create the pipeline, let's make one small addition to our high spender model. While we could do all of the previous steps without touching our original model code, we add the final step to the model code itself. Remember that once the model is trained, we save it to disk as outputs/highspender.pkl.

For this step, we'll make one Azure Machine Learning–specific addition: taking the trained model and storing it in the workspace. Add the lines in listing 7.19 to highspenders.py. It's important that you add this to highspenders.py (the model code) and not to pipeline.py (the pipeline automation we just put together).

Listing 7.19 Uploading the trained model to the Azure Machine Learning workspace

```
...
                              Gets the context of
                                the current run
# Register model
from azureml.core import Model
from azureml.core.run import Run                The context contains an experiment,
                                                which references the workspace.
run = Run.get_context()               ◄──
workspace = run.experiment.workspace  ◄──   Registers the model with the workspace
model = Model.register(               ◄──
    workspace=workspace,              ◄──
    model_name='highspender',         ◄──   Provides the workspace
    model_path=model_path)
                                      Sets the name under which
                                      we register the model
```

The model path on disk (this is
defined earlier in the script).

Note the call to `Run.get_context()` and how we use this to retrieve the workspace. In pipeline.py, we provided the subscription ID, resource group, and workspace name. That is how we can get a workspace from outside Azure Machine Learning. In this case, though, the code runs in Azure Machine Learning as part of our pipeline. This gives us additional context that we can use to retrieve the workspace at run time. Every run of a pipeline in Azure Machine Learning is called an experiment.

> **DEFINITION** Azure Machine Learning *experiments* represent one execution of a pipeline. When we rerun a pipeline, we have a new experiment.

We are all set! Let's run the pipeline.py script to publish our pipeline to the workspace. The following listing provides the command for this step.

Listing 7.20 Publishing the pipeline

```
python pipeline.py
```

The GUID matters! If we rerun the script, it registers another pipeline with the same name but a different GUID. Azure Machine Learning does not update pipelines in place. We have the option to disable pipelines so they don't clutter the workspace, but not to update them. Let's kick off the pipeline using Azure CLI, as the next listing shows.

Listing 7.21 Running a pipeline

**Reads the pipeline ID from the highspenders.id file
produced in the previous step to $pipelineId**

```
$pipelineId = Get-Content -Path highspenders.id
az ml run submit-pipeline `          ← Submits a new pipeline run
--pipeline-id $pipelineId `          ← Uses the pipeline ID we retrieved from the file
--workspace-name aml `               ←
--resource-group aml-rg              | Names the workspace
```

Sets the resource group containing the workspace

Check the UI at https://ml.azure.com. You should see the pipeline under the Pipelines section, the run we just kicked off under the Experiments section. Once the model is trained, you'll see the model output under the Models section. We accomplished quite a lot in this section. Let's pause for a quick recap before moving on.

7.2.5 *Azure Machine Learning recap*

We started with provisioning a workspace, which is the top-level container for all Azure Machine Learning–related artifacts. Next, we created a compute target, which specifies the type of compute our model runs on. We can define as many compute targets as needed; some models require more resources than others, some require GPUs, etc. Azure provides many types of VM images suited to all these workloads. A main advantage of using compute targets in Azure Machine Learning is that compute is provisioned on demand when we run a pipeline. Once the pipeline finishes, compute gets deprovisioned. This allows us to scale elastically and only pay for what we need.

We then attached a data store. Data stores are an abstraction over existing storage services, and they allow Azure Machine Learning connections to read the data. The main advantage of using data stores is that they abstract away access control, so our data scientists don't need to worry about authenticating against the storage service.

With the infrastructure in place, we proceeded to set up a pipeline for our model. A pipeline specifies all the requirements and steps our execution needs to take. There are many pipelines in Azure: Azure DevOps Pipelines are focused on DevOps, provisioning resources, and in general, providing automation around Git; Azure Data Factory pipelines are focused on ETL, data movement, and orchestration; Azure Machine Learning Pipelines are meant for ML workflows, where we set up the environment and then execute a set of steps to train, validate, and publish a model.

Our pipeline included a dataset (our input), a compute target, a set of Python package dependencies, a run configuration, and a step to run a Python script. We also enhanced our original model code to publish the model in AML. This takes the result of our training run and makes it available in the workspace. Then we published the pipeline to our Azure Machine Learning workspace and submitted a run, which in Azure Machine Learning is called an experiment. For now, we ran everything from our machine. Let's see how we can apply DevOps to ML, put everything in Git, and deploy with Azure DevOps Pipelines. That is the focus of the next section.

7.3 MLOps

We have a couple of Python scripts: our simple high spender model and our pipeline.py, which sets up an Azure Machine Learning pipeline. Let's start tracking these in Git and create an Azure DevOps pipeline to run the pipeline.py script, our automated deployment. Once we have this running, we'll talk a bit about scaling it out to multiple models.

7.3.1 Deploying from Git

First, let's add both Python scripts to our DevOps DE Git repository. By now, we should have several folders there:

- ADF (DevOps for Azure Data Factory)
- ADX (DevOps for Azure Data Explorer analytics)
- ARM (DevOps for Azure Resource Manager templates)
- Docs (documentation for self-serve analytics)
- Scripts (this contains our Azure Data Factory pull request validation)
- YML (the Azure DevOps pipeline definitions)

Let's create a new subfolder, ML, for storing our ML scripts. At a high level, our DevOps pipeline picks up the model code from Git and deploys it to our Azure Machine Learning workspace using an Azure DevOps pipeline as shown in figure 7.4.

We'll put both highspenders.py and pipeline.py under ML/highspenders as listing 7.22 shows. Note that if we have a branch policy on the master folder, we won't be

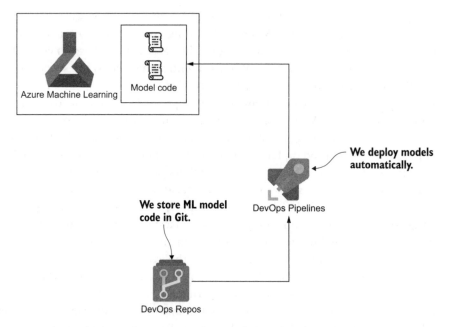

Figure 7.4   We store the code for our ML model in Git and deploy it automatically to our Azure Machine Learning workspace using Azure DevOps Pipelines.

allowed to push directly to master, rather, we need to create a new branch and submit a pull request. We won't cover the details of this here. We applied a branch policy in chapter 6 but reverted it for convenience.

Listing 7.22   Adding our ML scripts to Git

```
mkdir -p ML\highspenders

...            ⟵——— Copies the files to the new folder

git add *
git commit -m "Highspender model"
git push
```

Now let's look at the Azure DevOps pipeline that runs pipeline.py to deploy to our Azure Machine Learning workspace. This is straightforward: we just need to execute a Python script in the pipeline like we did in chapter 6 for the validation script. The following listing shows the pipeline definition.

Listing 7.23   Contents of YML/deploy-model-highspenders.yml

```
trigger:
  branches:
    include:
    - master
```

```
    paths:
      include:
      - ML/highspenders/*
```
Triggers the pipeline on changes under ML/highspenders

```
jobs:
  - job:
      displayName: Deploy High Spenders model
      steps:
        - task: UsePythonVersion@0
          inputs:
            versionSpec: '3.x'
```
Ensures that we use Python 3 to execute the Python script

```
        - script: python -m pip install azureml-sdk
        - task: PythonScript@0
```
Installs azureml-sdk dependency on the build agent

```
          inputs:
            workingDirectory: $(Build.SourcesDirectory)/
            ➥ ML/highspenders
            scriptPath: $(Build.SourcesDirectory)/
            ➥ ML/highspenders/pipeline.py
```
Runs the pipeline.py script in the ML/highspenders directory

```
          env:
            SP_PASSWORD: $(SP_PASSWORD)
```
Makes SP_PASSWORD available as an environment variable

This pipeline has multiple steps. First, we want to ensure that we run Python 3 on the build agent. We use the `UsePythonVersion` task for this. Next, we need to install the Python dependencies. We use a script to run `pip install`. Finally, we run the Python script. Remember, it needs an SP_PASSWORD environment variable. We use `env` to map that. More on this later.

Let's push this pipeline definition to Git and create an Azure DevOps pipeline based on it. First, we'll add the YAML definition to Git, then create the pipeline using `az pipelines create` as this listing shows.

Listing 7.24 Creating the model deployment pipeline

```
git add *
git commit -m "Deploy High Spenders model pipeline definition"
git push
az pipelines create `
--name "Deploy High Spenders model" `
--repository DE `
--repository-type tfsgit `
--yml-path YML/deploy-model-highspenders.yml `
--skip-run
```
Creates a new Azure DevOps pipeline

Names the pipeline Deploy High Spenders model

Sets the repository name and type for the pipeline

Defines the path to the pipeline definition file

By default, kicks off a pipeline once created. This flag prevents the pipeline from running.

We're almost done. The one thing we still need to take care of is making the service principal password available to the pipeline. Remember, we set an environment variable (SP_PASSWORD), and pipeline.py expects to retrieve the password from there. While this works locally, we need to ensure that the build agent on which our DevOps pipeline runs in the cloud also has the same environment variable.

It's also important to remember this password is secret. If it leaks, an attacker could use it to make changes to our Azure Machine Learning workspace. That means we can't store it in Git. Luckily, Azure DevOps has a provision for exactly this type of scenario. We can create a variable using Azure CLI, mark it as secret, and reference it in the pipeline. The next listing shows how to do this.

Listing 7.25   Creating a secret variable

The variable name in the pipeline; we reuse SP_PASSWORD.

```
az pipelines variable create `          ⟵ Creates a pipeline variable
  --name SP_PASSWORD `
  --pipeline-name "Deploy High Spenders model" `    ⟵ Sets the pipeline name and project
  --project DE `
  --secret true `                         ⟵ Hides secret variables to avoid leaks
  --value $env:SP_PASSWORD
```

Variable value; we pick it up from our environment.

We should be good to go. Let's kick off the pipeline, and it should update our Azure Machine Learning workspace. The following listing shows the command.

Listing 7.26   Running the pipeline

```
az pipelines run --name "Deploy High Spenders model"
```

Next, let's see what we can do about the published Azure Machine Learning pipeline ID.

7.3.2   *Storing pipeline IDs*

Remember that when we publish an Azure Machine Learning pipeline to the workspace, it generates a new ID. Our pipeline.py script stores this in the highspenders.id file. If we want to enable end-to-end automation from deployment to execution, we need a way to hand off the pipeline ID from the DevOps deployment to the orchestration service that runs the ML. For example, if we want to run our High Spenders model on a monthly cadence, how will we know which Azure Machine Learning pipeline ID to run?

We will extend our Azure DevOps Pipeline with an additional step to publish the pipeline ID. We can store this ID in any storage solution: an SQL database, an API, etc. In our case, let's keep it simple and upload it to our Azure data lake. We already have one set up, so we just need to move highspenders.id from the build agent to the data lake filesystem. Figure 7.5 shows our extended DevOps pipeline, which captures the ML pipeline ID in Azure Data Lake.

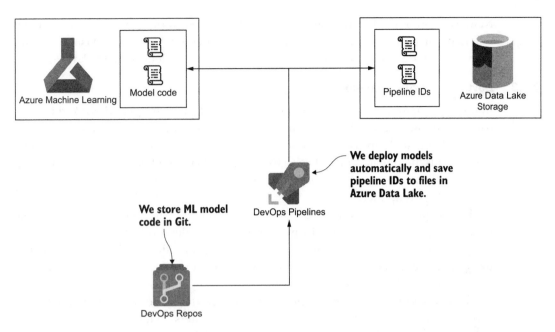

Figure 7.5 We deploy models automatically from Git using an Azure DevOps pipeline. The pipeline ID generated by Azure Machine Learning is saved to a file in Azure Data Lake Storage so we can reference it later.

We'll use an Azure CLI task and invoke the `az storage fs file upload` command, the same one we used earlier in this chapter to upload our input.csv file. Add the content of the following listing to the end of YML/deploy-model-highspenders.yml, after the PythonScript task.

Listing 7.27 Contents of YML/deploy-model-highspenders.yml

```
. . .
    - task: AzureCLI@2
  inputs:
    azureSubscription: 'ARM'
    scriptType: 'pscore'
    scriptLocation: 'inlineScript'
    inlineScript: 'az storage fs file upload
    --file-system fs1 --path "pipelines/highspenders.id"
    --overwrite
    --source "ML/highspenders/highspenders.id"
    --account-name "<your ADLS account>"'
```

Runs an Azure CLI script

Runs PowerShell Core

Uses the ARM service connection we created in chapter 3 to connect to our subscription

Uses an inline script

Uploads the file; remember to update <your ADLS account> with the name of your account, which has to be unique.

Now, when we redeploy, highspenders.id gets updated in our Azure data lake. Then other automation we might implement that would need to know this ID can pick it up from there. We'll look at that in the next section, but first, let's do a quick recap.

7.3.3   *DevOps for Azure Machine Learning recap*

In this section, we took our pipeline.py automation Python script and hooked it up to Azure DevOps, where it is stored in Git, next to the model code. When the model code updates, an Azure DevOps pipeline is invoked, which runs the script. The pipeline uploads the updated model code to the Azure Machine Learning workspace, and saves the ID of the new Azure Machine Learning pipeline in our data lake so other tools can look it up there.

This might seem like quite a lot of steps just to automate deployment of a simple Python script, but this benefits from economies of scale: most of pipeline.py can be extracted into a common module and reused to deploy multiple ML models. The few things that are different across models (like name, input datasets, and compute target) can be read from a configuration file.

We will want to keep separate pipelines for each model because an update to one model shouldn't have to trigger updates to the others. While we won't cover the details here, Azure DevOps does support templates for pipelines, so we can create a shared template for the deployment steps, then create lightweight pipeline-specific YAML files based on that.[2] Finally, let's look at the end-to-end. We'll use Azure Data Factory to run an Azure Machine Learning experiment.

7.4   *Orchestrating machine learning*

Our orchestration solution from chapter 4 is Azure Data Factory. We will use it to submit an Azure Machine Learning pipeline run to create an experiment. Azure Data Factory has a connector for Azure Machine Learning, so this type of flow is supported natively.

In a real-world context, our workflow would also include ETL for the ML inputs. We would copy and transform the input data for the model as a first step and, only after all inputs are available, train the model. Figure 7.6 shows a generic ML workflow as orchestrated by Azure Data Factory.

To keep things simple, we will skip the input ETL part because we already know how to implement that from chapter 4. We'll focus on the new parts: integrating with Azure Machine Learning and reading the pipeline ID from our data lake.

---

[2] See http://mng.bz/K4gX for details on Azure DevOps templates.

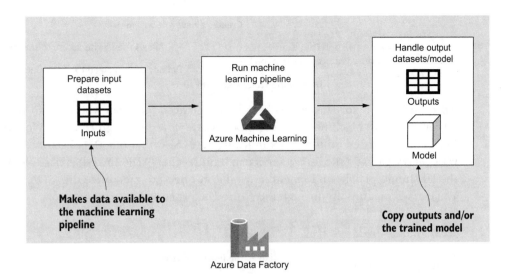

Figure 7.6 A generic ML workflow orchestrated by Azure Data Factory. First, we perform required ETL to get the data ready to run our model code. Then, we run the ML code using Azure Machine Learning. Finally, we copy the outputs—trained model or datasets—to their final destinations (if we use Azure Machine Learning to do batch scoring).

7.4.1 Connecting Azure Data Factory with Azure Machine Learning

As a quick reminder, Azure Data Factory uses linked services to connect to other Azure services. We'll want to set this up for our data lake and Azure Machine Learning workspace. We already saw this in chapter 4, where we created a couple of linked services to connect to the Bing COVID-19 open dataset HTTP service and our Azure Data Explorer instance. We used the `az datafactory linked-service create` command. This won't work anymore because now our Data Factory is connected to Git. Remember, once backed by Git, the UI loads the details from Git instead of the Data Factory instance itself, while Azure CLI still talks directly to the service. If we use Azure CLI, the Data Factory will get out of sync with Git, and we'll run into issues.

This time around, we'll set up the linked services differently. First, let's set up the data lake connection, then grant our Azure Data Factory access. Azure Data Factory itself comes with its own identity, called a *managed identity*. The following listing shows how we can retrieve it and grant it access to the data lake.

Listing 7.28 Granting data lake permissions to the Data Factory

```
$adf = az datafactory factory show `
--name "adf$suffix" `
--resource-group adf-rg `          Retrieves the details of the Data
| ConvertFrom-Json    ◁───         Factory and stores them in $adf

$acc = az storage account show -          Retrieves the details of the data lake
name "adls$suffix" | ConvertFrom-Json  ◁──  storage account and stores them in $acc
```

```
az role assignment create `        ◁────┤  Creates a new role assignment
--role "Storage Blob Data Contributor" `  ◁──── Allows read/write access to the data lake
--assignee $adf.identity.principalId `  ◁──┐
--scope $acc.id  ◁──┐                        │  Defines the managed ID of the Data Factory
                    │  Defines the storage account ID
```

Now the Data Factory has access to the storage account, from where it can read the IDs of the Azure Machine Learning pipelines deployed through DevOps. We create a linked service based on the JSON in listing 7.29. Now that our Data Factory is in sync with Git, we can add the linked service to it under the /ADF/linkedService folder, and the UI should pick it up. Remember, you don't need to memorize the JSON schema. You can also set this up through the Azure Data Factory UI.

Listing 7.29 Contents of /ADF/linkedService/adls.json

```
{
    "name": "adls",        ◁──┤  Names the linked service
    "type": "Microsoft.DataFactory/factories/linkedservices",
    "properties": {
        "type": "AzureBlobFS",   ◁──┐  Specifies an Azure Blob File System
        "typeProperties": {            (data lake) linked service
            "url": "https://adls<use $suffix>.dfs    │ Specifies the URL; replace this
            ➥ .core.windows.net"                     │ with your unique $suffix value.
        }
    }
}
```

When you push this to Git, you should see the new linked service in the Azure Data Factory UI. For Azure Machine Learning, at the time of writing, the linked service does not support a managed identity, so we will have to use a service principal. We'll let the Data Factory encrypt the service principal secret before storing in Git (because we don't want it leaked), so we need to configure this service through the UI. Figure 7.7 shows how to do this.

Go to the Manage tab. Select Linked Services and click + New, then fill in the subscription ID and service principal details. We use $sp because we already granted it access to modify the Azure Machine Learning instance. But, again, in a production environment, you should go for isolation and generate new service principals instead of recycling them. That's because if one of the principals gets compromised, it won't itself have access to multiple resources, so a potential attacker would gain less access. Contrast this with simply using a single service principal across all our systems. If that gets compromised, an attacker can get broad access.

As a side note, there are other options we could have used instead of the UI, but we're trying to keep things brief. The recommended approach is to store the principal key in an Azure Key Vault and load it from there. The reason we went through the UI this time is that before storing the service principal key in the linked service JSON in Git, Azure Data Factory encrypts it. Because we don't know how the encrypted password looks, we can't create the linked service JSON manually. Azure Key Vault would

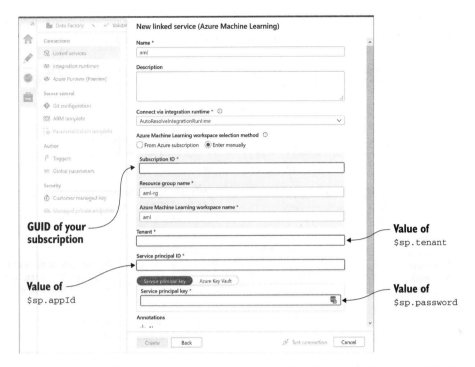

Figure 7.7 On the Manage tab, under Linked Services, click + New to configure a new linked service named `aml`. Fill in the form with your subscription ID, service principal tenant, app ID, and password.

have helped because we would only need to specify the name of the secret in the Key Vault. Again, we didn't do this so we can keep things short.

7.4.2 *Machine learning orchestration*

Now that we can both read the Azure Machine Learning pipeline ID and submit a run in Azure Machine Learning with the new linked services, the final step is to build a Data Factory pipeline for this. Figure 7.8 shows the steps. First, we'll look up the latest pipeline ID from where we uploaded it in Azure Data Lake Storage. Once we have the ID, we will submit a run to Azure Machine Learning.

In the previous section, we created linked services for both Azure Data Lake and Azure Machine Learning, so now it's just a matter of stitching things together. First,

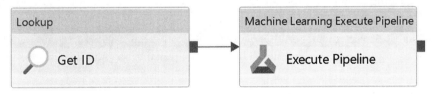

Figure 7.8 An Azure Data Factory pipeline for running ML. The first activity gets the pipeline ID, and the second activity submits a run to Azure Machine Learning.

we'll define a dataset for the model ID. The following listing shows the corresponding JSON definition, which you'll find in Git under the /ADF/dataset folder.

Listing 7.30   Contents of /ADF/dataset/HighSpendersId.json

```
{
    "name": "HighSpendersId",
    "properties": {
        "linkedServiceName": {
            "referenceName": "adls",                    ← Uses the adls linked
            "type": "LinkedServiceReference"              service we just created
        },
        "annotations": [],                              We call this delimited text as
        "type": "DelimitedText",            ←           CSV or TSV, but it's really just
        "typeProperties": {                              one value in the file.
            "location": {
                "type": "AzureBlobFSLocation",
                "fileName": "highspenders.id",          Defines the path to the file
                "folderPath": "pipelines",              /pipelines/highspenders.id
                "fileSystem": "fs1"                      in the fs1 filesystem
            },
            "columnDelimiter": ",",
            "escapeChar": "\\",                         Defaults for a CSV file, but
            "quoteChar": "\""                            we won't really use these.
        },
        "schema": []      ←         We don't define a schema, so the first (and
    }                                only) column has the default name Prop_0.
}
```

Defines a filesystem blob location (data lake) →

Now let's look at the pipeline definition. This uses two activities that we haven't used before: a Lookup activity and an ML Execute Pipeline activity. The Lookup activity allows us to read from a dataset and makes the read data available in the pipeline. In our case, we'll read the ID of the latest deployed High Spenders Azure Machine Learning pipeline. The ML Execute Pipeline activity, as the name implies, executes an Azure Machine Learning pipeline. We will use dynamic content to read the ID from the previous activity and pass it to Azure Machine Learning.

> **DEFINITION**   In Azure Data Factory, *dynamic content* is an expression language that enables us to build flexible, parameterized pipelines.

We briefly mentioned dynamic content in chapter 4, but now we get to use it. The following listing shows our pipeline JSON, which you'll find in Git under /ADF/pipeline.

Listing 7.31   Contents of /ADF/pipeline/runhighspenders.json

```
{
    "name": "runhighspenders",
    "properties": {
        "activities": [
            {
```

```
    "name": "Get ID",
    "type": "Lookup",          ◁─┐   The type of the first
    "dependsOn": [],             │   activity is Lookup.
    "policy": {
        "timeout": "7.00:00:00",
        "retry": 0,                       These are default
        "retryIntervalInSeconds": 30,     values for executing
        "secureOutput": false,            an activity.
        "secureInput": false
    },
    "userProperties": [],
    "typeProperties": {
 ┌─▷     "source": {
 │           "type": "DelimitedTextSource",
 │           "storeSettings": {
 │               "type": "AzureBlobFSReadSettings",
 │               "recursive": true
 │           },
 │           "formatSettings": {
 │               "type": "DelimitedTextReadSettings"
 │           }
 │       },
 │       "dataset": {
 │           "referenceName":
 └─▷     ➡ "HighSpendersId",
             "type": "DatasetReference"
         }
     }
 },
 {
    "name": "Execute Pipeline",           The type of the second activity
    "type": "AzureMLExecutePipeline",  ◁─┘  is AzureMLExecutePipeline.
    "dependsOn": [
        {
            "activity": "Get ID",
            "dependencyConditions": [
                "Succeeded"
            ]
        }
    ],
    "policy": {
        "timeout": "7.00:00:00",
        "retry": 0,
        "retryIntervalInSeconds": 30,     Uses default
        "secureOutput": false,            execution policy
        "secureInput": false              values
    },
    "userProperties": [],
    "typeProperties": {
        "mlPipelineId": {
            "value": "@activity('Get ID').output
 ┌─────▷ ➡ .firstRow.Prop_0",
            "type": "Expression"
        }
    },
```

```
        "linkedServiceName": {
            "referenceName": "aml",        ◁──┐ Uses the aml linked service
            "type": "LinkedServiceReference"
        }
    }
],                                    ┌─ If we don't disable our branch
    "annotations": []    ◁──┤ policies, we need to provide a link
                              └─ to the documentation here.
}
}
```

And that's it. When these activities run, they pick up the latest ID from the data lake, which is updated by our ML DevOps deployment. They then submit this to Azure Machine Learning. We can create a trigger and run this on whatever schedule we want. In practice, we would likely have additional ETL activities around this, but we're keeping things simple for this pipeline because we're focusing on the ML part.

7.4.3   *Orchestrating recap*

In this section, we looked at integrating Azure Machine Learning with Azure Data Factory for orchestrating ML runs. We saw how we can connect to all the required services and how to consume the pipeline ID from Azure Data Lake to make sure we always execute the latest version of an Azure Machine Learning pipeline. There are several advantages with this integration: we already have a solid DevOps infrastructure in place for Azure Data Factory, including monitoring. If the model run fails in Azure Machine Learning, the Azure Data Factory activity fails, and our monitoring triggers an alert.

We also defined some standards around who needs to review the code and what additional documentation is required in chapter 6, and we enforced them with branch policies. These policies would apply here too because we rely on Azure Data Factory for orchestration so we can reuse the setup. Also, training the model is just part of the story. We also need to gather all the required input data, clean it up, etc. This can be done using Azure Data Factory, which we already use for all our other data movement workloads. Figure 7.9 shows our complete DevOps setup with automated deployment from Git for both ML code and orchestration.

One DevOps aspect we omitted (for brevity) in this chapter but one which we would also automate in a real production scenario is the deployment of the Azure Machine Learning workspace itself. In section 7.2, we created a workspace using Azure CLI, which we then used throughout the chapter. Once created, we can export its ARM template, store it in Git, and deploy it from there, the same way we did with our Azure Data Explorer cluster. We won't go through the steps here because they are no different than the ones we saw in chapter 3 (section 3.3).

This is the final chapter on workloads. We covered data modeling, analytics, and now ML. For the remaining chapters, we'll switch our focus to governance and ensure that the platform we run all these workloads on is reliable, compliant, and secure.

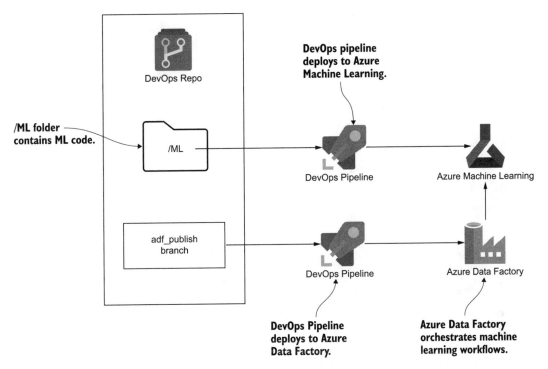

Figure 7.9 We deploy ML code from the /ML folder to our Azure Machine Learning workspace using a DevOps pipeline. We also deploy Azure Data Factory pipelines from our adf_publish branch (we discussed this in chapter 6). The Azure Data Factory orchestrates end-to-end ML workflows using our Azure Machine Learning instance.

Summary

- Machine learning (ML) models are usually developed in Python or R.
- Azure Machine Learning (AML) is the Azure PaaS (platform as a service) offering for running ML in the cloud.
- An Azure Machine Learning instance is a workspace that manages compute targets on which ML runs with data stores for input (and output) data.
- An Azure Machine Learning pipeline defines an ML pipeline containing one or more steps. Running a pipeline is called an experiment, which produces a trained model.
- Azure Machine Learning provides an SDK that makes it easy to deploy models using Python or R code. We can build an Azure DevOps pipeline to execute this code and deploy our models to Azure Machine Learning from Git.
- Each Azure Machine Learning pipeline deployment gets a unique GUID. We need to keep track of the latest version we deploy. We can do that by storing it after deployment succeeds.
- Using Azure Data Factory (ADF) to orchestrate machine learning enables us to leverage the infrastructure we already built to operationalize ML.

Part 3

Governance

Part 3 is all about governance. We'll cover this from a few different angles.

- Chapter 8 covers metadata (data about our data) and how this helps make sense of our data assets. In a big data platform, the ability to find and understand datasets becomes a necessity. In this chapter, we'll use Azure Purview as our metadata store.
- Chapter 9 talks about data quality. As data moves in and out of our platform and as we run various workloads, we need to keep an eye out for data quality issues. This chapter covers various types of data tests and data testing patterns.
- Chapter 10 looks at another important aspect of handling data: compliance. We'll talk about data classification and handling, access models, and supporting GDPR (General Data Protection Regulation) requirements. Compliance is a key aspect of governance.
- Chapter 11 discusses data distribution and various patterns of sharing data with other teams. We'll look at how we can share data through an API and how we can share it for bulk copy using Azure Data Share.

Metadata 8

This chapter covers

- Managing metadata for understanding data
- Introducing Azure Purview
- Maintaining a data dictionary and a data glossary
- Understanding advanced features of Azure Purview

This chapter is all about metadata: in other words, data about data. This is one aspect of data governance. We will cover two other important aspects in the following chapters: data quality in chapter 9 and compliance in chapter 10. Figure 8.1 highlights our current area of focus. We won't view this map of our data platform again until the last chapter, which covers data distribution.

We'll start by outlining the information architecture challenges a big data platform encounters and how metadata can help address them. We'll introduce two important concepts: data dictionaries and data glossaries. Using these, we can inventory our datasets and queries.

Next, we'll look at Azure Purview. Azure Purview is the Azure data governance service that helps us manage our metadata. We'll spin up a new instance of Azure Purview and go over some of its key features.

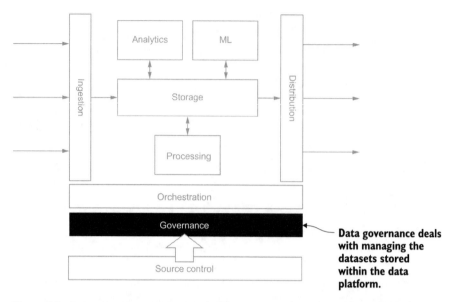

Figure 8.1   Data governance deals with multiple aspects of managing data, including metadata, data quality, access control, compliance with laws and standards, etc.

NOTE   At the time of writing, the Azure Purview service was recently launched, and there is no Azure CLI support for it yet.

Unlike other chapters, where we were able to automate via Azure CLI, this time around, we'll look at more of the UI. We'll see how we can create an inventory of our datasets in Azure Purview and how we can leverage its glossary capabilities to document our business space. Finally, we'll look at some of the more advanced features of Azure Purview, including tracking data lineage, automatic classification, and its REST API. Let's start by understanding the need for metadata in a big data platform.

8.1   *Making sense of the data*

As the volume of datasets in our platform grows, it becomes harder and harder for someone to figure out whether the data they are looking for is available. Even the small data platform we stood up to work through our examples consists of an Azure Data Lake Storage (ADLS) account and an Azure Data Explorer (ADX) cluster containing several tables.

A real-world data platform can easily span several data fabrics and can contain hundreds of tables spread across different databases. Once we add a layer of access control on top of that, most data scientists looking for datasets won't even be able to see all the data. This can lead to duplicate ETL; team members ingest the same data multiple times in different places because it's not obvious the data is already available. There needs to be a way to centrally document all available datasets in a searchable way to avoid this issue.

Another potential challenge is interpreting the data. Even if we know that a dataset is available, we might not know what each column means. Sometimes the name makes it obvious, oftentimes it doesn't, or there is too much room for misinterpretation. We need a place to describe what each column in a table means, what data we can expect in it, and how to associate it with the table. This type of data description, or data about the data, is called *metadata*. We've talked about a place to document what data each of our tables stores and what each of its columns represents. This is also known as a data dictionary.

> **DEFINITION**   A *data dictionary* contains descriptions of datasets. This includes the purpose of a table, what all of its columns represent, etc.

Data dictionaries must be searchable. If we want to check, for example, whether our data platform contains web telemetry, we should be able to go to the data dictionary, search for "web telemetry," and get back our PageViews table, including explanations of what each of its columns mean.

Even having this information might not be enough. In a complex business space, various metrics important to the business have precise meanings and shouldn't be left to interpretation. As an example, let's revisit our simple total page views report, developed by one of our data scientists. We looked at this example in chapter 3 when we covered DevOps, and saw how we can wrap the Azure Data Explorer query that produces this report into a function and deploy it from Git. The following listing shows the function.

Listing 8.1   Calling the `TotalPageViews` function

```
.create-or-alter function TotalPageViews() {
    PageViews
    | where Timestamp > startofmonth(now())         Excludes test traffic coming
      and UserId != 12345          <----------        from the known user ID 12345
    | count
}
```

In chapter 3, we said we also get some synthetic page view traffic from test automation, which shows up with a user ID of 12345. Our page view total explicitly excludes this. Now let's see what other issues might pop up, even with the `TotalPageViews` function stored in and deployed from Git.

First, not everyone might agree that this is the right way to report total page views. From a customer perspective, we want to exclude test traffic. But if we want to report on the load our servers can take, we might want to include the synthetic traffic.

Another issue raises a few questions. Does *monthly* mean from the beginning of the calendar month? Or does it mean looking one month back from today? We need some place to clearly define our metric, so we don't leave this up for interpretation. We can't have two data scientists report the same metric with different numbers! In our case, let's say our definition for total page views is *the total number of page views from the beginning of the month, excluding test traffic.* Our `TotalPageViews` function implements the canonical query that produces this metric.

DEFINITION   A *canonical query* is the definitive query to produce a given metric.

Having a clear definition for each metric important to the business and capturing the canonical query is critically important to avoid producing reports that contradict each other. We capture these definitions of business terms and their associated queries and datasets in a data glossary.

DEFINITION   A *data glossary* provides precise definitions for the various business terms relevant to the data platform and canonical queries and datasets associated with them.

Discovery is again important. Probably not everyone knows the `TotalPageViews` function is available in our cluster. A data glossary, like a data dictionary, needs to be searchable.

We identified two of the main tools used in metadata management: a data dictionary, describing the available datasets, and a data glossary, mastering business terms and associated canonical queries. Figure 8.2 shows how these map to the data layer.

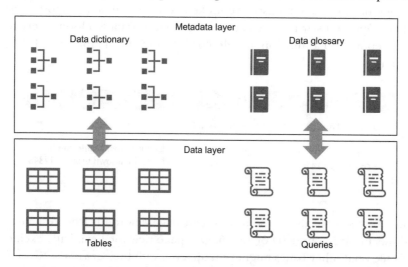

Figure 8.2   The metadata layer contains a data dictionary that captures information about the tables stored in the data layer and a data glossary that captures business definitions with links to the queries stored in the data platform.

Note that populating the metadata layer is done both by automation and by humans. Some tasks are easy to automate; for example, identifying all tables stored in a database and listing their schemas. Other are impossible to automate; for example, defining a business term requires someone with an understanding of the business context.

Now let's see how we can manage our metadata in Azure. Azure provides metadata as a service through the Azure Purview service, which we'll explore throughout the rest of this chapter.

8.2 Introducing Azure Purview

Azure Purview is a data governance service that lets you easily create and maintain an up-to-date map of your data landscape. It includes automated data discovery and data classification.

Let's start by deploying an instance of the service. First, you need to ensure your subscription registered the following resource providers: Microsoft.Purview, Microsoft .Storage, and Microsoft.EventHub. You can do this through the Azure Portal by navigating to your subscriptions, selecting Resource Providers from the left pane, and then searching for and registering the three providers. Alternately, you can use Azure CLI as in the following listing.

Listing 8.2 Registering required resource providers

```
az provider register --namespace Microsoft.Purview

az provider register --namespace Microsoft.Storage

az provider register --namespace Microsoft.EventHub
```

With this prerequisite satisfied, we can now deploy an instance of Azure Purview. First, we'll create a resource group for it, as the next listing shows.

Listing 8.3 Creating a resource group for Azure Purview

```
az group create `
--name purview-rg `
--location "Central US"
```

Because we don't have an Azure CLI extension, we'll deploy the service using an ARM template. The following listing shows the template, which you will need to update with a unique account name.

Listing 8.4 Viewing the Azure Purview ARM template

```
{
    "$schema": "http://schema.management.azure.com/schemas/2015-01-01/
    ➥ deploymentTemplate.json#",
    "contentVersion": "1.0.0.0",
    "resources": [
        {
            "name": "<use purview$suffix>",          ◁──┐  Uses a unique name for the resource.
            "type": "Microsoft.Purview/accounts",           Because we already have $suffix set up
            "apiVersion": "2020-12-01-preview",             to get the unique name, you can use
                                                            purview$suffix.
```

```
      "location": "CentralUs",
      "identity": {
        "type": "SystemAssigned"
      },
      "properties": {
        "networkAcls": {
          "defaultAction": "Allow"
        }
      },
      "dependsOn": [],
      "sku": {
        "name": "Standard",
        "capacity": "4"
      },
      "tags": {}
    }
  ],
  "outputs": {}
}
```

In listing 8.4, you can use `purview` and append your `$suffix` to form a unique name. You can get that by running `echo purview$suffix`. Save the template as purview.json, then use Azure CLI to deploy it. The following listing shows the command.

Listing 8.5   Deploying Purview

```
az deployment group create `
--resource-group purview-rg `        Target resource group for deployment
--template-file purview.json          ARM template file
```

Once the deployment completes, our Azure Purview instance is up and running. The service comes with its own UI, Purview Studio. Navigate to the resource in the Azure Portal. On the Overview tab, click Open Purview Studio. Figure 8.3 shows where to find the launcher.

Figure 8.4 shows the home page of the Purview Studio UI. As you can see, search is front and center. The search bar enables us to find data in our data platform. But because we just spun up the service, we haven't registered anything yet. That's why above the search bar we see No Data Sources, No Assets, and No Glossary Terms. Below the search bar, we see four titles for easy navigation:

- *Knowledge Center*—Opens the knowledge center that contains videos and tutorials on using the service
- *Register Sources*—Connects our storage services so Azure Purview can scan them and discover our assets (datasets)
- *Browse Assets*—Lets us browse the datasets tracked by the service
- *Manage Glossary*—Manages our data glossary

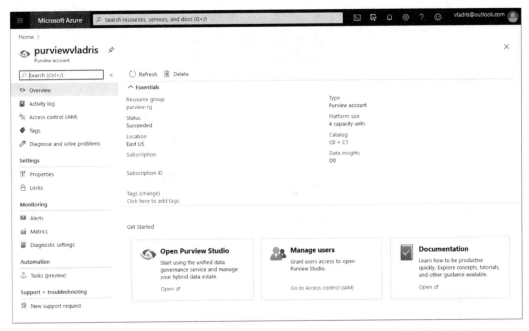

Figure 8.3 Azure Portal view of the Azure Purview instance, including a shortcut to Purview Studio

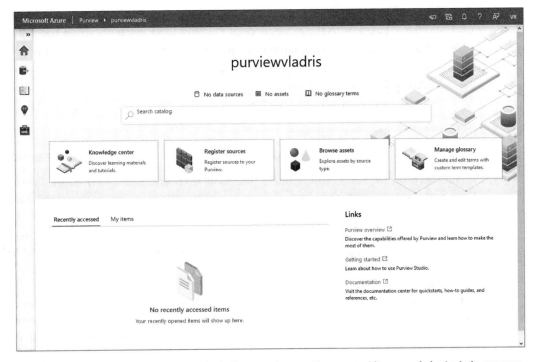

Figure 8.4 Azure Purview's home page, including search, recently accessed items, and shortcuts to common tasks

On the left navigation pane, we have five items. Figure 8.5 displays these.

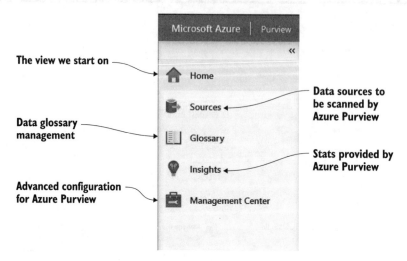

Figure 8.5   Left navigation pane with links to data sources, glossary, insights, and the management center

Here's where each link will take us:

- *Home*—The view we start on
- *Sources*—Takes us to the same place as clicking the Register Sources tile
- *Glossary*—Takes us to the same place as clicking the Manage Glossary tile
- *Insights*— Provides stats about the datasets, glossary terms, and scans performed by Azure Purview and so on
- *Management Center*— Provides advanced configuration settings for Azure Purview

Now, let's populate our catalog.

8.3   *Maintaining a data inventory*

In this section, we will connect our Azure Data Explorer cluster to Azure Purview. First, make sure to start the cluster if it is not running. Then, go to Register Sources and register a new source. Select Azure Data Explorer from the menu, leave the auto-generated name (should be `AzureDataExplorer-` followed by a few random characters), select your `adx$suffix` cluster, and for Select a Collection, choose None. Click Register to register the cluster with Azure Purview.

In case you are wondering, collections are simply a way Azure Purview organizes data. We can create new collections, group datasets in collections, and even provide a hierarchy because collections can have other collections as parents. We'll keep things simple, though, and won't use collections for our example. Once this step is completed, you'll end up in the Map View with an Azure Data Explorer source, as figure 8.6 shows.

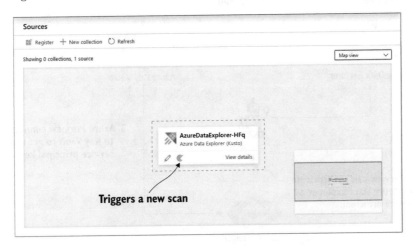

Figure 8.6 The Sources Map View. You can toggle to the Table View using the top right menu. Click New Scan to set up a scan of the cluster.

On the Sources screen, you can use the top right drop-down menu to switch to a Table View of registered sources. The Map View is valuable when we want to look at data lineage, which we'll cover later in this chapter. For now, let's continue setting up our data inventory.

8.3.1 Setting up a scan

We registered the source, but it hasn't been scanned yet. On the Sources screen, click the New Scan icon as shown in figure 8.6 to set up a new scan of the cluster, which ingests the data. This will take you to the Scan Configuration pane.

The newly opened pane has three fields: Name, Server Endpoint, and Credential. Leave the autogenerated name for the scan. The Server Endpoint (the URL of your Azure Data Explorer cluster) should be read-only because it comes from the registered source. Now we need to provide some way for Azure Purview to access Azure Data Explorer.

Leave your browser window open, and let's switch to PowerShell Core. We'll use Azure CLI to set up a new service principal and grant it access to our Azure Data Explorer telemetry database. Then we'll spin up a new Azure Key Vault and store the service principal key there as a secret. Once we have this done, we will provide the service principal to Azure Purview and set up a connection to the Key Vault. Azure Purview uses Azure Key Vault to manage secrets. Figure 8.7 shows how the services fit together.

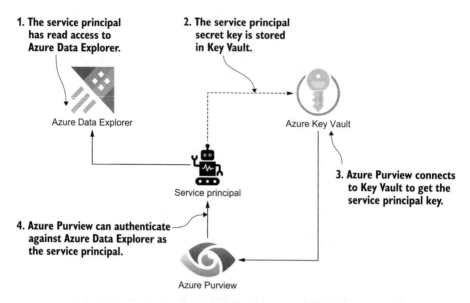

1. **The service principal has read access to Azure Data Explorer.**

2. **The service principal secret key is stored in Key Vault.**

Azure Data Explorer

Azure Key Vault

Service principal

3. **Azure Purview connects to Key Vault to get the service principal key.**

4. **Azure Purview can authenticate against Azure Data Explorer as the service principal.**

Azure Purview

Figure 8.7   The service principal has read access to Azure Data Explorer. We store its secret key in Azure Key Vault. Azure Purview connects to the Key Vault and retrieves the secret so it can authenticate against Azure Data Explorer as the service principal.

We'll create a new service principal and grant it read access to Azure Data Explorer. The following listing shows how to do this.

Listing 8.6   Granting a new service principal access to Azure Data Explorer

Creates a new service principal and
stores the result in the $sp variable

```
$sp = az ad sp create-for-rbac | ConvertFrom-Json

az kusto database-principal-assignment create `
--cluster-name "adx$suffix" `
--database-name telemetry `
--principal-id $sp.appId `
--principal-type App `
--role "Viewer" `
--tenant-id $sp.tenant `
--principal-assignment-name purview `
--resource-group adx-rg
```

Grants database
permissions to a principal

Specifies the cluster and
database we grant access to

The Viewer role grants
read-only access.

Names the assignment,
which we call purview

We used the commands in listing 8.6 before in chapter 4 when we connected Azure Data Factory (ADF) with our Azure Data Explorer cluster. We now have a new service principal with read-only access to the cluster; its details are stored in the $sp variable. Let's create an Azure Key Vault to store the principal's secret key, as the following listing shows.

Listing 8.7 Storing the service principal secret in Azure Key Vault

Names the vault purviewkv, followed by an unique $suffix

Creates a new Azure Key Vault

```
az keyvault create `
--location "Central US" `
--name "purviewkv$suffix" `
--resource-group purview-rg

az keyvault secret set `
--name purviewsppwd `
--value $sp.password `
--vault-name "purviewkv$suffix"
```

Puts the vault in the same resource group as our Azure Purview instance

Sets the key vault secret

Names the secret purviewsppwd

Sets the secret value, which we get from $sp

Let's go back to the browser window and finish the connection. We should be on the New Scan pane, configuring our Azure Data Explorer scan. Because we haven't registered any credentials with Azure Purview yet, select New from the Credential drop-down. Figure 8.8 shows how the New Credential pane looks.

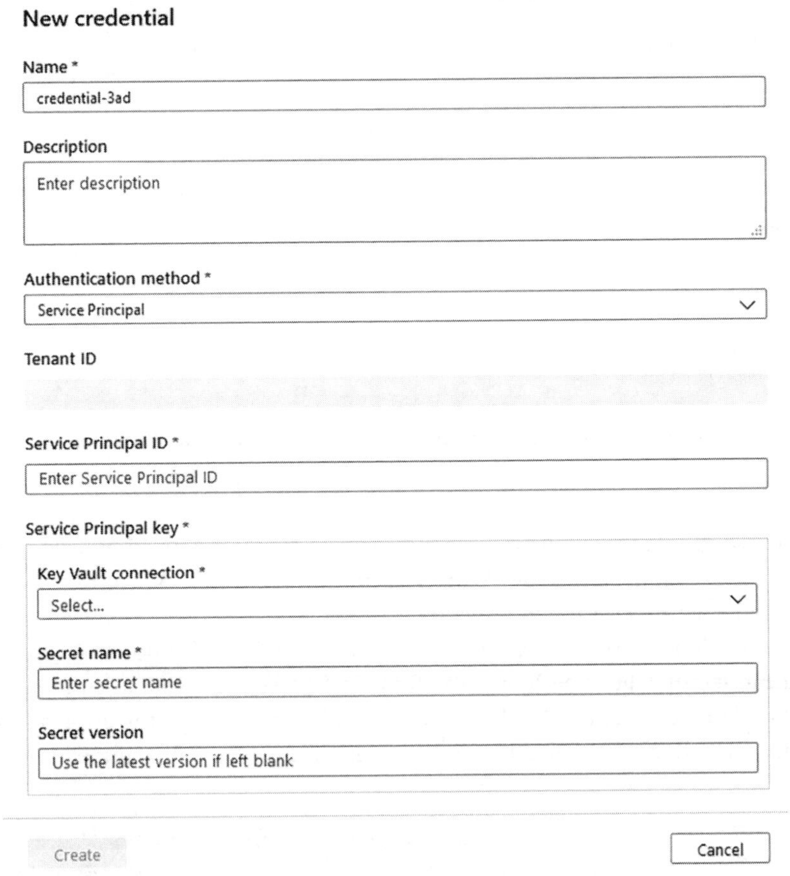

New credential

Name *

`credential-3ad`

Description

`Enter description`

Authentication method *

`Service Principal ▾`

Tenant ID

Service Principal ID *

`Enter Service Principal ID`

Service Principal key *

Key Vault connection *

`Select... ▾`

Secret name *

`Enter secret name`

Secret version

`Use the latest version if left blank`

Create   Cancel

Figure 8.8 New Credential pane. Use `$sp.name` for the Service Principal ID and `purviewsppwd` for the Secret Name. From the Key Vault Connection drop-down, select New.

In the New Credential pane, we can leave the Name with the default value (creden-tial- followed by some random characters) and the Authentication Method as Service Principal. For Service Principal ID, we'll use the name of our newly created service principal. You can get that name by typing $sp.name in PowerShell. Use pur-viewsppwd for the Secret Name because that is the name we gave it in listing 8.7. Finally, click to expand the Key Vault Connection drop-down and select New. Figure 8.9 shows how the New Key Vault pane looks.

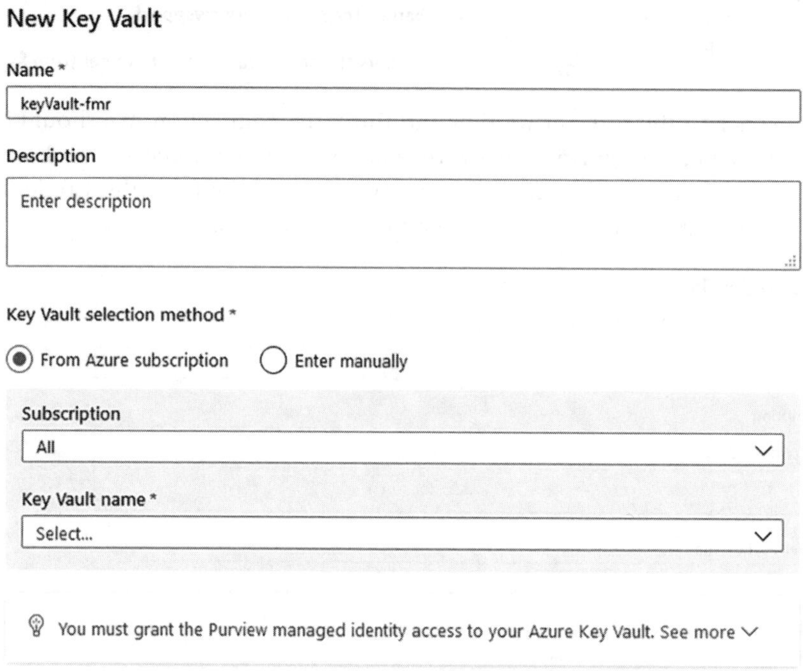

New Key Vault

Name *

    keyVault-fmr

Description

    Enter description

Key Vault selection method *

(•) From Azure subscription   ( ) Enter manually

    Subscription

    All   ∨

    Key Vault name *

    Select...   ∨

    💡 You must grant the Purview managed identity access to your Azure Key Vault. See more ∨

Figure 8.9   Creating a new Azure Key Vault connection. Click See More at the bottom of the pane to view the managed identity for the Azure Purview instance.

We're almost done. On the New Key Vault pane, select the Azure Key Vault we just created (purviewkv$suffix). Now Azure Purview knows which Azure Key Vault to connect to and which secret to get.

There's still one last missing piece: the Azure Key Vault should allow Azure Purview to read the secret. Click See More (see figure 8.9) to get the managed identity details. Copy the Managed Identity Application ID. (Make sure to copy the application ID, not the object ID.) Back at the shell, run the commands in the following listing.

Listing 8.8   Allowing Azure Purview to get the Key Vault secrets

```
$purviewId =
➥ "<use the managed identity application ID>"  ⟵
```
Replace this value with the Managed Identity Application ID of your Azure Purview instance.

```
az keyvault set-policy `          ◄─────┐   Sets a key vault policy
--secret-permissions get list `   ◄───── Grants get and list permissions for secrets
--name purviewkv$suffix `         ◄─────┐
--spn $purviewId                          Names the Azure Key Vault instance;
                                          we use purviewkv$suffix.
```

We can now click Create to finish setting up the Azure Key Vault connection for Azure Purview. Then use that connection for the new credential and create it.

We had to take quite a few steps. First, we created a service principal and an Azure Key Vault, then we stored the service principal's secret in the Key Vault, granted Azure Purview access to the Key Vault, and connected Azure Purview to it. Note this is just the initial setup. We can use the same Key Vault and Key Vault connection for other sources, maybe even the same credential (although, remember, a security best practice is to use different service principals for different connections in case one gets compromised). Now, configuring subsequent data sources should be much easier.

Now that we have our credential configured, we should be back on the Scan Configuration pane. Click Test Connection to verify that Azure Purview can indeed connect to Azure Data Explorer. This should work if everything is hooked up correctly. Click Continue to go to the next step. This shows a list of databases to scan. In our case, it should be only telemetry because the service principal only has access to that database. Click Continue again.

You should see the Select a Scan Rule Set Configuration. Azure Purview classifies data as it scans the datasets. By default, Azure Purview uses Microsoft's classification rules. We can specify custom rules and rule sets, but we won't do that now. Click Continue to proceed with the defaults.

Finally, we're at the Trigger Configuration step, where we can specify how often the scan should run. Let's pick Once for our example, although for a production system, we would most likely do this on a regular cadence. Click Continue, then Save and Run.

8.3.2   Browsing the data dictionary

Before we can browse our assets, we need to wait for the scan to complete. This takes a few minutes. Back on the Map View that shows Azure Data Explorer, click View Details. This takes you to a status page where you can check the progress of the scan. It shows up as Queued right after setup. You can click Refresh to refresh the latest status. At some point, the status changes to Scan In-progress and finally to Successfully Completed. The same status page should also show the number of scanned and classified assets (tables).

Once the scan completes, go back to Azure Purview's home page and from there click Browse Assets. You should be able to click through the Azure Data Explorer cluster, the telemetry database, and to any table in the database. Figure 8.10 shows the PageViews table.

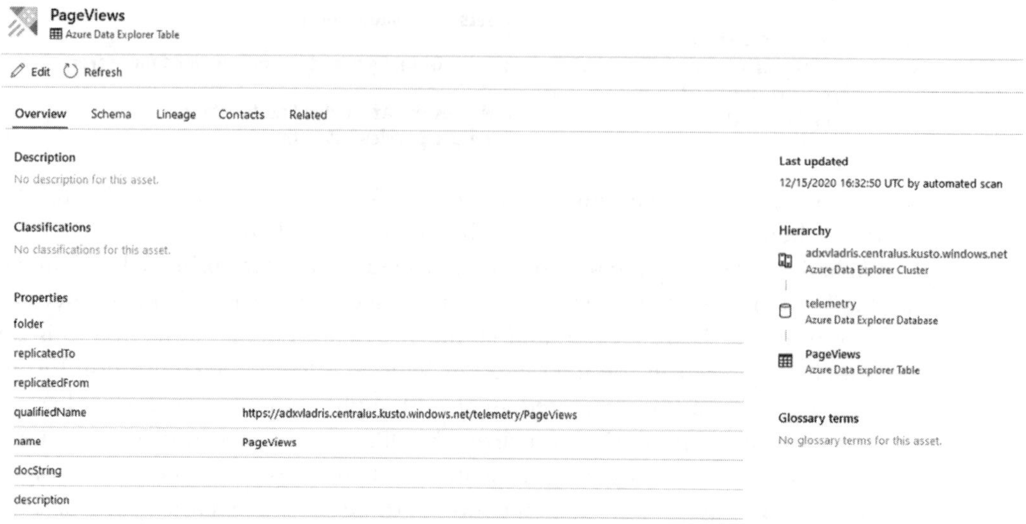

PageViews
⊞ Azure Data Explorer Table

🖉 Edit ↻ Refresh

Overview   Schema   Lineage   Contacts   Related

Description   **Last updated**
No description for this asset.   12/15/2020 16:32:50 UTC by automated scan

Classifications   **Hierarchy**
No classifications for this asset.   ⊞ adxvladris.centralus.kusto.windows.net
                                                                      Azure Data Explorer Cluster
Properties |
folder   ⬡ telemetry
                                                                      Azure Data Explorer Database
replicatedTo |
                                                                   ⊞ PageViews
replicatedFrom   Azure Data Explorer Table

qualifiedName   https://adxvladris.centralus.kusto.windows.net/telemetry/PageViews
                                                                   Glossary terms
name   PageViews   No glossary terms for this asset.

docString

description

Figure 8.10   PageViews table including properties, schema, contacts, and so on

We configured the automated part, which consists of scanning our data fabrics. The next step is to enhance this with meaningful descriptions. Clicking the Edit button at the top takes us to the Edit UI. This enables us to add descriptions for the table itself and for each individual column. It also allows us to list contacts, both owners and subject matter experts. We can also link to glossary terms (we'll cover the data glossary in the next section).

For a production data platform, we need to define a process to ensure descriptions are provided and kept up to date. A team member (data engineer, data scientists, project manager, etc.) would act as the curator, making sure that assets are properly documented. They would identify area experts and coordinate across the team to ensure information is high quality.

Before moving on to the data glossary, let's also check out the powerful search features. If we go back to the home page and enter `covid` in the search box, Azure Purview should suggest our Covid19 table. If we enter `user id`, it should suggest all tables that contain a User ID column. This is a powerful feature, and we are barely scratching the surface.

In a real-world scenario, we would scan multiple data fabrics, and being able to search across them is one of Azure Purview's unique features. Not only table names and columns get indexed, but so do descriptions. Once we provide descriptions for all our datasets, we can search for them too.

8.3.3   *Data dictionary recap*

In this section, we saw how we can use Azure Purview's data dictionary capabilities. We learned that

- A source in Azure Purview represents a data fabric it can connect to and scan for data assets. This can be Azure Data Explorer, Azure Synapse Analytics, Azure SQL, Azure Data Lake Storage, etc.
- A credential stores the configuration required to connect to a source. We used a service principal with a secret stored in Azure Key Vault.
- A scan tells Azure Purview what to read from a source and how often. Once a scan runs, the scanned tables become browsable and searchable as assets.
- Assets can be enhanced with descriptions, owners, and links to glossary terms.

We mentioned the word *glossary* several times so far. Next, we'll see what Azure Purview offers in terms of data glossary management.

8.4 Managing a data glossary

At the beginning of this chapter, we saw how even a simple metric like monthly page views can become confusing. Does it include test traffic? Is it from the first of the month or looking back one month from today? In this section, we will use the data glossary to capture this information. Let's add our monthly page views as an entry to the data glossary, see how these entries look, and talk a bit about managing glossaries.

8.4.1 Adding a new glossary term

Click Glossary on the left navigation pane or click the Manage Glossary quick navigation tile on Azure Purview's home page. This should take you to the Glossary view, which currently doesn't contain any entries. Let's add one by clicking New Term. You should see the New Term pane shown in figure 8.11.

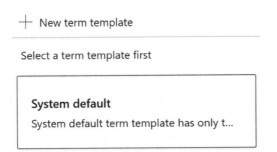

Figure 8.11 The New Term pane shows the first step in creating a new glossary term.

Glossary terms are highly customizable, so you can provide a template describing all the fields that a term should capture. Azure Purview comes with a default template. Let's use that for now, then we'll look at some other interesting fields we can add to a custom template.

Click Continue to accept the system default. You should see the next step for adding a new glossary item as figure 8.12 shows.

New term

Term template	System default ⌄
Status ⓘ	🗋 Draft ⌄

Overview   Related   Contacts

Name * ⓘ	
Definition	
Acronym ⓘ	Use commas to separate multiple values...
Resources ⓘ	Resource Name Resource link
	+ Add a resource

Figure 8.12   Adding a new glossary item using the default template

Let's go over the fields in the Overview tab:

- *Name*—The name of the term. Let's use "Monthly pageviews" for ours.
- *Definition*—Term definition. We'll fill in `Monthly pageviews from the first of the month, excluding test traffic`.
- *Acronym*—We'll leave this blank, but here is where we capture abbreviations (acronyms) for terms. For example, for a term like "Monthly active users," we could add MAU as an acronym.
- *Resources*—This is where we can link this term to other artifacts in our data platform. In this case, we can add a resource named `Canonical query` and a link to the canonical query that produces this metric. This can be either a link to documentation, a link to the canonical query in Git, or even a link to the query itself if the data fabric supports this type of deep linking.

Next, click the Related tab and let's go over the fields there. There should be only two:

- *Synonyms*—In a complex business domain, sometimes different teams or different departments end up referring to the same thing by different names. This is common enough that data glossaries support the concept of synonyms. We can use this field to link multiple terms that refer to the same concept.
- *Related Terms*—This enables us to link to other terms related to our current term. For example, if our term is "Monthly active users," we would say a related term is "Daily active users." Because this is the first term we add to our glossary (Monthly pageviews), we won't have other terms to link it to.

Finally, the Contacts tab lets us fill in the following two fields:

- *Experts*—The subject matter experts we should contact for the given term
- *Stewards*—People in charge of curating the definitions

Click the Create button to add our new term to the glossary. Note that terms have a status that curators can use for the term's life cycle:

- *Draft*—A term definition starts out as a draft. That is a proposed term that still needs review before becoming official.
- *Approved*—This represents a term that was reviewed and is now considered part of the standard.
- *Alert*—Curators can use this to flag a term and signal that it needs attention.
- *Expired*—This deprecates a term and signals that it should no longer be used.

After creating the term, the Glossary view should now show our new term under the letter *M*, as figure 8.13 illustrates.

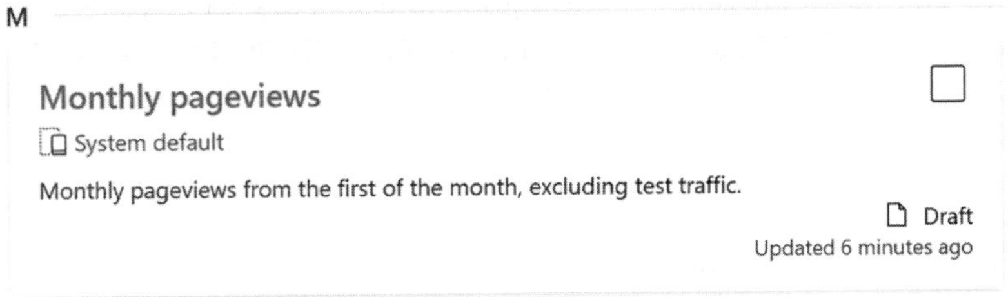

Figure 8.13   "Monthly pageviews" glossary term

We can link our data assets to glossary terms to capture relationships between our data dictionary and data glossary. For example, if we navigate to the PageViews data asset describing our PageViews table in our Azure Data Explorer cluster and click Edit, one of the options will be Glossary Terms. We can link the asset to our "Monthly pageviews" glossary term to indicate it is used to produce the metric.

8.4.2 *Curating terms*

As hinted by the Stewards field that we can associate with each glossary term, the team should designate one or more persons to be responsible for maintaining a high-quality data glossary. While we can automate many tasks, we still need humans to guarantee definitions are correct, to flag terms that are deprecated and no longer used, and to ensure new terms the business uses get added to the glossary. This is less about automation and more about process. We should make sure someone is on point to ensure the business domain is properly captured in the glossary and everything is kept up to date.

That doesn't mean a single person should handle all data entry. Rather, someone needs to ensure that everybody is doing their part. This is documentation-related work, and as we saw in chapter 6, making certain that documentation is kept up to date is notoriously hard. Having a good process in place is important.

For example, one way to approach this would be for the curators to work with the area experts to identify the key terms that should be captured, ensure that drafts for all of them show up in the glossary (initially in the Draft state), and maintain a rhythm to flesh out definitions, populate fields, and graduate terms to the Approved state at a good pace. The curators should be the ones who grant approval based on the standards a term should uphold.

An example of such a standard would be to mandate a link to the canonical query for every key metric, along with naming at least two area experts for each term, who can be reached in case there are any questions. Let's now look at some of the other capabilities provided by the data glossary: custom templates and bulk import.

8.4.3   *Custom templates and bulk import*

Custom templates allow us to configure what fields we want to capture with our glossary terms. The Azure Purview default is good and touches on all aspects of glossary management, including fields for acronyms, synonyms, related terms, etc. But in case your team needs to track some specific fields with these definitions, custom templates enable that.

We won't go through all the steps here, but if you go to the Glossary page and click Manage Term Templates, you will see how the system default template is defined (figure 8.14) and can then define your own custom template.

A template has a name, a description, and set of attributes. The attributes describe the fields to be filled in when adding new terms. Attributes have a name and a description, can be either optional or required, have a type (either text, single choice, multiple choice, or date) and, depending on type, can have some additional configuration (text can have a default value and choices have a set of values to select from). For example, we might want to tag a set of terms corresponding to key metrics for our business. We can use a custom template with the multiple choice options Key Metric and Not a Key Metric to keep track of this. Templates give us the flexibility to tweak the shape of glossary terms to fit our particular needs.

Another powerful feature of Azure Purview is the bulk import. This enables us to populate the glossary by uploading a CSV file containing term definitions. We need to specify the template we want to use, then Azure Purview translates the CSV file into glossary terms. We can use bulk import to migrate data from other systems or to enable stewards to enter data in a more familiar setting like Excel.

Manage term templates

System   Custom

Attribute name	Field type	Description	Display on
Name	Text	Term name	Header
Status	Choices	Term's status: Draft, Alert, Approved, Expired	Header
Definition	Text	What this term means.	Overview tab
Acronym	Text	An abbreviated version of this term.	Overview tab
Resources	Link	Hyperlinks to other resources that will be helpful for consumers of this term.	Overview tab
Related terms	Choices	Terms that are related to this one.	Related tab
Synonyms	Choices	Terms with the same or similar definitions.	Related tab
Stewards	Choices	The individual or individuals who define the standards for a data object or business term. They drive quality standards, nomenclature, rules.	Contact tab
Experts	Choices	These individuals are often in different business areas or departments. They could be business process experts or subject matter experts.	Contact tab

OK

Figure 8.14 The Manage Term Templates pane showing the system default template

8.4.4 *Data glossary recap*

In this section, we looked at Azure Purview's data glossary and added a new term to it. Data glossaries capture definitions of business terms and their associated queries and datasets. This ensures that everybody uses the same canonical definitions for the business domain, that metrics and reports are consistent, and that the business terms are easy to navigate.

A data glossary term has a name, a definition, and experts to contact as needed. A few other common fields that are part of the Azure Purview default template are synonyms (other names for the terms), acronyms, and related terms. Custom templates allow us to tweak the fields a term requires to fit our particular needs, while import capabilities make it easy to add terms to the glossary in bulk from CSV files.

Data glossaries are a common practice in information architecture. Regardless of whether you end up using Azure Purview in your data platform or an alternative solution, once the data volume is large enough and the business domain is complex enough, you will inevitably need to maintain some sort of glossary to ensure consistency within the system. Azure Purview also has a set of advanced features you should be aware of. We'll cover these in the next section.

8.5   *Understanding Azure Purview's advanced features*

We won't go too deep into these features, but you should be aware of them when integrating Azure Purview with your data platform. We'll look at the data classification capabilities and the REST API, which allows us to integrate Azure Purview with other services. We'll start with lineage.

8.5.1   *Tracking lineage*

So far, we saw how to inventory the datasets we have and how to describe their schemas. Sometimes, we need to know more about a dataset: not only what it contains, but also where it comes from. This is known as data lineage.

> **DEFINITION**   *Data lineage* includes the data origin, what happens to it, and where it moves over time.

One application of data lineage is in debugging issues. When we identify a problem with a dataset, being able to easily trace the data upstream and see where the issue originates is invaluable.

Another application of data lineage is compliance. As we'll see in chapter 10, in some cases when we collect data, the user consents to certain uses and, potentially, not others. For example, when gathering telemetry data, we might have told users we will only use this data to improve the product and not for targeted advertising. That means that not all data in our data platform can be used for all scenarios. We should know where the data comes from. This will inform us what we can do with it.

Azure Purview connects to two services commonly used to move data in Azure: Azure Data Factory and Azure Data Share. We covered Azure Data Factory in chapter 4 and used it for several examples in this book. Azure Data Factory is the cloud ETL solution for Azure. Azure Data Share is used to share data from various storage services with others. Azure Data Share handles access management and can share data across tenants. We'll take a more detailed look at Azure Data Share in chapter 11 when we talk about data distribution. Both Azure Data Factory and Azure Data Share are common ways through which datasets make their way into our data platform. Azure Purview can connect to both services and map out the data movement.

To connect to an Azure Data Factory, go to the Management Center (last icon on the left navigation pane). In the Management Center, select Data Factory under the

External Connections section. This takes you to the Data Factory Connections view that currently shows an empty list. Click New. Let's go through the steps of connecting our Data Factory. Figure 8.15 shows the New Data Factory Connections pane.

New Data Factory connections

Each Data Factory account can connect to only one Purview account.

Azure Subscription

All   ⌄

Data Factory *

Select...   ⌄

0 selected

Data Factory	Existing connection

No records found.

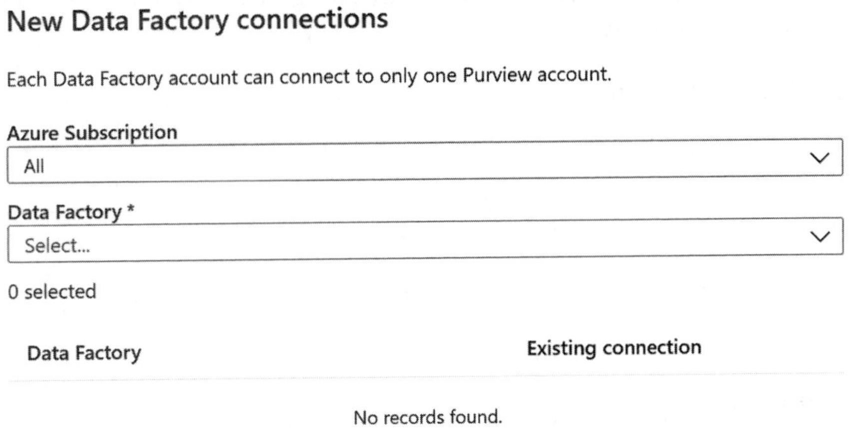

Figure 8.15 The New Data Factory Connections pane shows the Azure Subscription and Data Factory pickers.

Select your subscription and the `adf$suffix` Data Factory we used in the previous chapters, then click OK. Note that Azure Purview only supports a subset of Azure Data Factory activities: it understands Copy Data, Data Flow, and Execute SSIS Package. We used Copy Data to import the COVID-19 dataset in chapter 4, but remember, we copied the data to a temporary table and swapped it with the final one. That means Azure Purview won't be aware of the lineage of that particular dataset.

If you want to try out the feature, as an exercise, you can create a simple Azure Data Factory pipeline with a Copy Data activity between two storage services. Once they are scanned in Azure Purview (don't forget to run a scan), the Lineage tab for the asset should show where the data comes from; you should see a data flow map showing the data sources, the ETL steps, and the destinations.

8.5.2 Classification rules

When we set up our Azure Data Explorer scan, we used the default scan rule set. Let's zoom in on this to understand how classification rules work and how we can customize them.

If you go to the Management Center view, Metadata Management shows two options: Classification and Classification Rules. A classification simply has a name and a description. Azure Purview comes with over 100 default classifications. One example is the US Social Security Number (SSN). We can add as many custom classifications as needed. This is useful when our business space requires different classifications than those available by default.

A *classification rule* helps Azure Purview automatically classify assets during scans. Each of the default classifications has an associated classification rule. We can create custom classification rules to enable additional classifications. A classification rule tells Azure Purview when to consider a column as having a classification. Figure 8.16 shows the New Classification Rule pane.

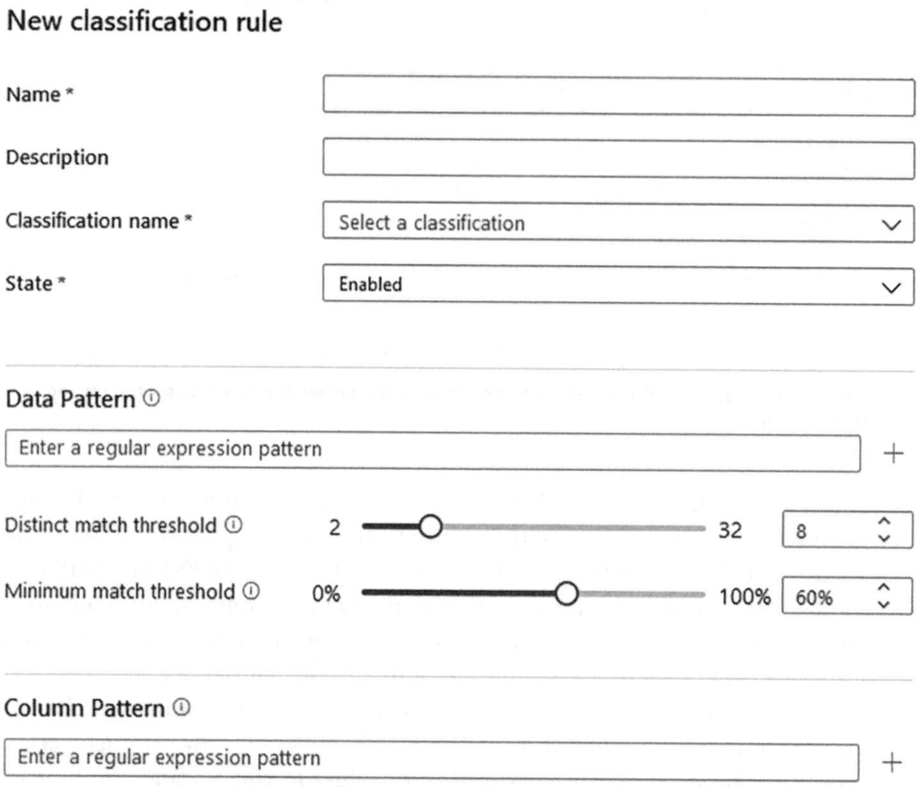

New classification rule

Name *

Description

Classification name *   Select a classification ⌄

State *   Enabled ⌄

Data Pattern ⓘ

Enter a regular expression pattern   +

Distinct match threshold ⓘ   2 ──O────── 32   8

Minimum match threshold ⓘ   0% ────O── 100%   60%

Column Pattern ⓘ

Enter a regular expression pattern   +

Figure 8.16 Creating a new classification rule. We can use patterns to classify data based on the shape of the rows, and column patterns to classify data based on the shape of the column names.

We can use both Data Pattern and Column Pattern to classify data. A *data pattern* is described by a regular expression the data should match, the minimum number of distinct matches in the column, and what percentage of rows need to match the pattern before we are confident the column has that classification. See the following sidebar if you are unfamiliar with regular expressions.

Assuming all user identities in our system start with *UID*, we can use the regular expression UID.* as our data pattern. A column pattern simply matches the name of the column. If our User ID column is usually named UserID or ID, we can use the UserID|ID regular expression to classify all these columns as containing a user ID.

Regular expressions

Regular expressions define search patterns in strings. Regular expression engines can interpret these patterns to perform powerful searches. Most programming languages have a regular expression language as part of their library and various tools also use regular expressions. Modern engines provide a rich syntax to describe searches. Although this is beyond the scope of this book, we will go over a few basic examples.

Most characters aren't considered special, so searches are performed literally. For example, the regular expression `data` matches "data" in "data engineering." The following shows the use of some of the regular expression special characters:

- `()` allow us to group terms and `|` represents an alternative (either/or). For example, the regular expression `data (science|engineering)` matches both "data science" and "data engineering" (either string is considered a match).
- `.` means any one character. For example, the regular expression `dat.` matches both "data" and "date."

We also have quantifiers that define how many times a term should repeat: `?` means zero or once, `*` means zero or more times, and `+` means one or more times. Let's see a few examples:

- `data( engineering)?` matches both "data" and "data engineering"; `( engineering)` repeats zero times or once.
- `data( engineering)*` matches any number of repetitions for `( engineering)` zero or more times; for example, this expression matches "data" and "data engineering."
- `data( engineering)+` is like the previous example, except `( engineering)` needs to appear at least once. In this case, it doesn't match "data."

Of course, we can combine these to create complex expressions. For example `data.*` matches any string that begins with "data." (We combined `.` with `*`, which means any character, zero or more times).

We'll stop here as this quick walkthrough should help you understand the examples in this section. Do look up regular expressions if you want to learn more about this powerful language.

Back in the Management Center, we can create new Scan Rule sets. A *scan rule set* allows us to specify for a data fabric which classification rules we want to apply during scanning. Defaults are provided, but we can create custom scan rules including our custom classifications. We can associate a scan rule set with one or more scans, so our data gets automatically classified by Azure Purview.

8.5.3   REST API

Azure Purview also exposes a REST API that grants programmatic access to the metadata. We won't go into the details of this; the API is well documented by Microsoft at http://mng.bz/O16j. Keep it in mind, though, as it enables you to connect custom services to it and make the metadata available to them. For example, in the following chapters, we'll look at data quality and compliance. Both can have tight integrations with a metadata store.

We'll cover data quality in chapter 9. Data quality automatically detects issues in our datasets. Once we identify a problematic dataset, a metadata store can help us identify which reports and metrics are impacted by the data quality issue. This is one scenario where we can leverage the REST API to query our metadata store and automatically report on the impact of a data issue.

We'll cover compliance in chapter 10. Data classification and handling is key to staying compliant. Leveraging the Azure Purview classification rules and data dictionary capabilities helps us easily identify which tables contain sensitive data. For example, we can automate compliance checks that ensure sensitive data only shows up in certain databases. The REST API lets us query this metadata from other services that deal with compliance tracking and enforcement.

We focused on metadata management using Azure Purview, but the same concepts apply regardless of the exact service we use. A big data platform needs a data dictionary and a data glossary. This metadata must be easily searchable and discoverable. An integration point (like the REST API in this case) allows us to leverage the metadata for other governance concerns such as tracking data quality and enforcing compliance.

8.5.4 *Advanced features recap*

Before wrapping up the chapter, let's quickly review the more advanced features we covered. We talked about lineage tracking. Azure Purview achieves this by connecting to Azure Data Factory and Azure Data Share instances (we'll revisit Azure Data Share in chapter 11). This allows us to track where data is coming from, which is important for several scenarios, including compliance. But keep in mind some of the limitations: Azure Purview understands only a small number of Data Factory activities.

We also covered data classification and how we would go about setting up a custom classification rule. This allows Azure Purview to identify the data within a dataset based on patterns defined as regular expressions. Having the proper data classification is another important aspect of compliance. Depending on what type of data we have, we need to apply different handling standards, as we'll see in chapter 10.

Finally, we briefly talked about the REST API. We didn't cover it in detail, but it is an important integration point if we want to enable access to the Azure Purview metadata catalog to other services. The key takeaway is that Azure Purview makes it easy for humans to search and browse the data assets and business space, but it can also serve as the metadata store for other services that make up your data platform.

In this chapter, we saw how metadata helps us make sense of our data landscape. This is a key part of data governance, but not the only one. In the next chapter, we'll look at another important aspect: data quality.

Summary

- Metadata is data about the data. It helps make sense of all the datasets in a big data platform.
- A data dictionary contains descriptions of datasets.
- A data glossary provides precise definitions for the various business terms relevant to the data platform and associated canonical queries.
- Azure Purview is the Azure service for metadata management.
- Azure Purview can connect to all Azure storage services (and some other third-party services), then scan and inventory the available datasets.
- Azure Purview has a data glossary in which we can add or import terms and link them to other terms, datasets, and other resources.
- Data lineage keeps track of where the data is coming from and how it is transformed.
- Azure Purview can connect to Azure Data Factory and Azure Data Share services to automatically discover lineage.
- Classification rules automatically classify datasets based on patterns in the rows and column names.
- A REST API enables other services to integrate with Azure Purview and query its metadata store.

Data quality

9

This chapter covers

- Testing data to ensure quality
- Different types of data quality checks
- Executing data tests
- Considerations for scaling out data testing

The insights generated by a data platform are only as good as the quality of the underlying data. A good data platform needs to provide some guarantees around data quality. In this chapter, we will focus on data quality.

At the time of writing, data quality testing isn't yet offered "as a service" by all major cloud providers. Unlike some of the previous topics we've covered in this book—such as storage, data processing, or machine learning (ML)—we don't have an out-of-the-box PaaS (platform as a service) solution, so we'll have to stitch something together ourselves.

We'll start by looking at what it means to test data and what are a few common types of data tests. Software engineering has a mature discipline of testing code. We'll draw an analogy to data engineering and testing data. Next, we'll look at what a data quality testing framework might look like and sketch a simple solution for our data platform. We'll see when we should run these data quality tests and how we can handle execution.

Finally, we will talk about some scaling considerations and how we would go about data quality testing in a real-world production system. This is a deep topic, so we won't be able to implement everything in this chapter, but we'll cover the necessary patterns and best practices. Let's start with the fundamentals of testing data.

9.1 Testing data

Testing code is part of the software engineering discipline. In the data engineering world, the equivalent is testing data. While conceptually similar, there is a major difference between the two. Once the code gets written and tested, we can expect the tests to keep passing unless the code is modified. On the other hand, in a data platform, data keeps moving. We might ingest bad data due to an issue upstream, or we might output corrupt data due to a processing issue. Data quality tests need to run all the time, as data moves, to uncover such issues.

Let's look at a few types of data quality tests and see how we would implement each on Azure Data Explorer (ADX). The list isn't exhaustive, but it is a good starting point. Start your Azure Data Explorer cluster if you stopped it to save on costs and open the Azure Data Explorer query UI.

9.1.1 Availability tests

The simplest type of data test is an availability test, which checks that data is available for a certain date. If, for example, we ingest COVID-19 data on a regular cadence using the pipeline we set up in chapter 4, we expect to have up-to-date numbers available in our system.

Let's check whether we have any COVID-19 data available for February 29, 2020. We will do this by querying the Covid19 table in Azure Data Explorer, looking for rows where the updated timestamp is 2020-02-29. If at least one row is returned, we'll consider the test passed. The following listing shows the query.

Listing 9.1 COVID-19 data availability

```
Covid19
| where updated == datetime(2020-02-29)
| take 1                                  ◁——— Takes one row from the result
                                              set that meets this criteria
```

This is a basic test we can run before running more complicated tests. It doesn't tell us whether the data we ingested is correct or even if we ingested all the data we were expecting to ingest. What it does tell us is that we have at least some data available for the date we are querying for, which means some ingestion happened. Knowing this, we can run more comprehensive tests.

Let's wrap this up in a function. Remember, in Azure Data Explorer, functions can wrap common queries to make reissuing them easier. Our function takes one parameter, the date we are checking for, and returns true if data is available; false, otherwise (this is the equivalent of pass/fail). The following listing shows the test function.

Listing 9.2 COVID-19 data availability test function

```
.create-or-alter
function Covid19Availability(
  testDate: datetime) {
    Covid19
    | where updated == testDate
    | take 1
    | summarize Result = count() > 0
}
```

Defines a datetime parameter that represents the date we want to test

Summarizes as a Result using count(), which gives us the number of rows and checks whether it's greater than 0

The final line of our function converts the result of the query into our pass/fail Boolean value by counting the number of rows. In our case, this can be at most 1 because we called take 1 on the previous line and checked if that value is greater than 0.

Let's call this function a couple of times to see what it returns. If you worked through the example in chapter 4, you should see some data for February 29, 2020. Checking a date in the future like January 1, 2030, for example, should return false. The following listing shows the two queries.

Listing 9.3 Checking for availability

```
Covid19Availability(datetime(2020-02-29))
// Should return true

Covid19Availability(datetime(2030-01-01))
// Should return false
```

In general, availability tests are quick sanity checks that we run before executing more comprehensive tests. Note that because we only check that at least one row of data is available, the query is inexpensive. Contrast this with a query where we perform some checks on each row.

> **DEFINITION** An *availability test* ensures that at least some data is available for a given date. Availability tests are cheaper to run than other types of tests.

Next, we'll look at a slightly more complex type of test: correctness tests.

9.1.2 *Correctness tests*

Ensuring data is available is just the first step. We also need to validate that the data is valid. What *valid* means depends on the dataset. Let's go back to our COVID-19 example and identify a few correctness checks we can apply. The data is reported by country/region, which is captured in the country_region column. We can make one check to ensure that some value is always present in this column. The next listing shows the corresponding query.

> **Listing 9.4   COVID-19 data correctness**

```
Covid19
| where isempty(country_region)
```

Another couple of checks would guarantee that the number of reported confirmed cases and fatalities is always greater than 0. We can separate each test in its own query or run the tests together. As long as we're not so compute-intensive that we reach the Azure Data Explorer query limits, running the queries together would be slightly faster because we are querying the same dataset. Running them separately, however, has the advantage of making it easier to pinpoint the exact issue. We would know exactly which check failed. We'll keep them together for our case, as the query in the next listing shows.

> **Listing 9.5   COVID-19 data correctness for multiple dimensions**

```
Covid19
| where isempty(country_region) or confirmed < 0 or deaths < 0
```

Let's wrap this query into a function as listing 9.6 shows, like we did with the availability test. We can have it return true or false, depending on whether the tests pass or fail. We'll introduce a testDate parameter again, so we can restrict testing to a specific date.

> **Listing 9.6   COVID-19 data correctness test function**

```
.create-or-alter
function Covid19Correctness(testDate: datetime) {
    Covid19
    | where updated == testDate
    | where isempty(country_region)
      or confirmed < 0 or deaths < 0
    | summarize Result = count() == 0
}
```

Filters by the date we want to test → (points to `| where updated == testDate`)

Checks that would indicate corrupt data (points to `| where isempty(country_region) or confirmed < 0 or deaths < 0`)

This time, we want no rows to be returned if the data is correct. (points to `| summarize Result = count() == 0`)

Running the test for February 29, 2020, should return true. Turns out that Switzerland reported -1 fatalities for February 24 and 25, 2020. If we run the test for one of those days, it returns false. The following listing shows the two queries.

> **Listing 9.7   Checking for correctness**

```
Covid19Correctness(datetime(2020-02-29))
// Should return true

Covid19Correctness(datetime(2020-02-24))
// Should return false
```

In general, correctness tests validate various dimensions of the data to ensure values are within expected ranges.

DEFINITION   A *correctness test* ensures that data is valid by checking that values are within allowed ranges. Allowed values are specific to each dataset and require domain knowledge to identify.

We can now check that the data is available and that it makes sense. The next thing to check for is whether the data is all there with nothing missing.

9.1.3   *Completeness tests*

Availability tests check that some data is present. Completeness tests check that all data is present. Like correctness tests, a completeness test depends on the dataset and what it means to be complete.

Continuing with our COVID-19 example, let's say that for a given date, we expect 52 entries for United Sates: 1 for each state, 1 for District of Columbia, and 1 aggregate for the whole country. Our query checks that the count of rows reported for United States for a given date is 52, as the following listing shows.

> **Listing 9.8   COVID-19 data completeness for United States**

```
Covid19
| where updated == datetime(2020-02-29)
| where country_region == "United States"
| summarize Result = count() == 52
```

We will wrap this query in a function. The function takes a `testDate` parameter, as the next listing shows.

> **Listing 9.9   COVID-19 data completeness for United States test function**

```
.create-or-alter
function Covid19CompletenessUS(testDate: datetime) {
    Covid19
    | where updated == testDate
    | where country_region == "United States"
    | summarize Result = count() == 52
}
```

We'll stick to United States for our example because this particular dataset contains various gaps; not all countries are reporting consistently. This can happen often in real-world scenarios, so we need to take that into account when designing our tests. We can't always guarantee an exact count, but we can set a threshold that is good enough to process the data. For example, another completeness test could ensure that for a given date, we have reports from at least 200 distinct countries or regions. The following listing shows the corresponding function.

Listing 9.10   COVID-19 worldwide data completeness test function

```
.create-or-alter
function Covid19CompletenessWW(testDate: datetime) {
    Covid19
    | where updated == testDate
    | distinct country_region
    | summarize Result = count() >= 200
}
```

We call this function `Covid19CompletenessWW` (the `WW` stands for worldwide). Turns out that when the virus was starting to spread, fewer countries reported cases. If we run this test for February 29, 2020, it fails. As more and more countries began testing and reporting their numbers, later dates have much more data. The following listing runs the test for a couple of dates.

Listing 9.11   Checking for completeness

```
Covid19CompletenessWW(datetime(2020-02-29))
// Should return false

Covid19CompletenessWW(datetime(2020-06-01))
// Should return true
```

In general, completeness tests ensure data is fully available and aim to identify data gaps and incomplete data loads.

> **DEFINITION**   A *completeness test* ensures that all the data is loaded by checking that the volume of data is what we would expect. If possible, we can check for an exact row count. If not, we can check that volume is above a certain threshold.

As we just saw, in some cases, we can't guarantee that the row count for a given date is going to be some exact number, so we must use some heuristics. Next, let's look at more sophisticated tests that look for anomalies in the data.

9.1.4   *Detecting anomalies*

Anomaly detection is a deep topic, so we'll just dip our toes here. When we looked at completeness tests, we checked that we have at least 200 countries/regions reporting COVID-19 data. We picked the number 200 as a reasonable volume, which is enough to use the data, but the number is fairly arbitrary. At the beginning of the pandemic, fewer countries reported data and, as time went by, more and more countries started reporting. We would have to adjust that number for our test, expecting more incoming data.

Let's see how we can create a test where we don't have to pick an exact row count. We can create a percentage difference test to check that day after day the data volume doesn't vary more than 5%.

Percentage difference

The formula for percentage difference is $\frac{|a-b|}{\frac{a+b}{2}} \times 100$. That's the absolute difference between *a* and *b* (it doesn't really matter which of the two values is larger) over the average of *a* and *b*, multiplied by 100. This tells us the percentage difference for two values. For example, if *a* is 95 and *b* is 105, the absolute difference is 10, the average is 100, so the percentage difference is 10:

$$\frac{|95 - 105|}{\left(\frac{95 + 105}{2}\right)} \times 100 = \frac{|-10|}{\left(\frac{200}{2}\right)} \times 100 = \frac{10}{100} \times 100 = 10$$

This type of difference measures the amount of change relative to the values, so it is a good way to measure drift without having to come up with exact expected row counts. We set a threshold, for example, 5%, and consider it an anomaly if data volume changes by more than 5%.

Let's see how we can measure this with Azure Data Explorer. We'll take the row count for two consecutive dates, convert them to doubles, then print the percentage difference. Azure Data Explorer deals with tabular data, so if we want a single value, we first need to convert to a scalar value and then, because we're going to divide, convert that value to a double (we don't want integer division). The following listing shows the query.

Listing 9.12   COVID-19 data percentage difference

```
let curr = todouble(toscalar(Covid19        ◁──┐ Converts data to a scalar value,
    | where updated == datetime(2020-06-01)  ◁──  then converts that to a double
    | count));
let prev = todouble(toscalar(Covid19              Specifies two
    | where updated == datetime(2020-05-31)  ◁──  consecutive dates
    | count));
print abs(prev - curr) * 100 / ((prev + curr) / 2) ◁──  Implements the percentage
                                                        difference formula (see the sidebar)
                                                        and calls print to output the result
                                                        for scalar values
```

As before, let's see how we can convert this to a function that takes a `testDate` parameter and returns true or false. The following listing shows the function.

Listing 9.13   COVID-19 data percentage difference test function

```
.create-or-alter function Covid19Anomaly(testDate: datetime) {
    let curr = todouble(toscalar(Covid19
        | where updated == testDate
        | count));
    let prev = todouble(toscalar(Covid19              datetime_add adds a value to a
        | where updated ==                            datetime. Here we subtract one day
        datetime_add("day", -1, testDate)  ◁──        from testDate to get the previous day.
```

```
        | count));
    let diff = abs(curr - prev) * 100 / ((prev + curr) / 2);
    print Result = diff < 5
```

**Checks that our percentage difference is less
than 5% and returns the value as Result**

Of course, we need to have some domain knowledge and explore the dataset to pick a good threshold. But if we pick one correctly, this makes the test much more resilient. For example, if the data volume slowly increases, our test remains valid and fails when we get an unexpected drop or spike in the data. Contrast this with a test that simply checks the row count is over a certain value. If the data volume increases, the test quickly stops being relevant.

> **DEFINITION** An *anomaly detection* test looks for statistical anomalies in the data. This type of test is more flexible than other types and can automatically adjust to changes over time.

In this section, we looked at a simple example: percentage difference day after day. Anomaly detection can be much more sophisticated than that. For example, if we consider website traffic, we might register a different volume between weekends and workdays. The same holds true for holidays and other important events.

For example, online shopping spikes during the holiday season, while job searches drop. For this, we can use AI-powered anomaly detection, which automatically learns from historical data and identifies anomalies, taking into account spikes and drops like weekends and holidays. We won't cover this approach here, but do keep in mind that there is a lot more we can do to raise the bar on data quality.

9.1.5 *Testing data recap*

In this section, we covered a few common types of data quality tests and looked at their corresponding implementations in Azure Data Explorer. We looked at

- Availability tests that ensure at least some data is present
- Correctness tests that check that various dimensions of the data are within allowed ranges
- Completeness tests that ensure that all (or enough) data is available
- Anomaly detection that checks for anomalies in the data based on historically observed metrics

There are various other types of tests we did not cover due to increasing complexity; for example, tests that ensure data is consistent across different tables or different storage solutions. We also barely scratched the surface on anomaly detection. Combined with AI, this can provide extremely powerful and flexible quality checks. Now that we have implemented a few tests for the Covid19 dataset, let's see how we can go about executing them automatically.

9.2   *Running data quality checks*

Implementing the tests is just part of the story. We also need a framework that handles executing the tests. We need to check the quality of our datasets in two ways: at rest and during movement.

> **DEFINITION**   *Testing data at rest* means we execute our data quality tests at some scheduled time to ensure that the data we have in some data fabric passes all checks.

We can think of testing data at rest like we expect data to be available at a certain time, conforming to certain characteristics. For example, if we ingest our Covid19 dataset every night at 2 A.M., we can expect to have all data available by 3 A.M. That would be the point where we run our tests.

One important characteristic for this type of testing is that we don't really care how the data makes it to our storage layer. We simply check that it is there when we expect it to be (and it is correct, complete, etc.). Contrast this with another type of testing, which is integrated in our ETL pipelines.

> **DEFINITION**   *Testing data during movement* means executing our data quality tests against the source before we start an ETL process or against the destination after an ETL process completes.

Testing during movement enhances our data movement pipelines so that if data is not good upstream, we won't move it. It also checks that data is in good shape at its destination after moving it. Both types of test execution, at rest and during movement, have their place in a data platform. We will again rely on our orchestration solution, Azure Data Factory (ADF), to implement test execution.

9.2.1   *Testing using Azure Data Factory*

We'll start by creating a simple Azure Data Factory pipeline to run our COVID-19 availability test, then see how we would go about running this on a schedule and as part of another pipeline. Figure 9.1 displays our test pipeline.

We'll look at the pipeline JSON in a bit, but before that, let's cover some important points that aren't obvious from figure 9.1. First, we define a `testDate` parameter for this pipeline, passing it to the Azure Data Explorer function. We saw another parameterized pipeline in chapter 5, when we looked at building an identity keyring. If you remember, the keyring ingestion step pipeline had a `FunctionName` parameter. This pipeline was embedded in the buildkeyring pipeline, which invoked it with various Azure Data Explorer function names. We'll do something similar here, letting whoever calls the pipeline provide the date we want to test.

Querying Azure Data Explorer like this requires that we create a Lookup activity, which wraps a query. A Lookup activity needs an Azure Data Factory dataset, even if we are just calling an Azure Data Explorer function. For that, we create a new TestResult dataset for Azure Data Explorer using the `adx` linked service already provisioned in

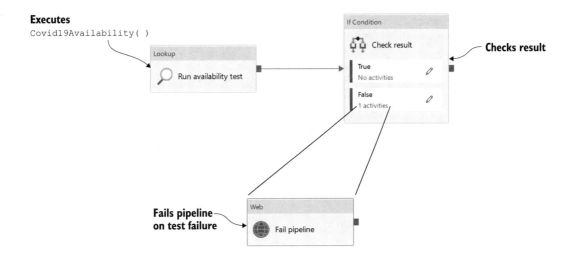

Figure 9.1   The Azure Data Factory pipeline that runs the `Covid19Availability` function and fails the pipeline on test failure.

chapter 4. The dataset will not point to any table, however, because we'll invoke a function instead, leaving its `Table` property with the default value `None`.

In the previous section, we ensured that all our test functions return a single column, Result, with a single row that can be either true or false. We can use this in the If Condition activity and branch based on the result. If the test succeeds, we don't need to do anything—the pipeline succeeds. If not, we need to fail the pipeline so we can trigger an alert. Remember, in chapter 4, we connected our Azure Data Factory instance to Azure Monitor, so if a pipeline fails, we'll receive a notification.

Unfortunately, at the time of writing, Azure Data Factory does not have a Fail activity to explicitly fail a pipeline. To work around this limitation, we'll use a Web activity and make a call to a URL that doesn't exist. The activity will fail, triggering a pipeline failure.

Now that we have covered some of the subtleties, let's look at the JSON files and highlight the important bits. First, the following listing shows the TestResult dataset definition.

Listing 9.14   Contents of ADF/dataset/TestResult.json

```
{
    "name": "TestResult",
    "properties": {
        "linkedServiceName": {          The TestResult dataset references
            "referenceName": "adx",  ◄── the adx linked service.
            "type": "LinkedServiceReference"
        },
        "annotations": [],
```

```
        "type": "AzureDataExplorerTable",
        "schema": []
    }
}
```

Remember that an Azure Data Explorer linked service provides two important things: the connection to the cluster (including the cluster URL and authentication details) and the database context to use (in our case, the telemetry database). This is all the information needed by the Lookup activity to execute a query. Next, let's take a look at the pipeline JSON in the following listing for the Covid19 dataset.

Listing 9.15   Contents of ADF/pipeline/testcovid19data.json

```
{
    "name": "testcovid19data",
    "properties": {
        "activities": [
            {
                "name": "Run availability test",
                "type": "Lookup",
                "dependsOn": [],
                "policy": {
                    "timeout": "7.00:00:00",
                    "retry": 0,
                    "retryIntervalInSeconds": 30,
                    "secureOutput": false,
                    "secureInput": false
                },
                "userProperties": [],
                "typeProperties": {
                    "source": {
                        "type": "AzureDataExplorerSource",
                        "query": "Covid19Availability(datetime(
                        '@{pipeline()
                        .parameters.testDate}'))",
                        "queryTimeout": "00:10:00"
                    },
                    "dataset": {
                        "referenceName": "TestResult",
                        "type": "DatasetReference"
                    }
                }
            },
            {
                "name": "Check result",
                "type": "IfCondition",
                "dependsOn": [
                    {
                        "activity": "Run availability test",
                        "dependencyConditions": [
                            "Succeeded"
                        ]
                    }
```

Uses an expression to pass the testDate parameter to the Azure Data Explorer Covid19Availability function as a datetime

The dataset provides the context in which to invoke the Azure Data Explorer function.

```
                            ],
                            "userProperties": [],
                            "typeProperties": {
                                "expression": {
                                    "value": "@activity('Run availability test')
                                    .output.firstRow.Result",
                                    "type": "Expression"
                                },
                                "ifFalseActivities": [
                                    {
                                        "name": "Fail pipeline",
                                        "type": "WebActivity",
                                        "dependsOn": [],
                                        "policy": {
                                            "timeout": "7.00:00:00",
                                            "retry": 0,
                                            "retryIntervalInSeconds": 30,
                                            "secureOutput": false,
                                            "secureInput": false
                                        },
                                        "userProperties": [],
                                        "typeProperties": {
                                            "url": "https://fail",
                                            "method": "GET"
                                        }
                                    }
                                ]
                            }
                        }
                    ],
                    "parameters": {
                        "testDate": {
                            "type": "string",
                            "defaultValue": "2020-01-01"
                        }
                    },
                    "annotations": []
                }
            }
```

The If Condition expression is the result of the Azure Data Explorer function call. → `.output.firstRow.Result`

Issues a GET request to https://fail to trigger a pipeline failure

Defines the testDate parameter of type string for the pipeline

You can try recreating the pipeline in the Azure Data Factory UI, or you can pick up the JSON files from the book's GitHub and push it to your DevOps instance. Put TestResult.json in the /ADF/dataset folder and testcovid19data.json in /ADF/pipeline. Because the Azure Data Factory instance is synced with Git, once the JSON describing the pipeline is in Git, it shows up in the UI. As an exercise, run the pipeline and provide different default values to the `testDate` parameter.

9.2.2 Executing tests

We can easily run this pipeline both on a schedule or as part of another pipeline. First, let's see how we can schedule the pipeline to run automatically. For that, we can create a new trigger. Let's call it test3am, which runs the test daily at 3 A.M. (UTC). The trigger also handles passing the `testDate` input to the pipeline as a *yyyy-MM-dd* string. We will use another expression to get the current date and format it as expected. The following listing shows the trigger.

Listing 9.16   Contents of ADF/trigger/test3am.json

```json
{
    "name": "test3am",
    "properties": {
        "annotations": [],
        "runtimeState": "Started",
        "pipelines": [
            {
                "pipelineReference": {
                    "referenceName": "testcovid19data",
                    "type": "PipelineReference"
                },
                "parameters": {
                    "testDate": "@{formatDateTime(utcnow(),
                        'yyyy-MM-dd')}"            ⟵──┐  Gets the current date
                }                                      │  formatted as yyyy-MM-dd
            }
        ],
        "type": "ScheduleTrigger",
        "typeProperties": {
            "recurrence": {
                "frequency": "Day",                    Sets the trigger recurrence, daily
                "interval": 1,                         at 3 A.M. UTC starting from June 6,
                "startTime": "2020-06-01T03:00:00Z",   2020. The Z at the end of the
                "timeZone": "UTC"                      timestamp denotes UTC time.
            }
        }
    }
}
```

In chapter 4, we created the pipeline to ingest the Covid19 dataset and scheduled a daily trigger to run at 2 A.M. UTC. We would expect the data to have arrived in our Azure Data Explorer cluster by 3 A.M., so this trigger runs our availability test to confirm that. This is our "at rest" execution, where we don't really care how the data comes in, but we can validate that it is there when we expect it to be.

We can just as easily execute the pipeline as part of the ingestion itself by extending our ingestcovid19data pipeline with a final step that executes testcovid19data. We won't show the implementation here because it is straightforward. Briefly, we can use the Execute Pipeline activity and the same expression as in the trigger to determine testDate:

```
@{formatDateTime(utcnow(), 'yyyy-MM-dd')}
```

The activity will run our test as soon as the data gets ingested and raise an alert if the data we ingested does not meet our quality bar.

Yet another option is to run the test at the source: we can run a test against the data source before we even start the ingestion and fail the ingestion if the source data is not in good shape. We can implement this as another Execute Pipeline activity that runs a test pipeline on the data source. All of these approaches are valid, and they all come with some trade-offs:

- Testing on a schedule has the advantage of being decoupled from the ingestion, but it might catch data issues later than the other approaches.
- Testing data as the final step of ingestion catches issues early on, but then testing becomes coupled with the ingestion. This means if we pause the ingestion pipeline, we no longer get data tests either.
- Testing data as the first step of ingestion catches issues upstream and avoids unnecessary ETL of bad data. On the other hand, it doesn't catch issues introduced during ETL, which might show up only after data reaches its destination.

9.2.3 *Creating and using a template*

What we have so far works, but if we want to invoke other tests, we end up repeating most of the pipeline: the `testDate` parameter, the If Condition activity, and our trick to fail the pipeline. The only thing that changes is the Azure Data Explorer function that we invoke.

We might want to invoke `Covid19Correctness`, `Covid19CompletenessUS`, any of the other functions we implemented in section 9.1, or some new functions yet to be authored. Fortunately, Azure Data Factory allows us to save a pipeline as a template and instantiate it with different parameters. Let's see how we can do this.

First, we'll parameterize not only the `testDate` parameter but the Azure Data Explorer function that we'll call. We can create a new `FunctionName` parameter for the pipeline and update the command from the original

```
Covid19Availability(datetime('@{pipeline().parameters.testDate}'))
```

to

```
@{pipeline().parameters.FunctionName}
➥ (datetime('@{pipeline().parameters.testDate}'))
```

We'll also rename the Azure Data Explorer Command activity from Run Availability test to Run Test. We can save this as a template from the UI by clicking Save As Template. Let's name the template runadxtest.

It should show up in Git as /ADF/templates/runadxtest/runadxtest.json. You should also see an /ADF/templates/runadxtest/manifest.json next to it. This file stores some additional metadata used by Azure Data Factory to represent the template in the UI. We won't show the full listing here because it is quite long, but feel free to take a look at it once you create the template. The template should show up on the left-hand side in the UI (under Factory Resources), as figure 9.2 shows.

After clicking the template, you will be prompted to select a linked service for the Azure Data Explorer connection. That is because the template is generic enough to

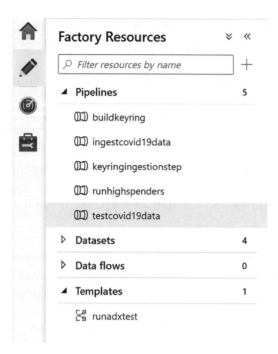

Figure 9.2   The Factory Resources pane contains the runadxtest template under Templates.

work for other Azure Data Explorer linked services, not just the one we use in the original pipeline. Once we select the linked service, a new pipeline is created as a copy of the original. This should make it easier to create multiple pipelines that consist of the same set of activities.

NOTE   One limitation of Azure Data Factory templates is that once instantiated, they produce a copy of the original without maintaining any connection. That means upgrading the template does not update any of the pipelines already created.

9.2.4   *Running data quality checks recap*

It's time for a recap. In this section, we looked at two ways in which we can execute data quality tests:

- *At rest*—Running tests on a schedule to ensure data is available and in good quality regardless of how the data arrived at its destination.
- *During movement*—Running tests as part of an ETL pipeline, whether against the source, before starting, or at the destination as a final step.

We saw how we can use Azure Data Factory to run a test and fail the pipeline if the test fails. We also saw how we can make our life easier by using Azure Data Factory templates to create multiple yet similar pipelines. This works for our small examples, but in the real world, we may have hundreds of datasets to test across multiple data fabrics. For the rest of this chapter, we'll talk about scaling data quality testing.

9.3 Scaling out data testing

Data testing is not yet offered as a service by all major cloud providers, so we need to stitch together data quality testing ourselves. We saw how we can implement a few different test types as Azure Data Explorer functions and how we can run them using Azure Data Factory. We could extend this to more datasets; after all, Azure Data Factory can scale to hundreds of pipelines. With that said, codeless infrastructure can take us only as far as the services cloud providers offer.

For data quality testing, we need to either deploy an existing third-party solution or implement something ourselves. Ideally, we would want to make test authoring and scheduling as simple as possible. In this section, we'll look at some of the common data quality testing patterns. You should either ensure the third-party solution you are considering implements these or implement them yourself with a custom-made solution. We'll show a possible Azure-native architecture for this.

9.3.1 Supporting multiple data fabrics

In our example, we authored a set of tests for Azure Data Explorer wrapped into an Azure Data Explorer function. A real-world data platform more often than not uses multiple data fabrics: upstream and downstream teams might use different storage solutions, and within our data platform, we might also pick different storage for different workloads. A good data quality test framework should support all the different data fabrics. Because the storage landscape is diverse, a plug-in model is the best approach. Figure 9.3 shows how this looks.

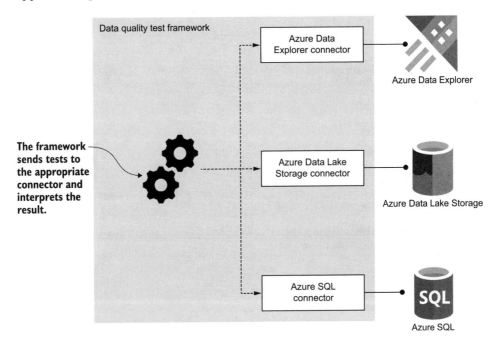

Figure 9.3 A data quality test framework with connectors for different data fabrics

These connectors handle query execution against the different data fabrics and translate the results back into a common format understood by the test framework. Different data fabrics execute things differently. Azure Data Explorer has its own query language that we use throughout this book. Azure SQL uses T-SQL, Microsoft's SQL dialect. Azure Data Lake Storage doesn't offer any compute, but we can read data from it and process it on other compute resources (for example, Azure Databricks).

> **DEFINITION**   A *plug-in connector model* abstracts storage away from the core data quality test framework and makes the framework extensible. We can add support for a new data fabric by adding a new connector, without having to touch the rest of the solution.

Azure Data Factory supports this through its different linked services and activities. If, for example, we standardize on returning a `Result` from any data fabric that is either true or false, we don't need to change the rest of our pipeline (the If Condition and so on). If we end up coding something ourselves, the connectors might become Azure Functions.

Azure Functions are Azure's serverless compute offering. They execute arbitrary code, scale automatically, and run on managed infrastructure that we don't have to worry about. Figure 9.4 shows an example implementation, where we use a different Azure Function for each data fabric and where the test framework sends POST requests to invoke tests.

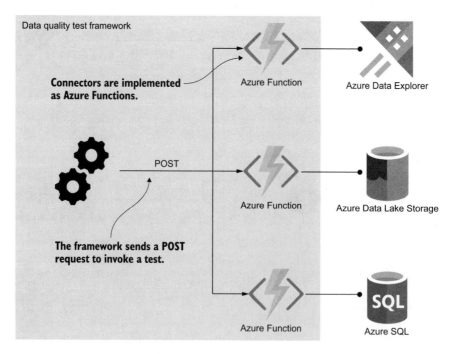

Figure 9.4   Each connector is implemented as an Azure Function that knows how to talk to a data fabric.

We won't go over the actual code here because implementing a data quality test framework from scratch would take a whole book by itself. We'll just cover the common patterns and possible implementations. The key takeaway is that we need some component to act as a connector for a data fabric, which can wrap the data fabric–specific logic. Then we can reuse common logic (for example, scheduling, what to do in case of failure, etc.) independently of whatever storage we test.

9.3.2 Testing at rest and during movement

We already talked about testing at rest (on a schedule) and testing during movement (as part of a pipeline), and we saw how we can implement these in Azure Data Factory. Abstractly, figure 9.5 shows what this looks like.

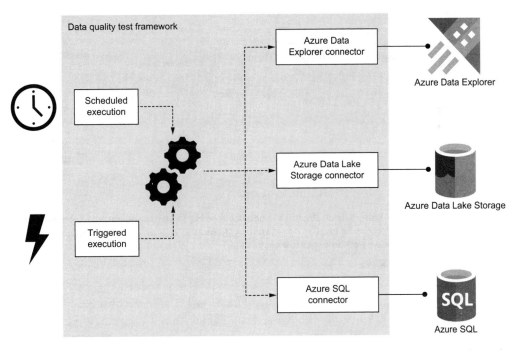

Figure 9.5   Scheduled execution tests data on a given schedule; triggered execution tests data on demand when invoked by some other system.

In our Azure Data Factory implementation, we scheduled execution through a schedule trigger and, for the on-demand execution, we used an Execute Pipeline activity. An alternative to Azure Data Factory is to provide an HTTP endpoint, where external systems can request on-demand test runs. We could also use an Azure Function for this. For scheduled execution, we can use an Azure Service Bus instance.

Azure Service Bus provides messaging as a service: message producers (other services) can enqueue messages, while consumers can read these messages. A key feature of Azure Service Bus is its ability to support scheduled messages. A scheduled message is only made available to consumers at a scheduled time, where the scheduled time is determined by the producer. We can schedule each test execution as a Service Bus message. Figure 9.6 shows how this looks.

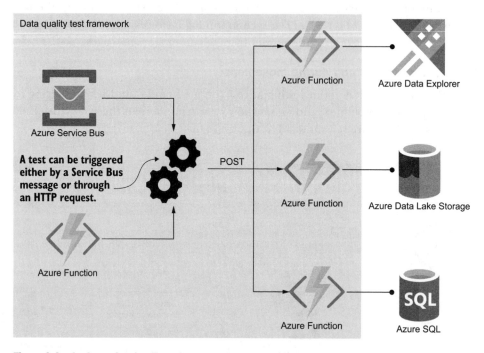

Figure 9.6   An Azure Service Bus with scheduled messages can act as our test scheduler, while an Azure Function can be invoked by external systems to trigger on-demand execution. Either of these get the framework to execute a test.

Another process that is part of our test framework schedules the tests by sending messages to the Service Bus. The Azure Function HTTP endpoint easily integrates with other systems. For example, Azure Data Factory has a native Azure Function activity that makes it easy to invoke Azure Functions. Note that while we are showing an architecture for a data quality testing alternative to Azure Data Factory, we should still use Azure Data Factory for ETL because it was meant for that.

9.3.3   *Authoring tests*

Now we are getting to the meat of the issue and why we are looking at alternatives to Azure Data Factory when it comes to data quality testing—we need to make it easy to author and deploy tests. A good data quality test framework makes it easy to add new tests. This is where we might hit some scaling issues with an Azure Data Factory–based solution. A new test involves creating a new Azure Data Explorer function or data fabric equivalent (for example, an SQL stored procedure) and hooking up new activities and triggers in Azure Data Factory. This is a lot of work, so let's explore some other ways we could implement this. We can create tests as stored queries, code, configuration, or a mix of these.

TESTS AS STORED QUERIES

Tests as stored queries are pretty much what we've used so far (the Azure Data Explorer functions implementing tests we created in section 9.1). For SQL, these would be stored procedures. For other data fabrics, it would be their equivalent. If we express tests as stored queries, we keep the tests on the data fabrics they test. Our test framework passes the arguments needed (like the `testDate` parameter) and interprets the results. There are two main challenges with this approach: code reuse and colocation with additional configuration.

Lack of code reuse comes from the fact that each test wrap is its own full-blown query, even though they have a lot in common. As an example, Azure Data Explorer availability tests differ only by the table they check and the date column. The following listing highlights the only parts where our COVID-19 availability test is different from other availability tests.

> Listing 9.17   Availability test

```
.create-or-
alter function Covid19Availability(
    testDate: datetime) {          ⟵─── The function implementing the test
    Covid19                        ⟵─── The table name
    | where updated == testDate    ⟵─── The date column name
    | take 1
    | summarize Result = count() > 0
}
```

Database engines are usually less flexible than general programming languages, so in some cases, it is hard to abstract some of this complexity into reusable code. Even if it is possible and we can create some helper functions, if we end up writing tests against two separate Azure Data Explorer clusters, we would have to replicate this in both clusters. This isn't an issue specific to Azure Data Explorer; the same holds for SQL. If we store all tests as SQL stored procedures, we end up duplicating both parts of the queries in the tests themselves and any helpers across different databases that we want to test.

The second limitation is colocation with additional configuration (for example, scheduling). We need some place to store common configurations like when to run the test, which this time is independent of the data fabric. Other examples include execution settings like timeouts, how many times we should retry on failure, or who to alert if the test fails. Having to store this somewhere else makes it harder to author tests; you would have to touch two places to get something running. This is pretty much where we are with our Azure Data Factory–based solution, but let's explore the alternatives.

TESTS AS CODE

Another option is to store tests as code like we would write tests if we were testing soft-ware. Of course, we wouldn't be completely removed from the data fabric's query lan-guage. We would still need to talk to our database engine. Instead of wrapping the query in a stored procedure, we would keep it with the code. The following listing shows an example of this, using the Azure Data Explorer Python SDK that you can install using `pip install azure-kusto-data`.

> **Listing 9.18   Python availability test for Azure Data Explorer**

```
from azure.kusto.data import KustoClient, KustoConnectionStringBuilder

cluster = '<your cluster URL>'

connectionBuilder =
➥ KustoConnectionStringBuilder.with_aad_device_authentication(cluster)

client = KustoClient(connectionBuilder)

database = 'telemetry'
query = 'Covid19 | where updated == "2020-02-29"
➥ | take 1 | summarize Result = count()'

result = client.execute(database, query)

...
```

This listing hardcodes the database and query, but you can imagine how we could parameterize all of this. Now that we have pulled the logic into a high-level program-ming language, we can refactor to reduce duplication. We can even use an existing unit testing framework and implement each data quality test as a unit test.

Most test frameworks use some form of reflection or introspection to enumerate the tests in a test module. We can do the same for our data quality checks. We can specify the additional required metadata (like when we want a test to run) in code. This approach addresses both issues we identified with our previous approach: we can build as much abstraction as needed so we don't duplicate anything, and we can keep both the actual test queries and additional configuration in the same place as code.

The main drawback of this approach is that it raises the bar for who can imple-ment tests. Anyone coming from a software engineering background is comfortable writing code, so making data quality tests more like unit tests seems simple. But other people using the data platform, like data scientists or analysts, are more comfortable writing queries. They may or may not be familiar with the programming languages the data engineers use. We should try as much as possible to make it easy for everyone to author tests, so let's explore yet another possible approach.

TESTS AS CONFIGURATION

With this approach, we express tests via configuration and let our test framework translate into queries. Configuration can be a file format like JSON, YAML, or XML. The following listing shows how the same availability test we looked at before would appear as a JSON file.

Listing 9.19   Content of Covid19DataAvailability.json

```
{
    "type": "availability",        ◁——— Indicates how to generate the actual query
    "dataFabric": "ADX",           ◁
    "queryParameters":                  Determines which connector
    {                                   should handle running this test
        "cluster": "<your cluster name>",
        "database": "telemetry",        A set of parameters
        "table": "Covid19",             generates the query.
        "dateColumn": "updated"
    },
    "executionParameters":
    {
        "retry": 3,                Specifies retry count and
        "timeout": "5m"            timeout parameters
    },
    "schedule":
    {
        "time": "2020-06-01T18:30:00Z",     Defines when
        "repeat": "daily"                   to run the test
    }
}
```

Our test solution can now read this configuration and generate the appropriate query. Because we determine how our code parses the file, we can extend the format as needed. We can also implement schema validation and even a UI to make it easier to specify tests.

We no longer express the actual test as a query or as code, rather we just list the parameters needed to generate the actual query. In the case of availability tests for Azure Data Explorer, these would be the cluster to connect to, the database context, the table to test, and the column capturing the date (in this case, updated). Additional configurations, like retry count and schedule, live in the same file. We can implement a UI to make most of the parameters configurable using drop-downs, lowering the barrier to author tests.

The main challenge with this approach is that it pushes a lot of the complexity into the code we need to write and maintain. Generating various queries from a set of parameters targeting various data fabrics can get complex. All of the approaches we discussed have advantages and drawbacks. There is some inherent complexity in the space of data quality that we can't eliminate; we just push it around. Either the tests themselves are complex (tests as stored queries), authoring them is harder (tests as code), or the test framework becomes complex (tests as configuration). But we can move the complexity slider by mixing these approaches.

TESTS AS A MIX OF STORED QUERIES, CODE, AND/OR CONFIGURATION

As a simple example, we can keep the easy-to-author configuration-based approach but reduce some of the framework complexity by embedding partial queries in the configuration itself. Let's see what our COVID-19 availability test used throughout this section looks like in this scenario. The following listing shows a potential JSON representation.

Listing 9.20   Contents of Covid19DataAvailability.json

```
{
    "type": "availability",
    "dataFabric": "ADX",
    "queryParameters":
    {                                                   Cluster and database context in which
        "cluster": "<your cluster name>",               to run an Azure Data Explorer query
        "database": "telemetry",
        "query": "Covid19 | where updated == @{testDate}
        ⇨ | take 1 | summarize Result = count() > 0"    ◁──  Query to run, which
    },                                                        takes a @{testDate}
    "executionParameters":                                    parameter
    {        "retry": 3,
        "timeout": "5m"
    },
    "schedule":
    {
        "time": "2020-06-01T18:30:00Z",
        "repeat": "daily"
    }
}
```

Now when our data quality testing solution processes this test, it doesn't need to generate a query; the query is already captured in the JSON file. It just needs to supply it a `testDate` parameter. This moves some of the complexity from the framework code (generate a test) to the developer (specify a query). With this approach, we are close to having the best of all worlds: when the test queries live together with the rest of the test configuration, it is easier to author than a test-as-code solution, and we can keep the framework code simpler.

We can tweak our expression language to push common query parts to the framework. For example, instead of having test authors specify the full query as

```
(Covid19 | where updated == @{testDate} | take 1 | summarize Result =
⇨ count() > 0)
```

we can ask them to supply just a query fragment like this:

```
Covid19 | where updated == @{testDate}
```

The supplied query fragment is different for different tests, while the common part can be appended by the framework:

```
| take 1 | summarize Result = count() > 0
```

We've covered the various ways in which we can define tests and their trade-offs. Let's look at one final aspect we've ignored thus far: storage.

9.3.4 Storing tests and results

We have two types of data to store: the test definitions and the results of test runs. We'll look at each in this section.

TEST DEFINITIONS

In the original implementation we covered based on Azure Data Factory, the tests are stored queries with additional configuration as Data Factory pipelines and triggers. Ultimately, all of these should end up in Git if we follow good DevOps practices. We should already have an Azure DevOps Pipeline to deploy Azure Data Explorer objects, so we could capture all our test definitions like `Covid19Availability`, `Covid19Correctness`, etc., as files in Git. Similarly, our Data Factory is synced up with Git, so pipeline and trigger definitions are also stored there.

If we go with a custom-made solution and implement the tests either as code or as configuration files, Git is still a good place to store definitions because these are text files (either source code or JSON). Git is great at tracking text files, and Azure DevOps can give us additional capabilities like enforced code review and automatic validation, as we saw throughout the book. Regardless of how we decide to represent tests, Git is a good place to keep track of them. Figure 9.7 shows how Git can act as test storage.

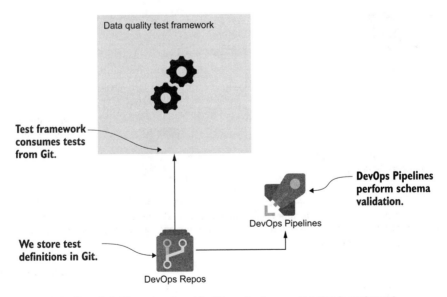

Figure 9.7 Test definitions are stored in Git, and schema validation is performed with DevOps Pipelines. The test framework consumes the tests from Git.

The data quality test framework can consume the tests from Git either directly by reading the Git repo or through an Azure DevOps Pipeline that deploys the tests, meaning it moves them to some other storage solution the framework uses, like Azure Blob Storage, for example.

TEST RESULTS

There is another type of data we need to store: the results of test runs. We overlooked this in our Azure Data Factory implementation to keep things simple. In our original implementation, a test failure fails the pipeline and raises an alert. In reality, we probably want a little bit more than that. We likely want a history of all test runs, on top of which we can build visualizations and perform analysis. For example, stakeholders might appreciate a dashboard showing the current status of all datasets and when they were last tested. An example of analysis could be identifying datasets that have issues at higher frequency than others and improving their reliability.

For this type of data, Git is not a good storage solution. We want a system where we can append rows as tests get executed. Because we should run hundreds of tests every day, we can append execution results to a table in Azure Data Explorer or Azure SQL. Once they land there, we can leverage the same analytics infrastructure to inspect test results. We can use solutions like Power BI to build interactive visualizations over this data. Figure 9.8 shows how storing test results in Azure Data Explorer would look.

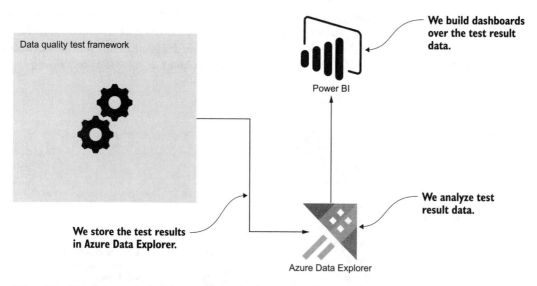

Figure 9.8   The data quality test framework tracks the result of test runs in Azure Data Explorer. From there, we can analyze test results like any other dataset in our platform, and we can build dashboards and visualizations using tools like Power BI.

We went through quite a lot in this section. Let's do another quick recap and touch on the main points we covered.

SCALING OUT DATA TESTING RECAP

Because not all cloud providers offer data quality testing as a service, we looked at what it means to implement data quality at real-world scale. Azure Data Factory is an option, but Azure Data Factory was meant for ETL (moving large datasets and complex orchestration). It might work as our data quality solution if we really want to be codeless, but this is an area where we might want to write some code to make our life easier (or, alternately, onboard a third-party solution).

We covered a high-level architecture of how we would implement a data quality test framework and went over some of the requirements and trade-offs. This is something to keep in mind if you ever decide to write the code. It should also help you evaluate a potential third-party solution to ensure it fits your needs. Here are the main points we covered in this section:

- *Plug-in support for different data fabrics*—We're likely to run tests against multiple data fabrics. Having the ability to reuse common code with plug-in data fabric–specific connectors is extremely valuable.
- *Testing at rest and during movement*—We'll want to run some tests on a schedule, while others can run before or after we move data. We should have a way to configure a scheduled run but also have a way to trigger an on-demand execution.
- *Authoring tests*—We went over the different ways we can author tests (as stored queries, as code, as configuration, or as a mix of these) and the pros and cons of each. Regardless of the approach we decide on, we should be aware of where the complexity lies and the trade-offs.
- *Storage*—We looked at where we would store the test definitions (Git is a good choice), and where we would store the test results. Results belong in our data platform because they are data we want to analyze and report on.

We didn't implement the whole solution because it would have taken us much more than a chapter to go through all the code. But we saw a few blueprints of how to do this that should, hopefully, make your life easier if you end up coding or evaluating a data quality framework.

We covered an important aspect of our governance layer: data quality. Without any data quality checking, we can't really trust the output of our platform. Standardizing data quality testing makes it easier to both author tests and get an overview of how healthy the data is across the platform. Unfortunately, today, data quality is not offered as a service by all major cloud providers.

The next chapter covers another important aspect of governance: compliance. Read on to learn about the different types of data, handling standards, access models, the famous General Data Protection Regulation (GDPR), and what it means to be GDPR-compliant.

Summary

- Some common types of data quality tests are availability, correctness, completeness, and anomaly detection.
- A test run can be implemented on our existing infrastructure using Azure Data Factory.
- Azure Data Factory templates simplify pipeline reuse.
- Scaling data quality testing might require us to write some code or adopt a third-party solution.
- A good data quality test framework supports multiple data fabrics, ideally through a plug-in model.
- Data quality tests need to run both on a schedule (against data at rest) or on demand (before or after data movement).
- Tests can be authored as stored queries, code, configuration, or a mix.
- Test definitions can be stored in Git, while test results can be stored in one of our data platform's storage solutions.
- Test results can be analyzed and reported on just like any other dataset.

Compliance

Data platforms, by definition, deal with data. While some types of data are harmless, other types carry liability. In this chapter, we will talk about compliance and data handling. First, we'll see some examples of data classification and data handling standards. Depending on the nature of the data we process, we will see where we can store it, who can access it, what we can do with it, how long can we keep it, and so on. We will also look at some techniques we can use to change the type of the data. This includes anonymization and pseudonymization of personably identifiable information, and aggregation of sensitive data.

Next, we'll look at implementing an access model that properly restricts access, including some advanced features provided by storage solutions, like row-level security and access control lists.

The General Data Protection Regulation (GDPR) is a famous regulation passed by the European Union with worldwide impact. We'll look at a few key points we need to be aware of and see how we can make our data platform GDPR-compliant. Before we dig in, please read the important note that follows.

NOTE Don't take the information presented here as legal advice. If you do end up dealing with sensitive data, work with a professional who understands the laws and can guide you through the measures you need to take to be fully compliant. This chapter is more about getting you to think about compliance and view the data platform through this lens. *Always work with an expert to ensure full compliance.*

10.1 *Data classification*

We'll go over a few examples to get an idea of some of the types of data we might end up with in our data platform. Let's say we run an online web store where customers can browse through our catalog of products and place orders. Some of the datasets we might end up storing include the following:

- A product catalog that contains all our products, prices, etc.
- Performance metrics for our website, page view telemetry, etc.
- Customer credit card information and shipping addresses for order fulfilment
- Financial data used by accounting, which includes monthly revenue

Not all of these types of data are the same. Our product catalog and prices are stored somewhere in our backend but are available to anyone on the internet when they browse our online store.

Data is also generated by our software, including various metrics and logs. Intuitively, most of it is harmless. While we probably don't want our competitors to know how many instances of our service we run and what is the average CPU usage, this type of data doesn't carry too much liability. Page view telemetry can be an exception though. If we keep track of which user visited which pages, that becomes personal information. We can use this data to provide value to our customers; for example, providing product recommendations based on what they are interested in. But if this data leaks, our customers would be upset to find their browsing history for sale on the internet.

Credit card information and shipping addresses are a whole new level of sensitivity. While this is something we must have in our system in order to charge our customers and deliver their products, if this data leaks, hackers can make purchases using the stolen credit cards.

Financial data is in another category. While our customers won't be directly impacted by mishandling of this type of data, our business would. Someone privy to how the business is doing can leverage this knowledge in the market through insider trading.

There are other categories missing from our examples. If, for example, we run an email service, the messages running through our platform are created and owned by our customers. In the previous examples, even when dealing with sensitive data, we always had a legitimate scenario to look at it, but in this case, we might never want to access this data. Our employees should never read our customers' emails. From our point of view, the emails should be opaque. Let's go over some of the considerations for a few data types and sketch out some handling standards.

10.1.1 Feature data

We'll start with the simplest, least sensitive type of data, feature data. Here's our definition.

> **DEFINITION** *Feature data* is data that is nonsensitive and doesn't come with any liability. This can be metadata about how our systems operate (metrics like CPU and memory usage), other data not critical to the business, or public data collected from the internet.

Nonsensitive data doesn't come with strict requirements. We might want to protect it to some extent so it's not available to everyone but only to the team members who have some business case for processing it. That being said, this type of data can be accessed and opened by anyone (or almost anyone) without incurring any risk.

10.1.2 Telemetry

Telemetry data is collected from website visits and from applications running on the user's computer or phone. In regard to telemetry, we need to answer a couple of important questions. First, can this data be connected to the user? (This depends on what identifiers we collect.) Are we collecting the user's account ID? Is it associated with other data points we collect such as which pages the user visits or which app features they use? (If so, this data might be considered user data, which we'll cover next.) Finally, what did the user consent to when giving us this data?

In some countries, it is required by law to inform the user of what data we collect and how we use it. A good example is when we start a new app and are prompted to share data to improve the product. It could be that the user agreed to help us improve the product, but nothing more. This could mean, for example, that we can't use this data to recommend other products to them because they haven't consented to that type of data use.

> **NOTE** The way we handle telemetry data depends on whether it can be tied to a particular user and on what the user consents to when they agree to share this data with us.

In this section, we briefly mentioned user data. Let's talk about that next.

10.1.3 User data

User data is data that can be directly tied to the user. This class of data is important because this is what GDPR covers, as we'll discuss in section 10.4. Citizens of the European Union have the right to request receipt of all the user data a company collects on them and to request that data be deleted. User data also comes in a couple of subcategories. One of them is End User Identifiable Information, or EUII.

> **DEFINITION** *End User Identifiable Information* (EUII) is information that can directly identify the user. Examples of EUII are name, email address, IP address, and location.

As data moves through our systems, we generate various IDs. We saw in chapter 5 how, in many cases, we need to generate a keyring to tie all these IDs together in order to get a complete picture of how consumers use our product. Any data that we have tied to such an ID (for example, order history or account ID) is called End User Pseudonymous Information or EUPI.

DEFINITION   *End User Pseudonymous Information* (EUPI) relates to IDs used by our systems that, in conjunction with additional information (for example, a mapping table), can be used to identify the user.

Note the important distinction between EUII and EUPI: when we look at EUII (for example, name and address), we can immediately identify the user. When we look at EUPI (for example, account ID), we need additional mappings to tell us which user owns the account ID. In general, we have one primary ID (or several) that directly identifies the user, which we consider EUII, and multiple other IDs that indirectly identify the user through their connection to the primary ID, which we consider EUPI.

10.1.4 User-owned data

Even more sensitive than the user data that we collect is user-owned data. Examples of user-owned data are emails (if we run an email service), documents (if we run a cloud storage service), and so on.

DEFINITION   *User-owned data* is data generated by our users and stored in our platform.

This is highly sensitive information because it has many privacy implications. What we can do with it depends on the privacy promises we make to our customers and the cost/benefit of accessing the data. For example, it might be reasonable to run AI that looks at the user's calendar and suggests when to schedule a meeting. On the other hand, users might feel their privacy is invaded if we read their emails to serve targeted ads based on message content. Think about the privacy statement, legal implications, and how users would perceive any processing of this data.

10.1.5 Business data

Business data is data that pertains to our business, which means it is also sensitive in nature, but for different reasons. While mishandling of user data exposes us to liability, mishandling of business data can directly impact the financials of our business.

DEFINITION   *Business data* is sensitive data that, if leaked, can directly impact the business. This not only includes, for example, financial information such as revenue, operational costs, etc., but also new products or features that haven't been launched yet.

If this type of information leaks, the business can be directly impacted. For example, if a new product leaks before it is officially announced, a competitor might start working on their own version of it. Similarly, if company financials leak for a publicly traded company, this can be exploited on the stock market.

10.1.6 *Data classification recap*

Let's quickly review the data classifications we covered in this section:

- Feature data, which is nonsensitive data
- Telemetry data, which could be user information, and could have restrictions on what the user agreed we can use it for
- End User Identifiable Information (EUII), which is data that allows us to directly identify a user
- End User Pseudonymous Information (EUPI), which consists of IDs that we can connect back to a user, given some additional information
- User-owned data, which is data generated by the user and stored in our system
- Business data, which is data that directly relates to our business

These are a few common data classifications most big data platforms end up dealing with. The list isn't exhaustive, by any means, and depending on your business, regulations you need to abide by, and so on, you may have to deal with different classes of data.

Do keep a few things in mind when working with data. Is it data collected from users? If so, what did the users agree to? Is it user data? If so, it needs to be GDPR-compliant, and mishandling it is a breach of trust. Is it business data? If so, it must be protected because it can impact the business. Next, let's look at a couple of techniques we can use to change the classification of the data.

10.2 *Changing classification through processing*

In general, we want to restrict the number of people who can access sensitive data. In most cases, access is on a need-to-know basis. For example, data scientists and engineers allowed to process the data have done some compliance training and understand the risks and liabilities. In some scenarios, however, we want to process data so that it becomes less sensitive. A good example is that we want to open it up for more data scientists to look at. In this section, we will look at a few techniques for achieving this. Let's start by defining two datasets, as figure 10.1 shows.

The first dataset, User Profiles, contains user accounts, including names, credit cards, and billing addresses. Here we omitted actual billing addresses to keep things short. This dataset also contains a User ID column that associates an identification number with each user. This is the primary ID in our system because we can use it to link back to a user's profile information. The second dataset, User Telemetry, contains telemetry data collected from our users. It contains the user ID, timestamp, and product feature the user engages with.

User Profiles dataset

User ID	Name	Credit Card	Billing Address
10000	Ava Smith	5105-1051-0510-5100	...
10001	Oliver Miller	5555-5555-5555-4444	...
10002	Emma Johnson	4111-1111-1111-1111	...
10003	John Davis	4012-8888-8888-1881	...

User Telemetry dataset

User ID	Timestamp	Feature
10002	2020-06-30 10:01:05	Search
10002	2020-06-30 10:01:10	Auto-translate
10003	2020-06-30 10:05:20	Search
10001	2020-06-30 10:07:11	Help
10002	2020-06-30 10:07:21	Auto-translate
10003	2020-06-30 10:08:03	Save

**Figure 10.1	A User Profiles dataset contains user accounts, and a User Telemetry dataset has telemetry gathered from the users. If needed, we can join the datasets on the User ID column.**

Let's create the equivalent datasets in Azure Data Explorer (ADX). Start your Azure Data Explorer if it is stopped, then go the Azure Data Explorer UI and run the command in the following listing in the context of our telemetry database.

**Listing 10.1	Creating user profiles and telemetry tables**

```
.create table UserProfiles(UserId: long, Name: string, CreditCard: string,
➥ BillingAddress: string)    #A

.ingest inline into table UserProfiles <|          Creates the User Profiles table
10000,'Ava Smith','5105-1051-0510-5100','...'      and ingests a few rows into it
10001,'Oliver Miller','5555-5555-5555-4444','...'
10002,'Emma Johnson','4111-1111-1111-1111','...'
10003,'John Davis','4012-8888-8888-1881','...'


.create table UserTelemetry(UserId: long, Timestamp: datetime,
➥ Feature: string)
                                                   Creates the User Telemetry table
.ingest inline into table UserTelemetry <|         and ingests a few rows into it
10002,datetime(2020-06-30 10:01:05),'Search'
10002,datetime(2020-06-30 10:01:10),'Auto-translate'
10003,datetime(2020-06-30 10:05:20),'Search'
10001,datetime(2020-06-30 10:07:11),'Help'
10002,datetime(2020-06-30 10:07:21),'Auto-translate'
10003,datetime(2020-06-30 10:08:03),'Save'
```

Per our classifications in the previous section, both of these tables contain EUII. We'll leave the User Profiles table as is for now because it contains user account data that we need to maintain for billing purposes. Instead, let's look at some techniques we can use on the User Telemetry table to change its classification to something less sensitive.

10.2.1 Aggregation

The first technique is aggregation, where we can take the EUII from multiple users, aggregate it, and get rid of the end user identifiable part. For example, if we collect telemetry from our users that captures which produce features they use, we can aggregate that data so we know how much each feature is being used, but not who uses what. Figure 10.2 shows how aggregation transforms EUII into data that can't be tied back to individual users.

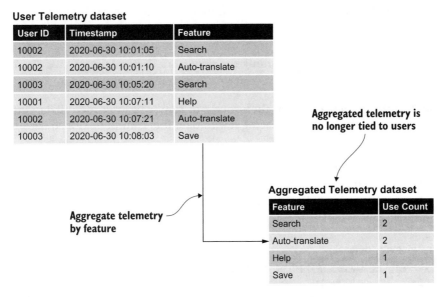

Figure 10.2 Aggregating telemetry data by feature usage yields data that can't be tied to individual users.

Before processing this data, we can see exactly what set of features an individual user uses, which has privacy implications. After aggregation, we can no longer tell that, but we still have valuable data. We know which product features are the most used, which ones are not that important to our customers, etc. We can store this data for analytics and ML purposes without having to worry about end user privacy. Listing 10.2 shows the corresponding Azure Data Explorer query to aggregate the User Telemetry dataset.

> **DEFINITION** Data *aggregation* is the processing of data into a summarized format. We can use this to transform the data so it no longer is tied to individual users.

Listing 10.2   Aggregating user telemetry

**Projects the columns to match
the table in figure 10.2**

```
UserTelemetry
| summarize count() by Feature
| project Feature, UseCount=count_
```

**Summarizes UserTelemetry by
Feature, counting how many
times each feature is used**

If we want to get rid of the EUII, we can ingest the result of this query into a new Aggregated Telemetry table and drop User Telemetry. But we might want to know more. For example, we might want to see when each feature is used or how our customers use different features in conjunction. Now, simply counting feature usage is not enough. We can use a different technique for that—anonymization.

10.2.2   *Anonymization*

We can use anonymization to unlink the data from the end user. Once the data is no longer connected to a user ID, we can't tell which user it comes from.

> **DEFINITION**   *Anonymization* is the process of removing user identifiable information from the data or replacing it with data that cannot be linked back to a user.

Going back to our telemetry example, if we want to know when features are used but don't care who uses them, we can get rid of the user identifier. Figure 10.3 shows how we can anonymize data by dropping the user IDs, and listing 10.3 shows the corresponding Azure Data Explorer query for this.

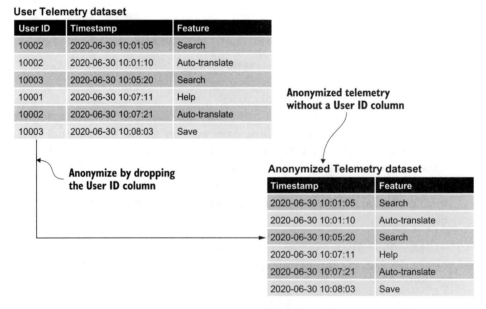

Figure 10.3   Dropping the User ID column from User Telemetry yields an anonymized dataset.

Listing 10.3 Anonymizing user telemetry by dropping User IDs

```
UserTelemetry
| project-away UserId        ◁——— Removes columns from the result
```

We could again ingest the results of this query into a new table and, if needed, drop the original table that contains EUII. But maybe this is not enough either.

Suppose we still need to see which features are used together by a user, but we don't really care who the user is. We can still anonymize by replacing user identifiers (that can be tracked back to the user) with randomly generated IDs. Figure 10.4 shows how we can anonymize the data by replacing each user ID with a randomly generated GUID. (See the following sidebar for a note on GUIDs.)

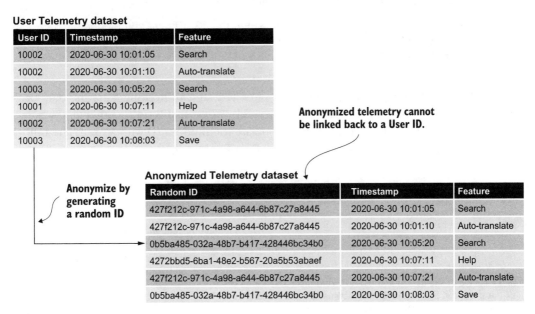

Figure 10.4   Replacing User ID with a Random ID (in this case a GUID) yields a dataset that can't be linked back to individual users.

Note that we intentionally do not persist a mapping between user IDs and corresponding random IDs. We generate the random IDs once, and then intentionally forget the association.

Globally unique identifiers (GUIDs)

GUIDs, also known as universally unique identifiers (UUIDs), are 128-bit numbers used to identify information. The algorithm to generate such a unique identifier is defined by the RFC 4122 standard.

(continued)

The great thing about GUIDs is that even without a central authority to issue them, the odds of generating the same GUID twice are extremely unlikely—one in a few quintillions. For all practical purposes, collision can be safely ignored.

GUIDs can be generated by most systems as they simply need to implement the algorithm defined by the RFC standard. These show up in many places, especially in distributed systems. For example, if we need unique identifiers for, say, website sessions for a high traffic website, we can have each node (assuming multiple servers are serving the website) generate a GUID to identify each session. Later, we can merge these into a common session table without running the risk of conflicting session identifiers, and we can do this without having to have the servers synchronize in any way when generating the identifiers.

This property of GUIDs is extremely useful, thus GUIDs are common in big data scenarios. Even with billions and billions of records generated across multiple systems, the values never coincide.

Because the original mapping is not persisted, we can no longer tie the data back to the user, so it is no longer user identifiable. We can still tie together datasets by the random ID, but there is no way to associate the random ID with a user. The following listing shows the corresponding Azure Data Explorer query.

Listing 10.4   Replacing user IDs with GUIDs

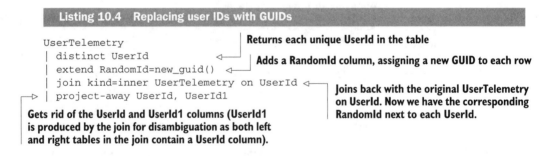

```
UserTelemetry                                      Returns each unique UserId in the table
| distinct UserId
| extend RandomId=new_guid()                 Adds a RandomId column, assigning a new GUID to each row
| join kind=inner UserTelemetry on UserId
| project-away UserId, UserId1
```
Joins back with the original UserTelemetry on UserId. Now we have the corresponding RandomId next to each UserId.

Gets rid of the UserId and UserId1 columns (UserId1 is produced by the join for disambiguation as both left and right tables in the join contain a UserId column).

As before, we can ingest the result of this query into a new table and drop the original table if needed. Note that this is a one-time processing. If we get new telemetry from our users, we won't be able to generate the same GUID when anonymizing. Each time we run this query, we will get different random IDs corresponding to our users. In some cases, this might not be enough. Or we might need to maintain the ability to link back to our original user IDs but restrict who can make that association. For these cases, we can use pseudonymization.

10.2.3   *Pseudonymization*

In the pseudonymization case, we have scenarios for which we need to know who the data belongs to, but it is not needed for all scenarios. For example, we might want to keep track of which user used which features so we can notify them of updates to those features. But, for other analytics, it is irrelevant who the user is. For the first case, we have a small set of people who can view this association. For analytics, we have a large team of people looking at the data, but from their perspective, it is anonymous. We can achieve this by pseudonymizing the data.

> **DEFINITION** *Pseudonymization* is the process of replacing user identifiable information with a pseudonym. The data can be linked back to a user, given some additional information.

The difference between pseudonymization and anonymization is that pseudonymization gives us a way to reconstruct the relationship. When we looked at anonymizing data, we swapped out the user ID with a randomly generated ID. Unless we explicitly stored which user ID got assigned with which random ID, we can no longer recover the link. For pseudonymization, we replace random IDs with something more deterministic. This can be either a hash of the user ID or an encryption of the user ID.

As a reminder, hashing is a one-way function: you cannot unhash the result of a hash to get the original value. Encryption is different, however. An encrypted value can be decrypted if we know the encryption key. Figure 10.5 illustrates the difference; then let's look at both approaches in this section.

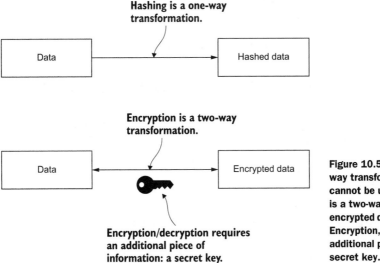

Figure 10.5 Hashing is a one-way transformation: hashed data cannot be unhashed. Encryption is a two-way transformation: encrypted data can be decrypted. Encryption, however, requires an additional piece of information, a secret key.

PSEUDONYMIZING BY HASHING

If we hash the user IDs and provide a dataset with just hashes, the only way to tie this pseudonymous data back to actual users is to take all the user IDs in our system and hash them to see where we can find a match. If we restrict the access to the user IDs, then anyone who can query the pseudonymized table can see all the connections (which features are used by which user) within the dataset, but with this approach, instead of seeing a user ID, they'll see a pseudonymous identifier. Figure 10.6 shows this transformation, and listing 10.5 shows the corresponding Azure Data Explorer query.

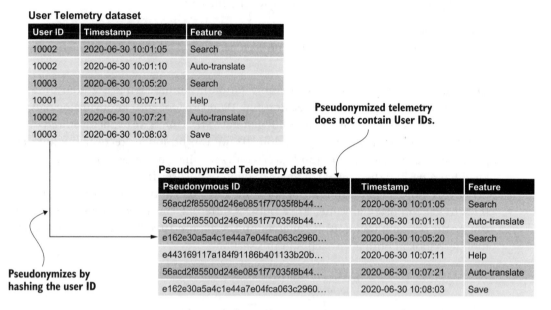

Figure 10.6   Replacing the User ID with a hash of its value produces a pseudonymized dataset.

Listing 10.5   Pseudonymizing by hashing the user ID

```
UserTelemetry
| project PseudonymizedId=hash_sha256(UserId),
  Timestamp, Feature
```
Replaces the User ID column with an SHA256 hash of UserId

SHA256 is one of the hashing algorithms available in Azure Data Explorer. The hash_sha256() function produces an SHA256 hash of a value. Note that if we only have a dataset consisting of Pseudonymous ID, Timestamp, and Feature, we can't produce a user ID. On the other hand, if we have a user ID, we can hash it and then link it to the pseudonymized data.

We can use this technique in cases where the data scientists processing the pseudonymized data don't have access to the unprocessed EUII. This way, they get a dataset that is, for all intents and purposes, just like the original except there is no mention of user IDs.

This approach doesn't work if the user IDs are visible because it is easy to hash them and produce the pseudonymous IDs. One option is to add a secret salt to our hash. In cryptography, a *salt* is some additional secret data mixed in to make it harder to recreate the connection. The following listing shows an alternative pseudonymization that adds salt to the mix.

Listing 10.6 Pseudonymization by hashing with salt

```
let salt=123456;                    ◁─── The salt number must be kept secret.
UserTelemetry
| project PseudonymizedId=hash_sha256(
➡ binary_xor(UserId, salt)),        ◁─┐ XORs the UserId with
  Timestamp, Feature                    └─ the salt before hashing
```

In our example in listing 10.6, we use a binary XOR to salt `UserId`. As a reminder, XOR (the exclusive OR operator) applied to 2 bits returns 1 when either of its inputs is 0 and the other is 1; otherwise, it returns 0. A `binary_xor` in our example XORs the `UserId` bits with the bits of the salt and produces a salted user ID. Now, as long as the salt stays secret, someone can't get from `UserId` to `PseudonymizedId` even if they know it is produced by an SHA256 hash. Let's now look at the alternative to hashing—encryption.

PSEUDONYMIZING BY ENCRYPTING

If we encrypt the user IDs and provide a dataset with encrypted values, the only way to tie the values back to actual users is to decrypt them. As long as the encryption key is secure and only available on a need-to-know basis, people that don't need to know can't recover the association.

This is similar to the hashing technique we just saw, except it is a two-way transformation. Even without having access to a user ID to hash, we can produce one by decrypting an encrypted pseudonymized ID. Figure 10.7 shows how this would look.

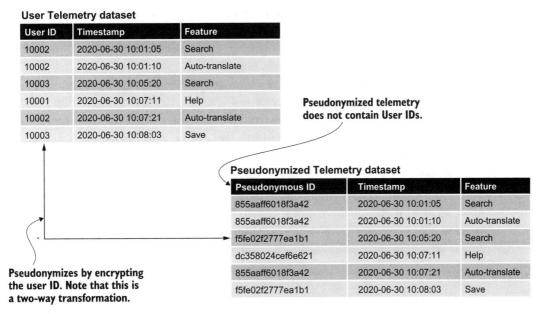

User Telemetry dataset

User ID	Timestamp	Feature
10002	2020-06-30 10:01:05	Search
10002	2020-06-30 10:01:10	Auto-translate
10003	2020-06-30 10:05:20	Search
10001	2020-06-30 10:07:11	Help
10002	2020-06-30 10:07:21	Auto-translate
10003	2020-06-30 10:08:03	Save

Pseudonymized telemetry does not contain User IDs.

Pseudonymized Telemetry dataset

Pseudonymous ID	Timestamp	Feature
855aaff6018f3a42	2020-06-30 10:01:05	Search
855aaff6018f3a42	2020-06-30 10:01:10	Auto-translate
f5fe02f2777ea1b1	2020-06-30 10:05:20	Search
dc358024cef6e621	2020-06-30 10:07:11	Help
855aaff6018f3a42	2020-06-30 10:07:21	Auto-translate
f5fe02f2777ea1b1	2020-06-30 10:08:03	Save

Pseudonymizes by encrypting the user ID. Note that this is a two-way transformation.

Figure 10.7 Encrypting the user ID produces a pseudonymized dataset. Note that the pseudonymized dataset can be transformed back to the original by decrypting the pseudonymous ID.

We'll skip the Azure Data Explorer sample because Azure Data Explorer doesn't have out-of-the-box encryption/decryption functions. This is not a hard limitation, though. Azure Data Explorer has a Python plug-in that allows us to implement arbitrary functions using Python and invoke them from our queries. We can easily add cryptography by enabling the Python plug-in and leveraging an encryption algorithm from the library. We'll skip this for brevity, but remember you have this capability at your disposal. You can learn more about it here: http://mng.bz/Pax8.

We can use encryption instead of hashing if we have a scenario in which we don't have the original dataset available, but we need a way to recover it. In this case, we can rely on the two-way transformation provided by encryption and restore the original dataset by decrypting the pseudonymized dataset.

Before moving on, a quick note on using cryptography in a real-world environment: cryptography helps us protect information but can be easily misused. When employed in a compliance scenario, make sure to follow best practices, which include the following:

- *Never hand-roll your own cryptography.* Always rely on libraries for this as there is complex math underneath, which is easy to get wrong.
- *Store secrets safely.* Azure Key Vault is a good place to store secrets.
- *Don't rely on security by obscurity.* This means considering something secure just because it is unknown.

    For example, if using a hash without a secret salt, and if we have both the original and hashed data, we can likely recreate the association even if we don't know the hashing algorithm used. We can do this by trying a few well-known algorithms until we find a match. In this case, obscurity (keeping the hashing algorithm secret) doesn't provide security.

- *If needed, use cryptographically secure hashing.* This means having an algorithm vetted to work in cryptographic scenarios.

    We used SHA265 in an earlier example, which is considered cryptographically secure. An example of a hashing algorithm that shouldn't be used in cryptographic contexts is MD5 (Azure Data Explorer also provides a hash_md5() function). MD5 hashing is fast, but suffers from multiple security vulnerabilities.

There are whole books written on cryptography, so we'll stop here. Do be careful when securing data and always think how an implementation could be exploited by an attacker that somehow gains access to your systems. An alternative to transforming data, which we'll cover more in depth in the next section, is masking.

10.2.4 *Masking*

Masking means hiding parts of the data from whomever accesses it, even if the data is fully available in our system. For example, think of how Social Security numbers are reduced to the last four digits: ***-**-1234. Masking sensitive data makes it less sensitive. Obviously, even with bad intent, someone can't do much with just the last four digits of a Social Security number, with just the city and state of a home address, or with the first few digits of a phone number.

> **DEFINITION** *Masking* leverages an additional layer between the raw data and query issuers, which hides sensitive information from nonprivileged access.

Masking the data requires an additional layer in between the raw storage and the people querying the data, which determines who gets to see the unmasked, full dataset, and who is restricted to a more limited view of the data. Figure 10.8 shows how masking looks for our User Profiles table.

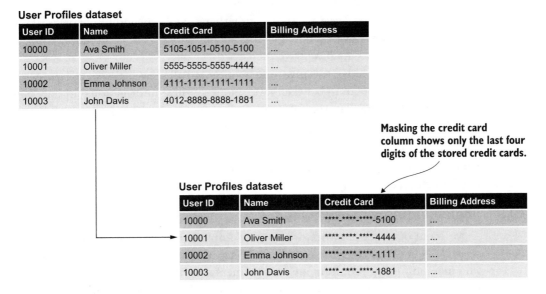

Figure 10.8 Masking the Credit Card column hides the sensitive credit card information and only reveals the last four digits of each credit card.

Unlike our previous techniques, which transformed the data, masking happens in place. In our example, we still have the full credit card number stored, but not everyone querying the table can see it.

The good news is many storage solutions and database engines offer such a layer out of the box. We'll cover an Azure Data Explorer implementation in the next section as part of implementing an access model for our data. Before we dig into that, though, let's do a quick recap of the techniques covered so far.

10.2.5 Processing classification changes recap

In this section, we looked at a few ways in which we can take sensitive data and make it less sensitive:

- Aggregating data makes it impossible to connect it back to individual users.

- Anonymizing data, while a bit more involved than aggregating, preserves the granularity of user-level data while removing the identifiable parts.

- We can use pseudonymization when we have legitimate scenarios in which we want to trace back the data to actual users. This makes the data partially anonymous and only restores the link to the real user ID on a need-to-know basis.

- Hashing is a one-way transformation of the data. For example, given `Pseudonymizedid`, we can't recover `UserId`. We can, however, restore the association by hashing `UserId` again and joining on `PseudonymizedId`.

- Adding secret salt to a hash makes it harder to restore the association, as one would need to also know the salt value.

- Encryption is a two-way transformation that requires an additional piece of information: a key. For example, given `PseudonymizedId`, we can recover `UserId` by decrypting the data if we have the key.

- Masking also hides sensitive information. In this case, the data is not transformed, rather, an in-between layer hides sensitive information and only makes it available when appropriate.

These are important techniques to know when dealing with sensitive data because all these processes allow us to make more data available to more analytical scenarios without compromising user privacy. Another important part of dealing with sensitive data is, of course, access control.

10.3   *Implementing an access model*

As we build our data platform, we need to implement an access model that ensures sensitive data is limited to the people who have a legitimate business case to use it and who meet any other requirements the business mandates. These requirements might include training on proper data handling, signing the right paperwork, and so on.

All Azure services have a layer of security enforced at the resource level. In Azure portal, you can configure this on the Access Control (IAM) blade, which shows up on most resources. This grants various rights on the whole resource. For example, granting Contributor-level access to someone on an Azure Data Explorer cluster allows them to create or delete databases, change the cluster configuration, and so on. There are three important roles common across all services, and various services have additional roles:

- *Reader*—Users with this role can view the resource but can't make any changes. Note that this includes, for example, viewing the access keys to a storage account.

- *Contributor*—Users with this role can both view and modify the resource, except they can't grant others permissions on the resource.

- *Owner*—Users with this role can do everything a Contributor can but, additionally, they can grant others permissions on the resource.

Access at the Azure resource level should only be granted to data engineers maintaining the platform. Access to production resources should be further restricted to the on-call engineers or SREs. This is a best practice straight from service engineering and is not specific to building a data platform.

The more interesting part comes next: storage solutions usually provide another layer of security for the objects they manage internally. For example, in Azure Data Explorer, we can grant permissions at the database level with roles like Viewer (can issue queries), User (can issue queries and create objects), Ingestor (can ingest data into existing tables but can't query), Admin (can do anything in the scope of the database), and so on. We touched on this in chapter 6, when we looked at an analytics workflow that moves objects between databases where different team members have access. This solution gives us more granularity than the previous layer: we can grant a few data scientists access to a database containing sensitive information, while others only get access to the databases containing nonsensitive data.

As another example, to access files stored in Azure Data Lake Storage (ADLS), we need either an account key or shared access signature (SAS). Azure Data Lake Storage also provides POSIX-like access control lists (ACLs), where we can set read/write permissions at the folder and file level to restrict access to the data. Figure 10.9 shows the two layers of access control.

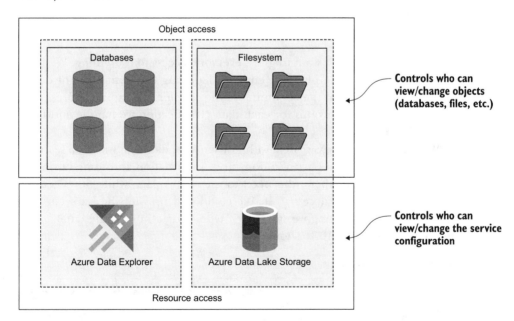

Figure 10.9 Resource access controls who can view or change the service configuration (Azure Data Explorer, Azure Data Lake Storage, etc.). Object access controls who can view or change the objects managed by the service (databases, files, etc.).

In this section, we will focus on the second layer of access control, object access, which protects the data in our data platforms. For the first layer, not data related, which protects our Azure resources, we can simply apply the same best practices as for other cloud-development projects: only grant access to engineering, grant just the level of access required to complete the task, etc. Let's start with security groups.

10.3.1 Security groups

The first important rule to remember is to never grant individual users access to a resource. Always use Azure Active Directory security groups and add users to a group instead. This is important for maintaining a compliant system.

Consider what happens if we have a set of databases in our Azure Data Explorer cluster, say, telemetry, analytics, and customers. When Alice joins the team, she needs access to all of them. If we grant her explicit access, we'll have to do that for each object. Then after a while, let's say Alice leaves the team. We should revoke her access, but by this time, we probably have more databases in our cluster and have lost track of which ones she needed for her work. We'd have to check permissions on each database and revoke hers if we find them. More than this, she might have gotten access to data stored in other services like Azure SQL or Azure Data Lake Storage.

Contrast this with having a security group, let's call it Data Scientists, which includes all members of our data science team. When Alice leaves the team, we remove her from this group, and she loses access to all the objects the group has access to.

Of course, we don't want to grant everyone access to everything. We'll need more granularity as our data platform ends up handling different types of data from the classifications we saw at the beginning of the chapter. We should address this by creating multiple security groups for each data classification we handle and for each role we need.

For example, let's say we deal with nonsensitive data that we'll call feature data, but we also have some end user pseudonymous information and some business data. We have some team members who need to query this data, while other team members only need read/write access to it. We could end up with the six security groups in table 10.1. And assuming we store each type of data in separate databases, we could grant access as figure 10.10 shows.

Table 10.1 Security groups

	Read-only security group	Read/write security group
Feature data	Feature data read-only access	Feature data read/write access
EUPI data	EUPI data read-only access	EUPI data read/write access
Business data	Business data read-only access	Business data read/write access

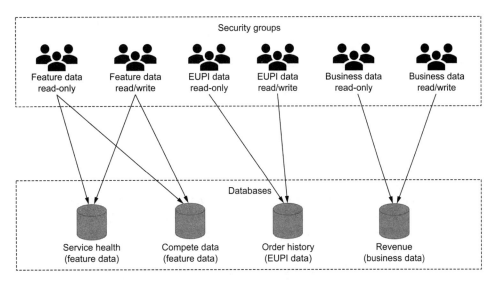

Figure 10.10 Different security groups have access to different databases, based on the classification of the data in each database.

Now when a new team member joins, depending on the type of data they can view, they join one or more of the security groups. When they leave, we only have to remove them from a small set of security groups.

Listing 10.7 creates the feature data and EUPI data read-only groups that we'll use in the following examples. We won't create all the groups in our examples to avoid being too repetitive, but the pattern is the same.

Listing 10.7 Creating the feature data and EUPI read-only groups

```
az ad group create `
--display-name "Feature data read only" `
--mail-nickname FeatureDataRO

az ad group create `
--display-name "EUPI data read only" `
--mail-nickname EUPIDataRO
```

With security groups, we also have a central place where we can audit who has access to what and against which we can automatically perform required checks. For example, we can check that all members of the EUPI data group have attended data-handling training. The following listing shows how we can list the members of our EUPI data read-only group using Azure CLI.

Listing 10.8 Getting the members of the EUPI data group

```
az ad group member list `
--group "EUPI data read only"
```

Now that we have a couple of security groups set up, let's see how we would secure an Azure Data Explorer cluster.

10.3.2 *Securing Azure Data Explorer*

While we focus on Azure Data Explorer here, most database engines have equivalent methods of securing their objects. You should be able to apply some of this regardless of which storage service you end up using. In Azure Data Explorer, we can secure databases, tables, and even certain rows or columns inside the tables. We'll cover all of these in order.

DATABASES

We already saw how to grant access to Azure Data Explorer databases in chapter 4, where we set up a service principal for an Azure Data Factory (ADF) to connect to our telemetry database. To do that, we used the `az kusto database-principal-assignment create` command.

In chapter 4, we wanted to stand up our Data Factory; we weren't thinking about our access model. Ideally, we would have created a security group with the minimum set of permissions required for our Data Factory workloads and then made the service principal a member of that group. You can try doing that as an exercise.

Let's create a couple of databases: orders will contain order history (EUPI) and servicehealth will contain service health signals from our platform (feature data). We'll grant the two Azure Active Directory (AAD) groups we just created access to these databases according to our access model. The next listing shows the steps.

Listing 10.9   Creating databases and assigning permissions

```
az kusto database create `        ◁──── Creates a new Azure Data Explorer database
--cluster-name "adx$suffix" `
--database-name servicehealth `   ◁────   The servicehealth database
--resource-group adx-rg `                 contains nonsensitive feature
--read-write-database location="Central US"   data.

az kusto database create `
--cluster-name "adx$suffix" `
--database-name orders `          ◁──── The orders database contains EUPI data.
--resource-group adx-rg `
--read-write-database location="Central US"

az kusto database-principal-assignment create `   ◁──── Assigns permissions to a database
--cluster-name "adx$suffix" `
--database-name servicehealth `   Specifies the cluster and database
--principal-id "Feature data read only" `
--principal-type Group `                  Grants rights to the ID and principal type.
--role "Viewer" `                         We use the name of the security group as
--principal-assignment-name               ID and the type is Group.
   servicehealthfeaturedataviewer `
--resource-group adx-rg            This role determines what the principal can do.
                                   For read-only access, we use the Viewer role.
```

Assignments must have a name.

```
az kusto database-principal-assignment create `
--cluster-name "adx$suffix" `
--database-name orders `
--principal-id "EUPI data read only" `
--principal-type Group `
--role "Viewer" `
--principal-assignment-name orderseupiviewer `
--resource-group adx-rg
```

Same as the previous command except we grant rights to a different group on a different database

Now members of the read-only Feature data group will be able to issue queries against tables in the servicehealth database but won't be able to see the orders database. Similarly, members of the read-only EUPI data group will be able to issue queries against the orders database.

We could make the EUPI data read-only group itself a member of the Feature read-only data group, so when we grant access to feature data, people who have clearance for more sensitive data (like EUPI) get access automatically. But, this approach doesn't scale well.

Sometimes people lose access to sensitive data due to a project change, etc., but they still need to view feature data. Revoking EUPI access in this case would remove their access from feature data too. Also, we don't always have a clear hierarchy of how sensitive data is: business-related data is a different type of "sensitive" than EUPI data and requires different standards when handling. In general, for a production scenario with many people accessing data, it's better to be explicit: for example, "If you want access to this type of data, you need to join this security group."

We looked at granting database-level permissions before. Now let's get more granular and see how we can secure tables within a database.

RESTRICTED-VIEW TABLES

At the time of writing, Azure Data Explorer doesn't support setting individual permissions on tables, but it does have the notion of restricted tables. If we enable the RestrictedViewAccess policy on a table, then only principals with the Unrestricted-Viewer role can query the table.

Let's add the policy to the User Profiles table in our telemetry database to understand how this works. We created the table in listing 10.1 and seeded it with some data. Open the Azure Data Explorer UI and run the command in the following listing.

Listing 10.10 Applying the RestrictedViewAccess policy

```
.alter table UserProfiles policy restricted_view_access true
```

Now if you try querying the table, you'll get an unauthorized error. A table marked as restricted (read/write privilege on the database) can't be queried even by database administrators or users. You need to become an UnrestrictedViewer to query this table. Run the Azure CLI code in the following listing to grant yourself Unrestricted-Viewer permissions.

Listing 10.11   Granting UnrestrictedViewer permissions

```
$me = az ad signed-in-user show --query objectId

az kusto database-principal-assignment create `
--cluster-name "adx$suffix" `
--database-name telemetry `
--principal-id $me `
--principal-type User `
--role UnrestrictedViewers `
--principal-assignment-name userprofilesmeunrestrictedviewer `
--resource-group adx-rg
```

You should now be able to query the table. The RestrictedViewAccess policy combined with the UnrestrictedViewer role allows us to split the data inside a database into unrestricted (any viewer can query) and restricted (only unrestricted viewers can query) data. This is a handy way to mix sensitive and nonsensitive data inside the same database while maintaining compliant access control.

The main problem with this approach is that it only works for two data classifications. If we want to store three types of data (for example, feature data, EUPI, and business data), this approach is not enough. Because of this, I don't recommend relying on this policy when building your access model in Azure Data Explorer. It is better to use separate databases, each containing a different type of data like we saw in the previous section. Or you can go even more granular and rely on row-level security, which we'll cover next.

Let's remove the restriction on the User Profiles table as we'll look at an alternative way of securing it. The following listing shows how to do this. Then all viewers of the database will again be able to query the table.

Listing 10.12   Removing the RestrictedViewAccess policy

```
.alter table UserProfiles policy restricted_view_access false
```

ROW-LEVEL SECURITY

Row-level security enables granular access control. We can filter our rows and/or columns from a table, depending on who queries it. This is implemented as a policy on a table, which effectively injects a query between the query the user is trying to run and the table being queried. This query can add additional filters on the data. Figure 10.11 shows how this works.

Azure Data Explorer has a couple of key functions that integrate with Azure Active Directory. These are as follows:

- `current_principal()` returns the ID and tenant of the principal who issued the query.
- `current_principal_is_member_of()` checks whether the principal who issued the query is a member of the list of provided principals. This can include user IDs, app IDs, or groups. For groups, group membership is checked.

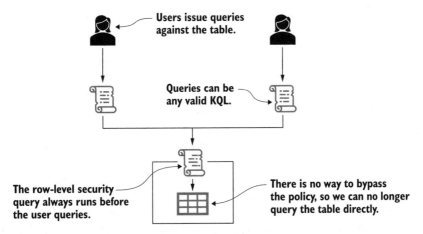

Figure 10.11 Different users issue queries against the table. The queries are arbitrary (they can be any valid KQL). The query set as policy always runs before the user queries so it can inject additional filtering. The table can no longer be accessed directly as the row-level security query always sits between other queries and the table.

Let's add a policy on our User Profiles table to check whether the current principal is a member of the EUPI data read-only security group we created. If not, we won't return any rows. First, let's grab the group ID and tenant ID using Azure CLI. We'll need them when we apply the policy in Azure Data Explorer. The following listing retrieves the group ID and tenant ID.

Listing 10.13 Group and tenant ID for EUPI data read-only security group

```
$group = az ad group show `
--group "EUPI data read only" | ConvertFrom-Json

$account = az account show | ConvertFrom-Json

echo "$($group.objectId);$($account.tenantId)"
```

Retrieves the details of the security group and stores them in $group

Retrieves the account details and stores them in $account

Prints the group's AAD object ID, a semicolon, then the tenant ID

Make a note of the output of the echo command from listing 10.13. We'll need to supply this to Azure Data Explorer. Then in the Azure Data Explorer UI, run the command in the following listing.

Listing 10.14 Applying row-level security to User Profiles

```
.alter table UserProfiles
  policy row_level_security enable
  "UserProfiles | where current_principal_is_member_of(
    'aadgroup=<group ID>;<tenant ID>')"
```

Enables the row_level_security policy on the table

Row-level security query. Replaces <group ID>;<tenant ID> with the values from listing 10.13.

Let's look at what happens here. First, we enabled the policy, then we used the following row-level security query:

```
UserProfiles | where current_principal_is_member_of('aadgroup=...').
```

This means any query issued against the User Profiles table runs against the result of this query instead. We effectively injected a `where` filter with a group membership check. If the principal issuing the query is a member of the group, the query returns all rows. If the principal is not a member of the group, `where` filters all rows. Try this out by querying User Profiles. Because you shouldn't be a member of the group, you should not get any rows back, even though the data still exists in the table.

Row-level security is powerful, but there are some restrictions around the injected query; for example, it must return the same columns as the underlying table. With that said, the filter we implemented in listing 10.14 is one of the simplest ones. We can do more complex filtering; for example, masking columns depending on group membership. Let's reimplement the policy so that it only shows the credit card number if the principal issuing the query is a member of the EUPI group; otherwise, it replaces the number with ****.

Listing 10.15 shows the new policy. We also implement the policy as a function, so it is easier to understand. We could have kept everything in the policy, but this approach is cleaner, especially for more complex row-level security queries.

Listing 10.15   Masking credit card numbers using row-level security

Replaces the group and tenant ID with your actual values

Implements the policy as a function to keep things clean

```
.create-or-alter function UserProfilesRLS() {
    let canViewCreditCards = current_principal_is_member_of(
       'aadgroup=<group ID>;<tenant ID>');
    UserProfiles
    | project CreditCard =
       iif(canViewCreditCards, CreditCard, "****")
}

.alter table UserProfiles
  policy row_level_security enable "UserProfilesRLS"
```

Uses an iif expression to replace the CreditCard column value with ** if the user isn't allowed to view credit card numbers**

Applies the function as the row-level security policy

This should give you a taste of the power of row-level security policies. This is a good mechanism to secure the data within the same database. But keep in mind a couple of downsides with this approach—complexity and performance.

As we saw, we can create complex policies to mask certain columns and hide certain rows, but we need to maintain these policies as schemas change and security groups evolve. Also, keep in mind the long-term maintenance cost.

Another thing to note is performance. We are effectively running a hidden query whenever someone tries to query the table. If this is not performant, all queries hitting the table will be impacted. Policies should be written such thay these run fast and scale well.

10.3.3 Access model recap

Before moving on to the next topic, let's quickly recap access model implementation. We can control access to Azure resources using RBAC (role-based access control) permissions. As a reminder, RBAC is the standard way to control access to Azure resources. This applies for all Azure resources, but it is not the main topic of this section. In general, only SREs should have access to modify Azure resources. The access model we discussed is implemented at a different layer than that of the storage solutions we use.

We talked about creating security groups for the various data classifications and permissions (read-only, read/write, etc.). Never assign permissions to users individually as it becomes hard to keep track of who can access what. Having a set of Azure Active Directory security groups that users join is the preferred approach. We can easily audit these groups and clean them up if users lose access (due to changing teams, for example).

We also looked at securing Azure Data Explorer. We went over the different ways we can achieve this. As a reminder:

- *We can keep data in separate databases depending on the data classification.* We can have one or more databases for storing feature data, one or more databases for storing EUPI, etc.
- *Instead of table-level permissions, Azure Data Explorer uses the RestrictedViewAccess policy to mark a set of tables in a database as restricted.* This only works for two data types (one restricted, one unrestricted) and doesn't scale beyond that. A big data platform usually handles more than just two types of data, so this approach might not be sufficient.
- *Row-level security enables much more granular access control.* We can filter out rows or mask columns depending on who queries a table.

The same concepts apply regardless of the storage services used by your platform. We looked at Azure Data Explorer in our example, but Azure SQL, for example, has similar capabilities, including support for row-level security. Azure Data Lake Storage is more like a filesystem: it supports access control lists (ACLs) for folders and files. We can secure folders and files using ACLs and assign only certain security groups permissions to read or write certain files.

In general, when we implement an access model, we secure objects within our storage solutions by data classification. This combined with security groups ensures that we don't have any data leaks and that we maintain compliance. Next, let's talk about GDPR, what it entails and what we need to do to comply with this regulation.

10.4   *Complying with GDPR and other considerations*

The GDPR legislation is quite complex, so we won't cover all of it in this section. Instead, we'll look at a couple of key points to consider when you have a data platform that handles any type of user data. We won't cover things like consent (when we collect user data, the user must be clearly informed about what we are collecting, why, and given the chance to opt out). Usually this happens upstream of the data platform, so we will consider it out of scope. We will, however, focus on data handling and data subject requests.

10.4.1   *Data handling*

GDPR doesn't prescribe any specific encryption requirements for user data, but strongly recommends keeping user data encrypted and using pseudonymization wherever possible. We covered pseudonymization in section 10.2.3. As a best practice, apply pseudonymization as much as possible and avoid keeping datasets with many non-pseudonymized datapoints. For encryption, Azure services offer encryption at rest. Most services have this enabled by default.

> **DEFINITION**   *Encryption at rest* provides data protection for stored data (at rest). Attacks against data at rest include attempts to obtain physical access to the hardware on which the data is stored and then compromise the contained data.

Data at rest is encrypted using Microsoft-managed keys when it is written to disk and decrypted when read. If needed, you can supply your own encryption keys to use instead of the Microsoft-managed ones. Both Azure Data Explorer and Azure Data Lake Storage encrypt data at rest by default. Same goes for Azure SQL and even for virtual machine (VM) disks. Another key requirement our data platform should be able to satisfy is honoring data subject requests.

10.4.2   *Data subject requests*

Under GDPR, a user has the right to request all personal data in a readable form, ask for corrections to the data, or exercise the right to be forgotten, which means removing all their data from the system. Honoring data subject requests is important for a data platform that stores user data. To support this, we'll bring together some of the components we covered in this book. We'll need to know all the tables where user data is stored, and we need to link together the different IDs we use to represent users in our system.

A metadata solution like Azure Purview gives us the complete list of tables containing user data. As we saw in chapter 8, we can use the data classification capabilities of Azure Purview to automatically tag our user identities across our data platform. Then we can use the Azure Purview REST API to retrieve them.

The other missing piece is how all the identities tie together. We discussed identity keyrings in chapter 5. An *identity keyring* connects all the various IDs in our platform,

IDs that sometimes come from different systems. With Azure Purview and an identity keyring, given a user ID, we can find all rows in all tables that contain user data under all IDs known by our system. Figure 10.12 shows how this works.

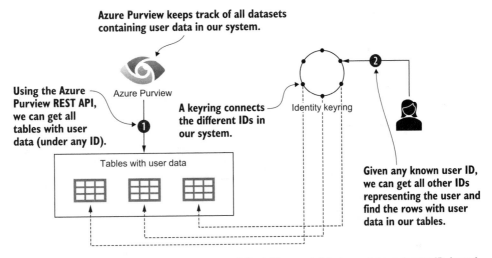

Figure 10.12 With Azure Purview, we can get all the tables containing user data under any ID, based on the data dictionary and classifications. From the identity keyring and given a user ID, we can get all other associated IDs in our system. We can then use those IDs to query the tables and identify all rows containing data associated with a given user.

We will need to write some code to achieve this, which we won't do here to keep things short, but an Azure Function should be enough to connect these components from our system and allow us to enumerate all data associated with a user. We can use this to honor both export and delete requests.

EXPORT REQUESTS

An *export request* means a user wants all data the company has on them. Note that this is a company-wide request, while our data platform might be only a small piece of the company's IT. The reason why this matters, especially in a large enterprise, is that many times data gets replicated across systems. For example, we might ingest some web telemetry data from the team operating our website and sales data from our payments team, and we might use this data to train an ML model for product recommendations. Figure 10.13 shows the data flow.

Because an export request is company wide, usually each department that handles user data needs to export the data it has. In this case, if we simply replicate data from upstream, upstream exports the copy. We would only worry about data that originates within our platform: our recommendations based on the ingested datasets.

In general, a best practice when dealing with export requests is for each department to export the data that originates from their system. If we implement this across the company, we don't need to worry about data we ingest from upstream (that

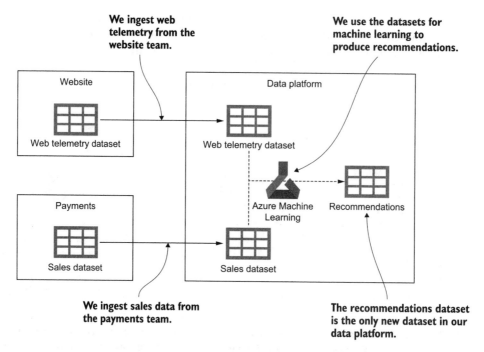

We ingest web telemetry from the website team.

We use the datasets for machine learning to produce recommendations.

We ingest sales data from the payments team.

The recommendations dataset is the only new dataset in our data platform.

Figure 10.13   The web telemetry and payments datasets come from upstream (the website team and the payments team). We use these datasets to provide ML-driven recommendations. In this case, only the recommendations are new to our data platform.

should already be handled upstream), and likewise, teams downstream need not worry about data consumed from us (we will export any new data we generate, like our recommendations).

DELETE REQUESTS

Delete requests are a bit trickier. If a user exercises their right to be forgotten, it is no longer enough to have the data removed from upstream. We need to ensure our data platform is also cleaned.

We have to honor a data subject request within 30 days. Here is where the different ways to ingest data, which we discussed back in chapter 2, and retention policies become important. As a reminder, in chapter 2, we talked about full load (always re-ingesting the full dataset) and incremental load (appending new data to the data we already ingested). If we perform a full load from upstream, and we do it on a cadence of less than 30 days, when upstream deletes the user data (they also need to honor a delete request), then we really don't have to do anything because the data automatically disappears from our platform on the next full load.

We also talked about retention policies in chapter 6. Putting a retention policy in place on a table in Azure Data Explorer ensures that data only lives for the set number of days and is automatically cleaned up afterward. If we have a retention policy of 30 days or less, we again don't need to do anything because data gets cleaned up for us.

For datasets that aren't fully loaded in a timely manner and are stored without a short retention policy, we need to remove the data. We can use the same combination of Azure Purview plus an identity keyring to pin down the records. While Azure Data Explorer is meant as an append-only store, it does have a `.purge` command,[1] which is used specifically for scenarios like GDPR to remove rows.

Going back to the data ingestion patterns from chapter 2, if we use a storage solution as our single source of truth, it is enough to clean up the data there and then restate the datasets stored in other data fabrics. Otherwise, we must explicitly clean up each data fabric, which requires additional automation.

In summary, full loads from upstream and retention policies reduce the amount of work we need to do to honor delete requests. Having one data fabric as our single source of truth also helps because we can clean it up and then refresh the data in other data fabrics. Azure Purview and an identity keyring together can enumerate all datasets associated with a user that we can export or purge as needed.

10.4.3 *Other considerations*

GDPR compliance is only one type of compliance. Depending on your problem space, there are many other regulations you might need to comply with and standards for which you might want to be certified. A few include PCI (Payment Card Industry) data security standard, HIPPA when dealing with health information, SOC (Service Organization Control), etc.

Data residency is another aspect to keep in mind. Depending on the data classification, some countries require data to stay within the country. For example, Microsoft has separate instances of the Azure cloud for Germany and China, using regional data centers.

You don't need to be an expert in data handling regulations, but you should know when to talk to an expert. When dealing with sensitive data, your team *should* work with an expert to ensure the applicable laws are properly interpreted and translated into clear handling standards and software requirements.

We covered three major aspects of data governance: metadata (in chapter 8), data quality (in chapter 9), and compliance (in this chapter). The last topic we will cover is data distribution or how data flows outside of our data platform. This is the focus of the next and final chapter.

Summary

- Data has different classifications depending on its nature. Different types of data require different handling standards. These standards are a combination of regulatory requirements and internal company policy.
- We can reduce the sensitivity of data through processing. User data can be aggregated, anonymized, or pseudonymized to make it less sensitive.

---

[1] For more information, see http://mng.bz/9N9j.

- Access models are implemented on top of the storage solution and provide different access controls than RBAC (role-based access control), which is common for all Azure resources.

- Always use Azure Active Directory security groups to control access, rather than granting access to individual users.

- We can secure objects at different levels. In Azure Data Explorer, we can use different databases (database-level access control), the RestrictedViewAccess policy (access control for a subset of tables), or row-level security (granular access control on rows and column values).

- Other storage services provide similar ways to secure objects. Azure SQL is similar to Azure Data Explorer, while Azure Data Lake Storage uses access control lists to secure files and folders.

- To comply with GDPR (General Data Protection Regulation), we can combine Azure Purview (which keeps track of all tables containing user data) with our identity keyring (which connects the different IDs in our system) to retrieve all data associated with a given user.

Distributing data

This chapter covers

- Sharing data through an API
- Sharing data for bulk copy
- Data sharing best practices

We've come a long way in this book: we've covered data ingestion and storage, all the different workloads a data platform runs, and multiple aspects of data governance. This final chapter is all about the output of our data platform or how data leaves our systems to be consumed by users or other systems. Figure 11.1 highlights this last focus area.

We'll start by talking about data distribution in general and then some common patterns for this. In some cases, this can be easily achieved with SaaS (software as a service) solutions like Power BI for publishing reports. Other times, we might need to stand up some infrastructure to support data distribution. Two common consumption patterns are low-volume/high-frequency and high-volume/low-frequency.

We'll talk about building a data API, how a data API can support low-volume/high-frequency consumption, the advantages of having an API layer, and some of the trade-offs. We'll introduce Azure Cosmos DB and show why it is a great option for a data backend. We'll also briefly touch on serving ML models specifically, as Azure Machine Learning (AML) offers this capability.

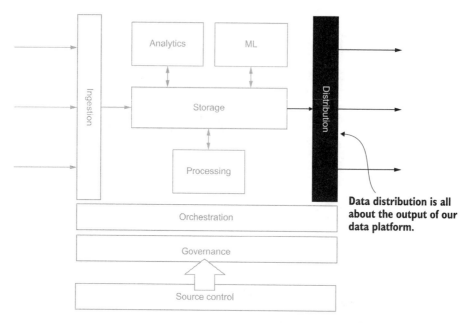

Figure 11.1   Data distribution covers the output of our data platform and how data leaves our system.

Next, we'll look at high-volume/low-frequency consumption, which usually means bulk copy of datasets. We'll talk about how separating compute resources, thereby ensuring data consumption by downstream teams, doesn't negatively impact our workloads. We'll introduce Azure Data Share, an Azure service specialized in data sharing. We'll wrap up with a few best practices for sharing data and talk a bit about the cost of moving data around. Let's start with an overview of data distribution.

11.1   Data distribution overview

We'll use a broad definition of data distribution: any consumption of data from our data platform by a consumer outside of our team. This includes other individuals and teams, and integration with other systems. In many cases, data platforms start with a handful of reports, which can easily be shared via email or a service like Power BI.

> ### Power BI
>
> Power BI is a SaaS offering by Microsoft. It provides interactive visualizations and business intelligence capabilities with a visual interface, which makes it easy for non-programmers to create reports and interactive dashboards.
>
> Power BI can connect and query all Azure storage services and is a popular solution when building on the Microsoft ecosystem. If you build a data platform on Azure, it's likely that one of your outputs will be a set of Power BI reports.

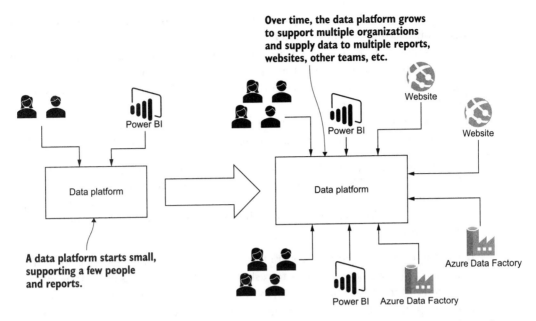

Figure 11.2 A data platform starts small but, over time, grows to support more and more reports and websites, supplying data to other teams and people. Scaling out becomes an important engineering challenge.

This is perfectly fine in the initial stages, and no additional engineering is required. Problems arise once the platform grows and more parts of the business take dependencies on it. Figure 11.2 shows this evolution.

Once we reach a certain scale, we can't efficiently satisfy all these data needs with a single data fabric: some systems require low latency (for example, serving data to a website) and some require high throughput (for example, copying large datasets). We need to ensure we have enough compute resources to support our internal workloads like data processing, analytics, and machine learning.

At this stage, we need to implement solutions to support downstream consumption without impacting our ongoing workloads. Broadly speaking, there are two patterns for consuming data: low-volume/high-frequency and high-volume/low-frequency.

> **DEFINITION** *Low-volume/high-frequency* data consumption means consuming small amounts of data (usually one or a few records) at a high frequency. This is common for websites.

An example of this pattern is data for a website (for example, showing a user their order history). While we may have hundreds of thousands of users, a website just needs to retrieve the order history of one of them at a given point in time (when the user wants to view it). This is a low-volume request, but potentially high-frequency. Multiple users can request similar data through the website, so for a high-traffic website, requests could come in quite often.

Another example of this pattern is consuming ML model predictions. As users browse our website, we show them recommendations from our ML model. Again, this is low-volume (predictions for just the current user), but high-frequency (multiple users might be browsing the website at the same time), so many requests can come in a short time span. This type of data consumption is best served by a data API, which we'll discuss in the next section.

The other common type of data consumption is high-volume/low-frequency. This is what we did when we covered data ingestion in chapters 2 and 4.

> **DEFINITION**   *High-volume/low-frequency* data consumption means copying large datasets (GBs or TBs of data) at a low frequency (with a specified time span—daily, weekly, etc.). This is common for downstream data platforms ingesting our data or downstream systems that want to perform additional batch processing.

If another data team wants to consume our data, they would usually perform this type of load. Similarly, if a team wants to reshape the data before using it, they might want to copy it in bulk first. For example, as an alternative to our team maintaining an API that integrates with a customer-facing website, the team specializing in running the website might simply copy our data in bulk, then optimize it for serving web traffic.

This type of data consumption is best served by sharing data using a storage solution that doesn't include compute. We'll cover this in section 11.3. Figure 11.3 shows the two patterns side by side.

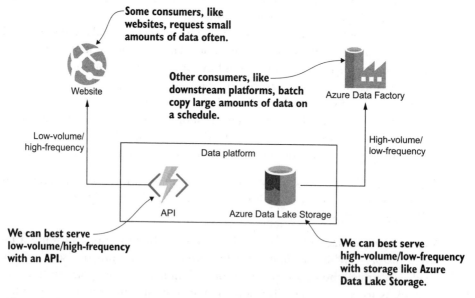

Figure 11.3 For low-volume/high-frequency requests, we can share data via a data API that our downstream can call. For high-volume/low-frequency requests, we can share data by placing it in storage and letting downstream systems pick it up from there.

There are two combinations we didn't cover because they are less common: low-volume/low-frequency and high-volume/high-frequency. Low-volume/low-frequency is not a big concern; this usually means occasionally refreshing a report. This pattern can usually be absorbed by our systems at no great cost. High-volume/high-frequency is in the realm of streaming data, usually in the world of IoT sensors or other live signals.

In this case (high-volume/high-frequency), data would be consumed from the event stream directly, which sits upstream of our data platform. There are rare situations in which we would process a large volume of data in real time and also have to serve it to a downstream system. This requires specialized infrastructure outside the scope of this book. For this type of workload, I recommend looking into Azure Stream Analytics (https://azure.microsoft.com/en-us/services/stream-analytics/) and Azure Event Hubs (https://azure.microsoft.com/en-us/services/event-hubs/). We'll start by looking at the low-volume/high-frequency scenario and talk about data APIs.

11.2 Building a data API

First, let's define data API. By data API, we mean an HTTPS endpoint that clients can call to retrieve data. This can be implemented as an Azure App Service or an Azure Function App. The protocol can be anything: REST, GraphQL, or something else. While not a main topic of this book, see the following sidebar for a quick overview of these protocols.

> ### Web APIs
>
> We mentioned two services we can use to build web APIs, Azure App Service and Azure Function App. We also mentioned two protocols, REST and GraphQL. We'll provide a quick overview of each in turn, starting with the Azure services.
>
> Azure App Service is a fully managed, platform-as-a-service (PaaS) solution for building web applications. It abstracts away the virtual machine (VM) and web server management and allows us to focus on developing the application code. We can use Azure App Service to build websites and web APIs.
>
> Azure Function App is the Azure serverless, compute-on-demand solution. It executes short-running functions (up to a few minutes) on various triggers. A trigger can be a timer, a message in an Azure Service Bus queue, or an HTTP request. Functions are pay per use, and we can use them for any stateless processing. We can also use them to implement a web API. Next, let's describe the two protocols.
>
> Representational state transfer (REST) is the most common protocol for web services to talk to each other. It relies on resource identifiers and HTTP verbs (GET, POST, PUT, DELETE) to read and write resources. For example, the common way to retrieve the data associated with user ID 5 is to issue an HTTP GET request at the URL: `<base URL>/user/5`. This returns a JSON object with the user details.

(continued)

GraphQL is an open source query language and runtime developed by Facebook as an alternative to REST. GraphQL allows clients to specify exactly what data they want to retrieve from the service. This is one of the key advantages compared to REST. When dealing with a lot of data, a REST request for user ID 5 returns all of the user's details, even if the client only needs to know a subset (for example, we only need the name). With GraphQL, we tell the service exactly which fields we need, so we end up moving less data from service to client.

We can use either Azure App Service or an Azure Function App to implement a data API, and we can make the API "speak" either REST or GraphQL, or potentially some other protocol. A discussion on the trade-offs, advantages, and disadvantages of each is outside the scope of this book, but I encourage you to look them up when you need to build an API to serve data.

Using an API between our consumers and our storage layer brings this set of advantages:

- *We can use this middleware to control what data we expose and to whom.* In general, even with a solid security model, if we get too granular, it becomes extremely hard to maintain (for example, having a security group for each table). That's why, in chapter 10, we looked at having security groups per data classification.

  Someone getting access this way has access to multiple datasets in the system, which is desirable in some cases, like a data scientist from another team exploring the data and trying to create a new report. But this might not be desirable in other cases, especially when integrating with other systems. Someone might start to consume datasets that we weren't planning to maintain or that we were planning to modify. An API allows us to add another layer of control and abstraction on top of what we expose.

- *The API abstracts away the storage.* External systems are no longer tightly coupled with our storage layout. We are free to move things around, switch data fabrics, etc.

- *We can get great insights on how the data is used.* If we simply hand off the data in bulk to another system, there is no way to tell how that system uses our data. With an API, on the other hand, we can keep track of how many records are being requested, who requests them, etc. This gives us some good insights into how our data is being leveraged.

- *We can optimize for low-volume/high-frequency.* Because consumers no longer connect directly to our storage layer, we can make things a lot more efficient. We can copy our data to a data fabric better suited for this access pattern and, if needed, throw in a cache to optimize performance.

Let's zoom in on one data fabric better suited for this type of scenario: Azure Cosmos DB.

11.2.1 Introducing Azure Cosmos DB

We looked at a few storage services throughout this book and mentioned many others in passing. Azure Data Explorer (ADX), which we used in our examples, is optimized for quickly ingesting large volumes of data and querying them at impressive speeds.

Azure Synapse Analytics, the evolution of Azure SQL Data Warehouse, brings limitless compute capabilities to query data across data warehouses and data lakes. Azure Databricks is a managed version of Apache Spark, offering hyperscale data processing capabilities. Azure Data Lake Storage provides cheap storage for extremely large datasets.

All these solutions can store and/or process petabytes of data. In fact, these services were all created to support specific big data scenarios. None of these was optimized for serving low-volume/high-frequency requests, though. Processing a billion rows is different from quickly finding and retrieving one record. Enter Azure Cosmos DB. Azure Cosmos DB is a managed NoSQL database service that offers a few key features, making it the best choice for an API backend:

- *It has 99.999% availability.* When processing data within our data platform, we can recover from any glitch by rerunning the failed workflow. This shouldn't have any visible impact. Contrast this with serving data to a customer-facing website. In this case, high availability is critical as any issue would degrade the user experience.
- *Querying a single record is guaranteed (in the 99th percentile) to return within less than 10 milliseconds.* Other storage solutions can't provide this guarantee because they are geared towards processing large volumes of data rather than retrieving individual records.
- *It offers turnkey geo-replication.* We can replicate a Cosmos DB in multiple regions through a configuration change. This becomes important when we have global websites serving traffic from around the globe. In those scenarios, we want data to be replicated in multiple regions and served to users depending on where it is requested from, thus reducing latency by avoiding roundtrips around the globe.

You've probably heard of NoSQL databases, which are non-relational or document databases. Instead of storing data as rows in tables, NoSQL databases store each record as a separate document. Documents are usually stored in a format like JSON, and a common property of NoSQL databases is a lack of schema: different documents might contain different fields within the same dataset.

Let's sketch out a data API backed by Cosmos DB. We'll start by spinning up a Cosmos DB account. Listing 11.1 shows how to do that. Note that the `create` command might take a bit of time to run. You can grab a cup of coffee in the meantime.

> **Listing 11.1 Creating a Cosmos DB account**

```
az group create `
--location "Central US" `
--name cosmosdb-rg
```
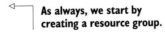
As always, we start by creating a resource group.

```
az cosmosdb create `
--name "cosmosdb$suffix" `
--resource-group cosmosdb-rg
```

Creates a Cosmos DB account

Uses cosmosdb and our unique **$suffix** as the account name

For our examples, we will use a single region, but note that we can enable geo-replication of the database with a single configuration setting. You can explore this in the Azure Portal by navigating to the resource and selecting the Replicate Data Globally blade.

Cosmos DB structures data in a set of databases. Each database contains a set of containers. Each container contains a set of documents. Figure 11.4 shows the hierarchy.

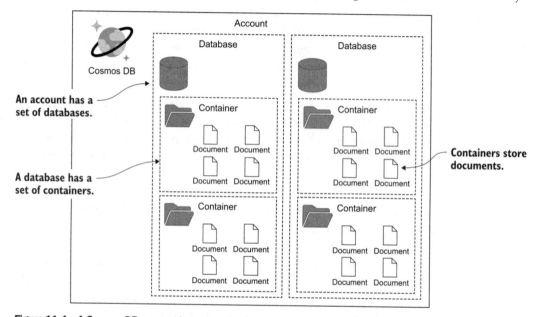

Figure 11.4 A Cosmos DB account has a set of databases. Databases have a set of containers. Each container stores documents.

A database is simply the outer wrapper for our data. A neat feature of Cosmos DB is that it can "speak" multiple languages. We can interact with Cosmos DB using an SQL API (a subset of the T-SQL language), a MongoDB API (Cosmos DB can pretend to be a MongoDB instance), the Apache Gremlin API (used for graph queries), a Cassandra API (Cosmos DB pretending to be an Apache Cassandra instance), and more.

We'll use the SQL API going forward, but note that we have all these other options. We can decide which API we want to use when we create the database. The following listing creates the distribution database.

Listing 11.2 Creating a Cosmos DB database

```
az cosmosdb sql database create `
--name distribution `
```

Creates a new Cosmos DB database using the SQL API

Names the database distribution

```
--account-name "cosmosdb$suffix" `
--resource-group cosmosdb-rg
```
| **Specifies the target Cosmos DB account and resource group**

In the Azure Portal, you can navigate to the Cosmos DB resource and select the Data Explorer blade. This is the portal UI for navigating Cosmos DB, which you can use to create databases, containers, and documents, and to issue queries. We'll stick to Azure CLI in our examples, but I encourage you to use the Data Explorer blade to play with the capabilities.

Next, let's create a container. Besides a name, we must also supply a partition key when we create a container. In order to be able to respond to queries with millisecond latency, Cosmos DB does a lot of work under the hood, including partitioning data in order to easily scale horizontally. That said, Cosmos DB doesn't know what a good partition key is because it is data dependent.

A *partition key* needs to be some field in your data that does not change, has a wide range of possible values, with evenly distributed values. *Evenly distributed* means given all our values, we can split these in any number of groups, and the groups should be of roughly the same size. For example, if we partition users by their unique IDs, then we should have many possible values (each user has a different ID), and we can split all our users into any number of groups that should be roughly similar in size. On the other hand, if we partition users by country, we would have few possible values (only the countries our users are from), and the values might not be evenly distributed (we likely have a lot more users from the U.S. than from Luxembourg, for example).

Let's say we are going to use `UserID` as our partition key. In this case, we will specify it as the `/UserID` document path. The following listing creates the container.

Listing 11.3 Creating a Cosmos DB container

Creates a new CosmosDB container with the SQL API

Names the container (users, in this case)

```
az cosmosdb sql container create `
    --name users `
    --partition-key-path "/UserID" `
    --database-name distribution `
    --account-name "cosmosdb$suffix" `
    --resource-group cosmosdb-rg
```

Sets the partition key path in the document

Targets the resource group, account, and database

If you refresh the Data Explorer, you should now see the new users container under the distribution database. We're all set. We now have a Cosmos DB account, a database, and a container. We can populate this container with documents as long as they contain a `UserID` field, and then we can retrieve them in milliseconds.

With our storage set up, let's see how we can use Azure Data Factory to copy a dataset from Azure Data Explorer to Cosmos DB. In our data platform, we ingest data into Azure Data Explorer (our single source of truth), which we use for our internal processing. We then copy data we want to distribute via the API to Cosmos DB.

In general, your data platform might ingest data in any of the storage solutions optimized for big data ingestion and processing. For serving, you might want to copy this data to a serving-optimized storage.

11.2.2 *Populating the Cosmos DB collection*

We can use Azure Data Factory to copy data from any other Azure Data Factory–compatible service to Cosmos DB. We won't go through all the steps again in this chapter because we already covered ETL in depth in chapter 4. If you want, you can do this as an exercise.

As a reminder, building a data ingestion pipeline in Azure Data Factory consists of the following items. Figure 11.5 shows the pieces involved.

- *A source linked service*—Tells Azure Data Factory how to connect to the source service. In chapter 4, we created the bingcovid19 linked service to connect to the Bing COVID-19 open dataset and the adx linked service to connect to our Azure Data Explorer cluster. We can reuse the adx linked service for the source in this example.
- *A source dataset*—Uses, for example, a table in Azure Data Explorer.
- *A sink linked service*—Tells Azure Data Factory how to connect to the destination service. We can easily create a Cosmos DB using an SQL API linked service in Azure Data Factory, like we set up all our other linked services.
- *A sink dataset*—Tells Azure Data Factory where to move the data. In the Cosmos DB case, this would be our users container.
- *A pipeline with a copy activity*—Connects the source with the sink.
- *A trigger*—Kicks off the pipeline on a regular schedule.

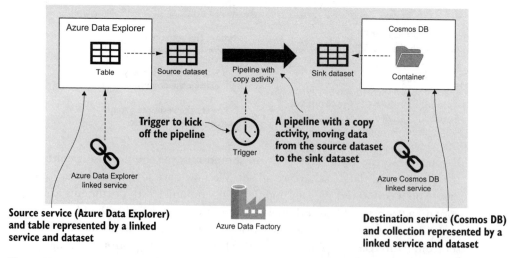

Figure 11.5   A source Azure Data Explorer service and source table are represented in Azure Data Factory by a linked service and a dataset. The Cosmos DB account and destination collection are represented by another linked service and dataset. A pipeline with a copy activity copies data from the source dataset to the sink (destination) dataset. A trigger determines when the pipeline will run.

Because we won't be creating an ETL pipeline to move the data, we'll just create a couple of documents directly in Cosmos DB instead. We'll use the documents through the rest of this section. Remember that in a real-world scenario, we would ingest the data from one of our other storage solutions by using an Azure Data Factory pipeline.

We'll create two dummy JSON documents containing a `UserID` and a couple of other fields: `Name` and `BillingAddress`. The following listings (listings 11.4 and 11.5) show the two files.

Listing 11.4 user1.json

```json
{
    "UserID": 10000,
    "Name": "Ava Smith",
    "BillingAddress": "..."
}
```

We keep the two JSON files separate. This is because each represents a different Cosmos DB document.

Listing 11.5 user2.json

```json
{
    "UserID": 10001,
    "Name": "Oliver Miller",
    "BillingAddress": "..."
}
```

To upload our dummy data directly to Cosmos DB, let's go to the Cosmos DB resource in the Azure Portal and open the Data Explorer blade. Navigate to the database and collection as shown in figure 11.6, then click Upload Item.

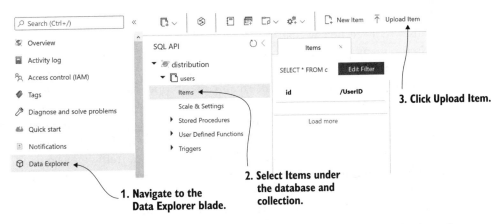

Figure 11.6 In the Azure Portal, navigate to Data Explorer. Select the distribution database, the users collection, and choose Items. Next, click Upload Item. This uploads our dummy data to the Cosmos DB.

Select both JSON files (Upload allows selecting multiple files). These should be added to the collection. If you refresh the view, you should see the two new items. Figure 11.7 shows one of the documents viewed in Data Explorer.

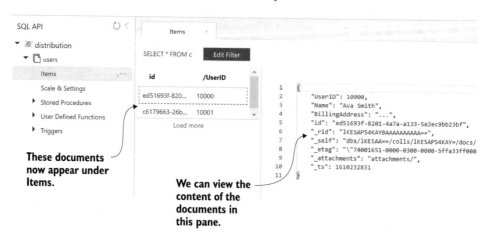

Figure 11.7   The uploaded documents show up under Items. We can view the content of any document in the collection in Azure Data Explorer.

You will notice that when the files are uploaded, Cosmos DB automatically adds a few more fields to the document that we didn't have in our JSON files. The id is a unique ID (GUID) that Cosmos DB generates for the document. The remaining fields, all prefixed with an underscore (_) represent various properties used by the Cosmos DB engine. We now have a Cosmos DB account provisioned and populated with some data, so let's quickly see how we can build a REST API over it.

11.2.3   Retrieving data

Building REST APIs is not a main focus of this book, so we won't go too deep into the details. We'll see how we can query our collection using Python. Microsoft provides SDKs for many popular programming languages (including C#, Java, Python, and JavaScript) to connect to Cosmos DB. We'll write a small script to query Cosmos DB and retrieve a user's details. This small code snippet can be embedded in an Azure Function App or Azure App Service to expose an API that clients can connect to.

We won't cover Function App or App Service development because we wouldn't do justice to the topic in a few pages. Building a robust web API includes DevOps, telemetry (using App Insights), concerns like geo-replication, traffic management, authentication, and so on. There are many resources that cover these in depth. Let's instead focus on querying Cosmos DB from Python. First, we need to install the azure-cosmos Python package. The following listing shows the command.

Listing 11.6   Installing the azure-cosmos Python package

```
pip install azure-cosmos
```

Next, we need to make note of our Cosmos DB endpoint and access key. The endpoint is the URL where clients connect to the account. The access key is a secret key. This ensures only clients who know the key can issue queries. We'll retrieve both in the next listing.

Listing 11.7   Retrieving the endpoint and access key

```
$acc = az cosmosdb show --name "cosmosdb$suffix" `     ⟵  Retrieves the Cosmos DB
    --resource-group cosmosdb-rg | ConvertFrom-Json       account details and stores
                                                          them in $acc

$keys = az cosmosdb keys list --name "cosmosdb$suffix" `
    --resource-group cosmosdb-rg | ConvertFrom-Json  ⟵  Retrieves the access keys
                                                         and stores them in $keys

echo $acc.documentEndpoint               ⟵
echo $keys.primaryReadonlyMasterKey          Prints the endpoint, a URL
```

**Prints an access key, a long string of
letters and digits, ending with ==**

Make a note of the endpoint URL and access key, as we'll put these in our script. The following listing shows the Python script we'll use to query Cosmos DB.

Listing 11.8   Querying Cosmos DB from Python

Gets a collection client from the database client

```
from azure.cosmos import CosmosClient    Updates the endpoint with the two
from sys import argv                     values retrieved from listing 11.7

                                                 Creates a Cosmos DB client
endpoint = "<your endpoint URL>"                 using the endpoint and key
key = "<your access key>"
                                                       Gets a database client from
client = CosmosClient(endpoint, key)       ⟵         the Cosmos DB client
database = client.get_database_client("distribution")  ⟵
container = database.get_container_client("users")

                                      Retrieves the Name field of the given UserID,
query = f"SELECT c.Name FROM c WHERE   passed as a command-line argument
  c.UserID = {argv[1]}"           ⟵
                                          For each item in the result
for item in container.query_items(query):  ⟵  (should be one or zero)...
    print(item["Name"])   ⟵
                                  ... prints the name.
```

You can now run queries from the command line. You should see the name of the users stored in the collection. Running `python query.py 10000` prints Ava Smith, and running `python query.py 10001` prints Oliver Miller, the two users in our database. We'll stop here with a couple of notes on security and scaling out.

To keep things simple, we wrote a small Python script. Bringing this script to production, we would not store the secret key in the source code, of course. We would store it in a Key Vault and retrieve it from there at run time. Remember, never store secrets in code (especially as we are implementing good DevOps practices and storing all code in source control). Accidentally pushing secrets to Git is a good way to leak them. In general, few people should have access to these secrets, whereas more people (sometimes, if developing on GitHub, the whole world) would have access to the source code.

On scaling out, as mentioned, we could wrap this function into an Azure Function App or Azure App Service to provide a web API clients can call, passing in the user ID and retrieving the associated data, for example. App Services and Function Apps can be scaled out, deployed in multiple regions, etc. We would then store everything in Git and use Azure Pipelines to deploy the services. We would also add telemetry with Azure App Insights and alerts, if anything goes wrong with Azure Monitor.

As you can see, there is a lot of additional work to do for building a web API at scale. Unfortunately, we don't have space to cover all of it here, but figure 11.8 shows how a final product would look.

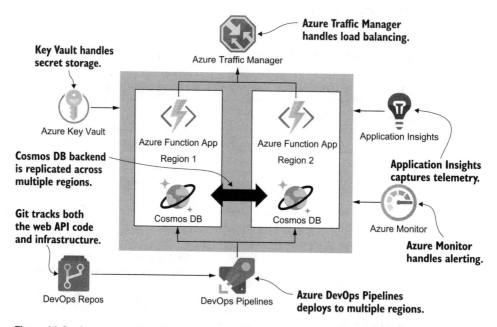

Figure 11.8   A more complete picture of the services involved in a web API. Code and infrastructure is stored in Git and deployed to multiple regions using Azure DevOps Pipelines. A Cosmos DB backend replicated across multiple regions is queried by Azure Function Apps. Azure Key Vault stores the secrets involved, Application Insights is used for telemetry, and Azure Monitor provides alerts. Azure Traffic Manager directs traffic to the multiple regions.

Let's do a quick recap. We went over a lot of material in this section.

11.2.4 Data API recap

We have scenarios in which our data is consumed in low-volume/high-frequency (many requests reading small bits of data). A common scenario for this pattern is when serving data to a website or some other service. We can use a data API for these scenarios. Data APIs allow us to add another layer of control, abstract away storage, add caching if needed, and get insights into who is consuming our data. All this goodness comes at the cost of us having to maintain a web service.

Cosmos DB is a document database service optimized to serve as a backend for an API. Some of its key features include guaranteed uptime, low-latency for queries, and turnkey geo-replication. With a simple configuration change, data gets replicated in different regions to support APIs deployed around the globe.

A Cosmos DB account has a set of databases. A database has a set of containers. Containers store documents. Cosmos DB can use multiple query languages to access data, including a subset of SQL, MongoDB and Cassandra APIs, Apache Gremlin (a graph query language), and Azure Table API.

We can use Azure Data Factory to transfer data from our other data fabrics to Cosmos DB and serve it from there. We can also use the Cosmos DB SDK to query data from code. For this, we looked at a Python sample script. The Cosmos DB SDK is also available for multiple languages, including Python, C#, Java, and JavaScript. Before moving on to the high-volume/low-frequency data distribution pattern, a brief note on serving ML models.

11.3 Serving machine learning

We won't cover this in depth here, but do note that Azure Machine Learning provides a built-in capability to package a trained model into a Docker container and to deploy it as a web service endpoint (see http://mng.bz/Jvlz). For this specialized scenario, we have a trained model that we want to expose as an API that can perform inference. We can leverage this feature of Azure Machine Learning instead of standing up a web API from scratch.

We won't go through all the steps, but remember this option if your team ends up needing to stand up an API for serving ML. Instead of zooming in on this specialized scenario, we'll switch to our other major data distribution pattern: high-volume/low-frequency, which means bulk copy of large datasets.

11.4 Sharing data for bulk copy

In section 11.2, we looked at Cosmos DB, a storage service optimized for serving individual documents with minimum latency. This works great when our data ends up backing a website or feeds into some other service that consumes it item by item. There is another set of scenarios in which a downstream team or service wants to consume whole datasets from us. This could be another data science team that wants to bring our data to their platform or it could be a team that wants to do some additional processing and reshape our data before using it for their scenario.

While we can, of course, create an API to serve data in bulk, this is not optimal once we reach a certain scale. In these cases, we don't need to optimize for low latency, rather, we need high throughput. Another key factor, which we alluded to before, is that we don't want to share compute resources with the downstream team. Let's expand on that.

11.4.1 *Separating compute resources*

We talked about network, storage, and compute all the way back in chapter 1. This is a common way to categorize cloud services based on their function. Storage is all about data at rest, maintaining data in various formats. Compute is all about processing data and performing calculations.

Some services we looked at, like Azure Data Lake Storage, are purely storage. Some are purely compute. For example, Azure Databricks and Azure Machine Learning can connect to storage services but don't store data, rather, these provide capabilities to process data. Others have a combination of storage and compute, like most database engines. Azure SQL, Cosmos DB, and Azure Data Explorer are examples of this. They both store data within the service and provide processing capabilities (we can run queries, joins, etc. over the stored data).

From the perspective of sharing data with other teams, pure storage solutions are the easiest. If we have a big dataset in Azure Data Lake Storage, we can grant permissions to the downstream principals to read the data, and we're done. But things get a bit more complicated for services that include compute.

Let's take Azure Data Explorer as an example. As we saw in chapter 2, Azure Data Explorer is deployed on a set of VMs, the cluster's SKU. We can specify the size of the VM that we want and the number of nodes. We don't have to deal with VM management; Azure Data Explorer handles this for us. Notice, however, there is a set of compute resources we need to deal with.

If we simply grant access to other teams to our cluster, when their automation tries to retrieve a large dataset, it can impact other queries running on the cluster. There is a limit on how much CPU and how much bandwidth to move data we have available. An expensive query can eat up enough resources on the cluster to make everyone else's queries run slow or time out. That's why we don't want to share data directly from these types of services.

> **NOTE**   If our data service includes both storage and compute, and if we need to share data, we must ensure not to also share compute.

We have two ways to achieve this. One is to simply copy the data to a better-suited storage solution. For example, we can copy the data from Azure Data Explorer to a data lake. Of course, this copy can also impact other processing running on the cluster, but now this is fully in our team's control. We can guarantee this copy happens at a time when the cluster isn't under heavy load, and we can ensure that we don't do it more often than necessary.

Another way to ensure that we don't share compute resources is to use a replica. Most database engines support this in one form or another. A *replica* is a copy of the data, but copying and ensuring consistency is handled by the database engine itself. This is highly optimized because the database engine knows how to best create this. Instead of us having to create an Azure Data Factory pipeline, we can simply configure our database to provision a replica. Let's see how this works in Azure Data Explorer.

FOLLOWER DATABASES IN AZURE DATA EXPLORER

Azure Data Explorer allows a cluster to follow databases from other clusters. A follower database is a read-only replica of the leader database. Data gets replicated automatically, with low latency. Figure 11.9 shows a cluster following a database from another cluster.

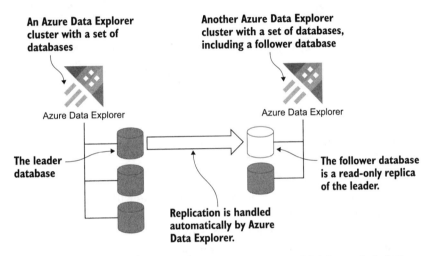

Figure 11.9 An Azure Data Explorer cluster contains a set of databases, including a leader database. Another cluster contains another set of databases, including a follower database, which is a read-only replica of the leader database. Replication is handled automatically.

Because the follower database is read-only, the policies applied on the leader can't be modified. There are a few exceptions, however:

- *Caching policy*—In Azure Data Explorer, the caching policy on a table tells the engine how many days back it should keep the data in the cache. This makes queries within that time range more efficient but requires higher-end SKU VMs, which is more expensive. We can tweak this on the follower database in case the queries have different requirements than the ones on the leader.
- *Permissions*—We can grant access to additional users, apps, and groups on the follower. This makes it possible to allow someone to query the follower but not have access to the leader.

A cluster can follow databases from any number of other clusters. Clusters can even follow (different) databases from each other, as figure 11.10 illustrates.

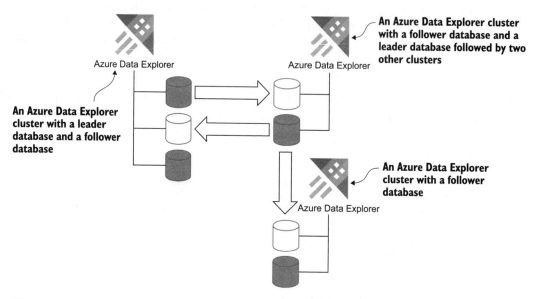

Figure 11.10   A more complex leader/follower setup involving three clusters. Clusters can follow each other's databases, and the same database can be followed by multiple clusters.

The one limitation with this setup is that both the cluster that has the leader database and the cluster following that database must be in the same region. There is no way to follow a database from a different region. Contrast this with Cosmos DB, which was purposefully built to support multiregion endpoints.

Using a leader/follower setup, we can isolate workloads on a dedicated compute: both the leader and each follower cluster have their own compute, which we can scale up and down independently. An expensive query running on a follower database has no way of impacting other queries running on the leader or another follower.

The same principle applies for SQL replicas and, in general, for any storage solution that supports replicas. We can use this feature to design our system in such a way that workloads can't interfere with one another. Normally, we would go through the steps of setting up a follower database, and this is something we could do with Azure CLI, but Azure provides a better way to share data that handles the follower setup for us—Azure Data Share.

11.4.2 *Introducing Azure Data Share*

Azure Data Share is an Azure service dedicated to sharing data for bulk consumption. It works with all Azure data fabrics and, depending on the data fabric, allows two ways to share data:

- *Copy based*—Takes a snapshot of the source data and copies it to the destination account.
- *In place*—Provisions a read-only replica. This is the sharing scenario for Azure Data Explorer, where Azure Data Share sets up the follower automatically.

Azure Data Share allows sharing data across tenants, so sharing isn't limited to your organization. You can share data with other companies. Azure Data Share also handles configuring permissions and even includes terms of use we can configure for consumers to agree to before receiving the data. In this section, we'll look at how we can share our telemetry database using Azure Data Share. First, let's go over the anatomy of Azure Data Share. Figure 11.11 shows the different concepts.

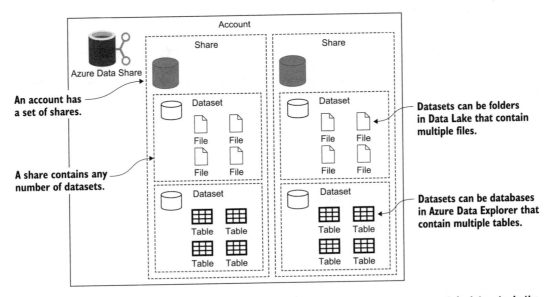

Figure 11.11 Anatomy of Azure Data Share. An account contains a set of shares. Shares contain datasets. In the case of Azure Data Lake Storage, a dataset corresponds to a folder containing multiple files. In the case of Azure Data Explorer, a dataset corresponds to a database containing multiple tables. Azure Data Share also supports Azure Blob Storage, Azure Synapse Analytics, and Azure SQL.

An instance of the service is called an *account*. An Azure Data Share account contains any number of sent shares and received shares. A *share* is the unit of sharing data. This is where we specify the terms of use (if any) and invite others to get the data.

A share consists of one or more datasets. Datasets are databases, folders in Azure Data Lake, etc. Note that Azure Data Share uses a slightly different definition of dataset than Azure Data Factory. We used the Azure Data Factory definition throughout the book and considered a dataset to be, in the Azure Data Explorer case, a table. In Azure Data Share, for Azure Data Explorer, a dataset is the entire database.

We email an invitation for a share to other users. The email receivers get a link through which they can pick the destination Azure Data Share and other required services. For example, if sharing an Azure Data Explorer database, the receiver has to provide an Azure Data Explorer cluster in the same region on which the database can be followed. Figure 11.12 shows the workflow.

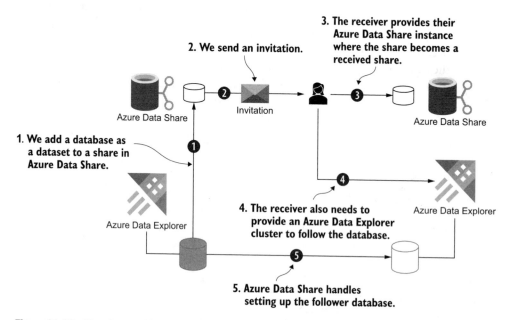

3. The receiver provides their Azure Data Share instance where the share becomes a received share.

2. We send an invitation.

Azure Data Share

Invitation

Azure Data Share

1. We add a database as a dataset to a share in Azure Data Share.

Azure Data Explorer

4. The receiver also needs to provide an Azure Data Explorer cluster to follow the database.

Azure Data Explorer

5. Azure Data Share handles setting up the follower database.

Figure 11.12   Step 1: we add a database as a dataset to a share in Azure Data Share. Step 2: we send an invitation for the share. Step 3: the receiver of the invitation selects an Azure Data Share account to receive the share. Step 4: the receiver of the invitation also needs to supply an Azure Data Explorer cluster to receive the dataset. Step 5: Azure Data Share handles the leader/follower setup under the hood.

Now that we covered the concepts, let's go ahead and invite someone to a share of our telemetry database. We'll provision an Azure Data Share and send an invitation. First, we need to register the Data Share provider with our Azure subscription.

At the time of writing, this is not enabled by default, so we won't be able to provision a data share without this. We also need to install the Azure Data Share Azure CLI extension. The following listing shows how to do this.

Listing 11.9   Registering the Data Share provider and installing the Azure CLI extension

```
az provider register --namespace Microsoft.DataShare
```
◁── Registers the Data Share provider with our subscription so we can create data shares

```
az extension add --name datashare
```
◁── Installs the Azure CLI extension

Registering the provider might take a few minutes. We need to wait for this to complete before we can proceed with creating our Azure Data Share account. To create an account, we will, as always, create a new resource group, then provision the resource. Listing 11.10 creates the Azure Data Share account.

At the time of writing, Azure Data Share is not available in Central US, the region where we deployed all our other resources, so we'll create this in the West US 2 region. This is common for new Azure services: they begin as a preview with limited region availability and eventually graduate to general availability.

Listing 11.10 Creating an Azure Data Share account

```
az group create `
--name datashare-rg `          Creates the datashare-rg resource
--location "West US 2"         group in the West US 2 region

az datashare account create `  ◁─── Creates an Azure Data Share account
--name "datashare$suffix" `    ◁─┐
--resource-group datashare-rg     We need a globally unique name, so we
                                  use the $suffix variable in the name.
```

You can navigate to the resource in the Azure Portal and explore the capabilities offered. As always, we can set up the share using the UI, but we'll stick to Azure CLI to see how this can be automated. Currently we don't have any incoming or outgoing shares. The next step is to create a share for our database. We'll call it share, and we'll set it up as an in-place share. The following listing shows the steps.

Listing 11.11 Creating a share

```
az datashare create `     ◁─── Creates a new share
--name share `
--description distribution `      Names and describes the share
--share-kind InPlace `
--account-name "datashare$suffix" `   Supplies the account and resource
--resource-group datashare-rg         group containing the share

kind can be InPlace or CopyBased.
```

You should be able to see the share in Azure Portal under the Sent Shares blade. Of course, we aren't sharing anything yet. Next, we'll share our telemetry database. First, we need to retrieve the resource ID of the database as the following listing shows.

Listing 11.12 Retrieving the resource ID of the telemetry database

```
$telemetry = az kusto database show `
--cluster-name "adx$suffix" `          Stores the details of the
--database-name telemetry `            telemetry database from our
--resource-group adx-rg | ConvertFrom-Json   ADX cluster in $telemetry

echo $telemetry.id      ◁─── Prints the resource ID to the console
```

The last line, `echo $telemetry.id`, prints the resource ID to the console. Make a note of it, as we'll use it later.

Azure Data Share handles setting up permissions for us, so when the share receivers set up the destination on their side, they will automatically get permissions to read the data. In order for Azure Data Share to do that, though, it needs permissions on the shared resources. Remember, the way the Azure security model works, if Azure Data Share doesn't have permissions on our telemetry database, it can't grant access to others either.

We'll need to retrieve the service principal ID of our Azure Data Share instance. We'll then grant it Contributor rights on the Azure Data Explorer database as the following listing shows.

Listing 11.13   Granting Contributor rights to the Data Share account

```
$datashare = az datashare account show `
--name "datashare$suffix" `
--resource-group datashare-rg | ConvertFrom-Json       <─── Stores the details of the
                                                              Azure Data Share account
                                                              in $datashare

az role assignment create `                  <─── Creates a new permission assignment
--assignee $datashare.identity.principalId `  <───
--role Contributor `                                  Grants permission to the Data Share
--scope $telemetry.id  <───                           account by providing its principal ID
                            Sets the permission scope
Grants Contributor permissions   to the telemetry database
```

Now Azure Data Share can set up a follower database to share the data. Let's go ahead and create the dataset corresponding to the telemetry database in our share. Because datasets are defined as JSON objects, we'll create a telemetrydataset.json file as in the following listing. Here is where we need to use the database resource ID we retrieved in listing 11.12.

Listing 11.14   Contents of telemetrydataset.json

```
{
    "kind": "KustoDatabase",       <─── Shares an Azure Data Explorer database
    "properties": {
        "kustoDatabaseResourceId":      Replace with the resource ID
"<value of $telemetry.id>"  <───        we retrieved in listing 11.12.
    }
}
```

We'll create a dataset named telemetry based on the telemetrydataset.json file. The following listing shows the command.

Listing 11.15   Creating a dataset inside a share

```
az datashare dataset create `   <─── Creates a new dataset
--name telemetry `
                                <───  Defines the dataset name, telemetry
```

```
      ┌─▷   --dataset telemetrydataset.json `
      │     --share-name share `
      │     --account-name "datashare$suffix" `
      │     --resource-group datashare-rg
```
> **The share, account, and resource group containing the dataset.**

JSON describing the dataset; we use the telemetrydataset.json file.

In the Azure Portal, you should now be able to see the dataset if you navigate to the share. The final step is to send an invitation. You can use the email address associated with your Azure account, so you can receive the invitation and see how it looks. The next listing sends a data sharing invitation.

Listing 11.16 Creating an invitation

Creates an invitation | **Names the invitation "invitation"**

```
      ┌─▷  az datashare invitation create `
      │      --name invitation `                          ◁─────
      │      --target-email "<use your email address>" `  ◁─────
      │      --share-name share `
      │      --account-name "datashare$suffix" `
      │      --resource-group datashare-rg
```

> **Uses the email associated with your Azure account**

> **The share, account, and resource group containing the dataset**

You should receive an email inviting you to share data. If you click the link, you'll end up in the Azure Portal UI, where you will be asked to pick the Azure Data Share account to receive the share. We won't cover all the steps to receive the share because they are self-explanatory. We'll also need to set up additional infrastructure if we are to accept the share because we need to provide another Azure Data Explorer cluster where we can attach this database.

Azure Data Share is a great solution for sharing data as it uses the same concepts (shares, datasets, invitations) regardless of the data fabric on which our data resides. It also makes it easy to see in a centralized place exactly what data we're sharing and with whom. Using Azure Data Share is better than implementing data fabric–specific sharing. Let's do a quick recap of our high-volume/low-frequency data sharing.

11.4.3 Sharing data for bulk copy recap

When we share data for bulk copy, an API is not the best option. Rather, we want to serve it from a service optimized around reading large amounts of data. While we could share our data platform storage directly, this is not always optimal. It works for storage services that don't involve compute, like Azure Blob Storage and Azure Data Lake Storage, where we can grant permissions to other teams to read the data.

If we do the same thing for storage solutions that include compute, like Azure SQL or Azure Data Explorer, we run the risk of external queries (queries outside of our control) interfering with the workloads running on our platform. To avoid this, we need to offload external queries to replicas. For example, Azure Data Explorer supports follower databases. These are read-only replicas of a database queried on another cluster's compute.

Sharing data includes granting permissions, provisioning resources for the receiver, etc. Azure Data Share is an Azure service that specializes in sharing data regardless of the data fabric. An Azure Data Share account can send and receive shares, both in place or as a snapshot copy (depending on the data fabric). Shares consist of one or more datasets.

11.5   *Data sharing best practices*

Before wrapping up, let's cover a few best practices to keep in mind beyond the low-volume/high-frequency and high-volume/low-frequency patterns we covered throughout this chapter. There is one important trade-off to keep in mind, which we haven't discussed so far: network costs.

Besides storage and compute, network is another important piece of the cloud infrastructure and is not free. Moving large volumes of data through our platform incurs costs in terms of network bandwidth. Keep this in mind when creating a new ETL pipeline as an additional datapoint to evaluate your architecture.

It is great to have a dataset in multiple data fabrics, each optimized for a particular workload, but copying that dataset around is not free. Don't think of this as going against what we just covered in this chapter, rather, that this is an opposing force that creates tension in our system; something we shouldn't completely ignore.

> **NOTE**   Don't ignore the cost of copying data. This creates tension with repli-cating a dataset across different data fabrics to optimize for different workloads.

Another best practice to keep in mind is to not provide pass-through data. What we mean by this is that our data platform ingests datasets from upstream. If a dataset is available upstream, we shouldn't share it ourselves with a downstream team. We would rather point them to the source. If we don't enhance the data in any way, our data platform simply becomes an extra hop, a potential source of failure, and introduces latency. We end up supporting an additional scenario with no real added value. For these situations, when there is a data request, redirect it to the upstream team that provides the same dataset to our platform.

> **NOTE**   Don't share pass-through data. If a dataset is available upstream and we ingest it into our platform, redirect requests for the dataset upstream to the source.

Finally, we have scenarios where a downstream team doesn't want to yet commit to consume data from our platform, but they would still like access to it. For example, they might want to create a prototype before committing to supporting a production ETL pipeline, or they might want to simply create a couple of Power BI reports for which it is not worth copying large datasets around.

For these situations, we can still isolate the compute to protect the core workloads of our data platform. We can create a replica just as if we were sharing the data with another team, but we can manage the replica and grant access to it to multiple other teams. Figure 11.13 shows the setup for Azure Data Explorer.

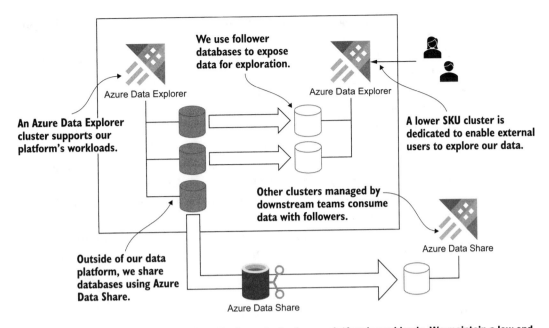

Figure 11.13 We have a main Azure Data Explorer cluster for our platform's workloads. We maintain a low-end cluster for data exploration. This protects our workloads from external queries. Other teams can explore our datasets in the low-end cluster for non-production scenarios. For production scenarios, other teams bring their own cluster to which we can attach databases using Azure Data Share.

In this case, we maintain the cluster dedicated to exploration, but we can scope this to a low-end, cheap SKU because it isn't meant to support business-critical processes. If a team connecting to it realizes they need more compute or if they support a production scenario, we can transition them off this replica and to a data share.

> **NOTE** A low-end SKU replica for exploration protects our compute workloads and provides a stepping stone toward a data share scenario.

These best practices should help optimize the cost of distributing data and avoid unnecessary data movement. And this brings us to the end of the book. I hope you enjoyed the journey and learned something new. We covered all major aspects of a big data platform built on the Azure cloud, including infrastructure, common workloads, and governance. We explored a variety of services, techniques, processes, and patterns that I hope you find useful and that you can apply to your problem space. Thank you for reading!

Summary

- Distributing data is a data engineering challenge for a big data platform.
- We need to ensure that the compute workloads of our data platforms aren't impacted by downstream data copy.

- For low-volume/high-frequency data requests, we can use a data API to share data.
- Cosmos DB is a document database storage solution optimized to serve as an API backend.
- Azure Machine Learning has built-in capabilities to package models into Docker containers and expose these as APIs.
- For bulk data copy, we can either share data from storage accounts (no compute) or provision database replicas.
- Azure Data Share is an Azure service specializing in sharing data that uses common concepts (share, dataset, invitation) regardless of the data fabric.
- Always keep in mind the cost of copying data and avoid pass-through sharing (data that is also available upstream).
- A low-end replica is a good way to enable other teams to explore the datasets available in your data platform without impacting other workloads and with a small additional cost.

appendix A
Azure services

This appendix provides a short description of some popular Azure data services you might encounter as components of a data platform. The list is by no means exhaustive.

AZURE STORAGE
Azure Storage services are the foundational Azure data stores. They come in several flavors: Azure Files that are fully managed file shares, Azure Disk for VM disk storage, Azure Blob for unstructured object data storage, and more. Azure Data Lake Storage (Gen2) builds on top of Azure Blob and adds a hierarchical file system and file-level security. None of these services offers any compute; they are purely storage. You will need other services to process data. That said, Azure Storage provides cost-effective, hyperscale storage.

AZURE SQL
Azure SQL is a managed cloud database. It comes in several flavors: SQL Server on Azure VM helps migrate on-premises Microsoft SQL Server workloads to the cloud; Azure SQL Managed Instance is a cloud-based managed version of Microsoft SQL Server; Azure SQL Database is a serverless version of an SQL database. Depending on how much on-premises legacy your enterprise has, you can ease your way into the cloud with one of the managed SQL Server offerings or start with a cloud-native serverless database. Azure SQL provides all the familiar benefits of a relational database. Azure offers cloud-based versions of other popular database engines: Azure Database for PostgreSQL, Azure Database for MySQL, and Azure Database for MariaDB.

AZURE SYNAPSE ANALYTICS
Azure Synapse Analytics is the evolution of Azure SQL Data Warehouse. The technology aims to handle a higher volume of data than traditional SQL databases and decouples storage from compute so they can scale independently. Compute scales

elastically so more CPU becomes available as needed. Azure Synapse Analytics provides a unified experience across different data fabrics (SQL, Azure Data Lake Storage, streaming data, etc.) and analytics runtimes (SQL and Apache Spark), making it easy to integrate and query various datasets across an enterprise.

AZURE DATA EXPLORER

Azure Data Explorer is a big data analytics and exploration service. It is optimized to quickly ingest and index large amounts of data and queries this data with low latency. A common use case for Azure Data Explorer is log and telemetry analytics at web scale. In general, it is a great platform for ad hoc data exploration because it automatically indexes all ingested data. Azure Data Explorer is meant to be used as an append-only service; data can be added but not updated, and deletions are not granular (we cannot delete individual rows). Azure Data Explorer comes with its own query language called KQL (Kusto Query Language).

AZURE DATABRICKS

Azure Databricks provides an Azure-managed version of Apache Spark, the open source big data processing framework. Azure Databricks can quickly spin up and deprovision Apache Spark clusters and supports processing implemented in Python, Scala, R, Java, and SQL. This service is a great option for standing up or moving a solution based on the Apache ecosystem into the Azure cloud.

AZURE COSMOS DB

Azure Cosmos DB is a managed NoSQL database for Azure. It exposes multiple APIs to clients (either SQL, Apache Gremlin, MongoDB, or Cassandra), making it easy to swap other NoSQL databases with it when moving to the Azure cloud. It also provides turnkey geo-replication and response time guarantees measured in milliseconds. This makes it an ideal option for a backend storage solution for a web API.

appendix B
KQL quick reference

Common query reference

The following table shows some common queries running against the PageViews table we created in chapter 2. The PageViews table has three columns: UserId, Page, and Timestamp.

Table B.1   Common queries

Query	Description
`PageViews`	Returns all rows from the PageViews table.
`PageViews` `| take 5`	Returns five rows from the PageViews table. `take` is useful for limiting the size of the output of a query.

`PageViews`
`| where UserId == 12345 or`
`UserId == 10001`
	Returns all rows where `UserId` is either `12345` or `10001`. `where` filters the data. Filters can be combined using logical operators (like `or` in this example).

`PageViews` `| where Timestamp >= ago(1d)`	Returns all rows with a timestamp newer than 1 day ago. Azure Data Explorer is optimized for time series analysis. `ago()` subtracts the given amount of time from the current time.

`PageViews`
`| where Timestamp >= ago(1d)`
`| project Url=Page, Timestamp`
	Returns the Page column as `Url` and the Timestamp column. `project` restricts the number of columns returned and, optionally, renames them.

`PageViews`
`| where Timestamp >= ago(1d)`
`| project-away UserId`
	Returns rows without the UserId column. `project-away` discards columns from the query result.

`PageViews`
`| where Timestamp >= ago(1d)`
`| summarize count() by UserId`
	Returns page view count by `UserId`. `summarize` aggregates data. `count()` is one of the possible aggregation functions; other examples are `min()`, `max()`, `sum()`, `avg()`, and `stdev()`.

Table B.1   Common queries *(continued)*

Query	Description

`PageViews`
`| where Timestamp >= ago(1d)`
`| join kind=inner`
➥ `UserProfiles on UserId`
`| project Page, Name`
	Joins the PageViews table with the User Profiles table on the User ID column, using an inner join. Other join types are `innerunique`, `leftouter`, `rightouter`, `fullouter`, `leftanti`, `rightanti`, `leftsemi`, and `rightsemi`.

Checkout Microsoft's online documentation at http://mng.bz/w0PB for a comprehensive reference.

SQL to KQL

Azure Data Explorer uses KQL as its main query language, but it also supports a subset of SQL. If you are more familiar with the traditional SQL syntax, you can leverage this knowledge in two ways. First, you can write a SQL query against Azure Data Explorer. While KQL is the preferred query language, Azure Data Explorer supports a subset of SQL. For example, you can use

```
SELECT * FROM PageViews WHERE UserId = 12345
```

instead of the KQL equivalent:

```
PageViews | where UserId == 12345
```

Second, use `EXPLAIN` to have Azure Data Explorer translate an SQL query to a KQL query. For example, running

```
EXPLAIN SELECT * FROM PageViews WHERE UserId = 12345
```

outputs the KQL translation of the query:

```
PageViews | where (UserId == int(12345)) | project UserId, Page, Timestamp
```

> **NOTE**   `EXPLAIN` is especially useful if you are familiar with SQL because you can use it as a translation tool.

appendix C
Running code samples

The cloud evolves at an extremely fast pace. This book contains many code samples that were reviewed and tested at the time of writing. In case you encounter any issues running the code samples, one of several things might have happened: an error snuck through the rigorous review process, or the command syntax changed after the book went to print. Also, most of the code examples leverage Azure CLI, including extensions that are, at the time of writing, experimental and subject to change.

If you encounter an issue with any of the code samples, first check the book's GitHub repository at https://github.com/vladris/azure-data-engineering for the latest code sample. For Azure CLI, check the following in case you encounter an error:

- If the command includes `$suffix`, ensure you have this set up in your environment. If `echo $suffix` doesn't print anything, make sure to update your PowerShell profile as described in chapter 1.
- Make sure you have the extension installed. For example, all Azure Data Explorer samples require the Kusto Azure CLI extension installed in listing 2.1 with `az extension add -n kusto`. Check that you didn't skip an extension installation step.
- As mentioned, some extensions are experimental, and their syntax might change after the book goes to print. All Azure CLI commands accept a `--help` flag. Run with `--help` to see the latest syntax and adjust if needed.

Finally, we use the command line as much as possible, but remember we can also achieve everything through the UI, be it the Azure Portal UI, the Azure Data Factory UI, or the UI of some other service. That's another option in case you can't get a command to work.

index

RELATED MANNING TITLES

Azure Storage, Streaming, and Batch Analytics
by Richard L. Nuckolls

ISBN 9781617296307
448 pages, $49.99
October 2020

Designing Cloud Data Platforms
by Danil Zburivsky and Lynda Partner

ISBN 9781617296444
336 pages, $59.99
March 2021

Cloud Native Patterns
by Cornelia Davis
Foreword by Gene Kim

ISBN 9781617294297
400 pages, $49.99
May 2019

*Learn Azure in a Month of Lunches,
Second Edition*
by Iain Foulds

ISBN 9781617297625
368 pages, $49.99
June 2020

For ordering information go to www.manning.com

A new online reading experience

liveBook, our online reading platform, adds a new dimension to your Manning books, with features that make reading, learning, and sharing easier than ever. A liveBook version of your book is included FREE with every Manning book.

This next generation book platform is more than an online reader. It's packed with unique features to upgrade and enhance your learning experience.

- Add your own notes and bookmarks
- One-click code copy
- Learn from other readers in the discussion forum
- Audio recordings and interactive exercises
- Read all your purchased Manning content in any browser, anytime, anywhere

As an added bonus, you can search every Manning book and video in liveBook—even ones you don't yet own. Open any liveBook, and you'll be able to browse the content and read anything you like.*

Find out more at www.manning.com/livebook-program.

*Open reading is limited to 10 minutes per book daily

MANNING

The Manning Early Access Program

Don't wait to start learning! In MEAP, the Manning Early Access Program, you can read books as they're being created and long before they're available in stores.

Here's how MEAP works.

- **Start now.** Buy a MEAP and you'll get all available chapters in PDF, ePub, Kindle, and liveBook formats.

- **Regular updates.** New chapters are released as soon as they're written. We'll let you know when fresh content is available.

- **Finish faster.** MEAP customers are the first to get final versions of all books! Pre-order the print book, and it'll ship as soon as it's off the press.

- **Contribute to the process.** The feedback you share with authors makes the end product better.

- **No risk.** You get a full refund or exchange if we ever have to cancel a MEAP.

Explore dozens of titles in MEAP at www.manning.com.